365 Yummy Holiday Candy Recipes

(365 Yummy Holiday Candy Recipes - Volume 1)

Adele Chun

Copyright: Published in the United States by Adele Chun/ © ADELE CHUN

Published on December, 02 2020

All rights reserved. No part of this publication may be reproduced, stored in retrieval system, copied in any form or by any means, electronic, mechanical, photocopying, recording or otherwise transmitted without written permission from the publisher. Please do not participate in or encourage piracy of this material in any way. You must not circulate this book in any format. ADELE CHUN does not control or direct users' actions and is not responsible for the information or content shared, harm and/or actions of the book readers.

In accordance with the U.S. Copyright Act of 1976, the scanning, uploading and electronic sharing of any part of this book without the permission of the publisher constitute unlawful piracy and theft of the author's intellectual property. If you would like to use material from the book (other than just simply for reviewing the book), prior permission must be obtained by contacting the author at publishing@crumblerecipes.com

Thank you for your support of the author's rights.

Content

CHAPTER 1: EASTER CANDY RECIPES . 8

1. Batty Bark 8
2. Bird Nests 8
3. Bird's Nest Treats 9
4. Bird's Nests 9
5. Bunny Tails 9
6. Candied Lemon Peel 10
7. Candied Pecans 10
8. Candy Easter Eggs 11
9. Caramel Cashew Clusters 11
10. Caramel Pretzel Bites 11
11. Caramel Pretzel Sticks 12
12. Cherry Chocolate Bark 13
13. Chocolate Basket 13
14. Chocolate Cherry Truffles 14
15. Chocolate Easter Eggs 15
16. Chocolate Mascarpone Truffles 15
17. Chocolate, Peanut & Pretzel Toffee Crisps 16
18. Chocolate Covered Eggs 16
19. Chocolate Mallow Peanut Candy 17
20. Christmas Candy Bags 17
21. Coconut Almond Candy 18
22. Coconut Cream Eggs 19
23. Coconut Creme Chocolates 19
24. Coconut Egg Nests 19
25. Coconut Rocky Road Treats 20
26. Coffee Pecan Marshmallows 20
27. Contest Winning Brown Sugar Angel Food Cake 21
28. Cookies & Cream Truffle Balls 22
29. Cranberry Cashew Fudge 22
30. Cranberry Pistachio Truffles 23
31. Creamy Chocolate Fudge 23
32. Creamy Coconut Snowballs 24
33. Creamy Pastel Mints 24
34. Crunchy Chocolate Eggs 25
35. Date Pecan Coconut Candy 25
36. Dragonfly Snacks 26
37. Easter Egg Candies 26
38. Easy Peanut Butter Truffles 27
39. Eggnog Creams 27
40. Favorite Dipped Pretzel Rods 28
41. German Chocolate Pecan Truffles 28
42. Gianduja 29
43. Gingerbread Caramels 29
44. Halloween Layered Fudge 30
45. Holiday Marshmallows 30
46. Homemade Chocolate Easter Eggs 31
47. Homemade Holiday Marshmallows 31
48. Honey Caramels 32
49. Jelly Bean Bark 32
50. Jelly Bean Brittle 33
51. Kahlua Truffles 33
52. Lemon Bark 34
53. Lemon Fudge 34
54. Marbled Orange Fudge 35
55. Marshmallow Easter Eggs 35
56. Mine Run Candy 36
57. Mini S'mores 36
58. Nana's Rocky Road Fudge 37
59. Neapolitan Fudge 37
60. Nut Fruit Bark 38
61. Nutty Chocolate Truffles 39
62. Old Fashioned Lollipops 39
63. Orange Gumdrops 39
64. Orange Jelly Candies 40
65. Orange Truffles 41
66. Pastel Almond Bark 41
67. Peanut Butter Coconut Balls 42
68. Peanut Butter Easter Eggs 42
69. Peanut Butter Eggs 43
70. Peanut Butter And Marshmallow Chocolate Eggs 43
71. Pineapple Coconut Snowballs 44
72. Pretzel Bark Candy 44
73. Salted Soft Caramels 44
74. Semiformal Evening Truffles 45
75. Shamrock Toffee Fudge 45
76. Sugary Orange Peel 46
77. Three Chip English Toffee 46
78. Tiger Butter Bark Candy 47
79. Truffle Cherries 47
80. Truffle Eggs 48
81. White Chocolate Easter Egg Candies .. 48
82. White Chocolate Easter Eggs 49

CHAPTER 2: HALLOWEEN CANDY RECIPES 49

83. Black Widow Bites 49

84. Bloodshot Eyeballs 50
85. Butterscotch Candy 50
86. Caramel Lollipops 51
87. Caramel Pecan Candy 51
88. Caramel Nut Candy Bars 52
89. Cherry Mice 53
90. Cherry Peanut Butter Balls 53
91. Chocolate Marshmallow Peanut Butter Squares 54
92. Cinnamon Pumpkin Truffles 54
93. Crispy Peanut Butter Cocoa Cups 55
94. Dracula Cookies 55
95. Evil Eye Truffles 55
96. Fingers Of Fright 56
97. Flying Broomstick Cats 56
98. Four Ingredient Tumbleweeds 57
99. Gingerbread Truffles 57
100. Halloween Candy Bark 58
101. Halloween Chocolate Spiders 59
102. Homemade Peanut Butter Cups 59
103. Hosts Of Ghosts 60
104. Licorice Caramels 60
105. Lollipop Ghosts 61
106. Magic Wands 61
107. Maple Ginger Fudge 61
108. Marshmallow Ghosts 62
109. Marshmallow Witches 62
110. Martian Marshmallows 63
111. Marzipan Harvest Table Topper 63
112. Midnight Mice 64
113. Mother Lode Pretzels 65
114. Mounds Of Bugs 65
115. Nutty Caramels 66
116. Peanut Butter Cups 66
117. Peanut Butter Pretzel Bites 67
118. Peanut Goody Candies 67
119. Pumpkin Pie Marshmallows 68
120. Salted Peanut Squares 68
121. Scary Eyeballs 69
122. Spiced Chocolate Truffles 69
123. Spider Nest Candies 70
124. Spiderweb Candy 70
125. Stained Glass Lollipops 71
126. Trail Mix Clusters 71

CHAPTER 3: AWESOME HOLIDAY CANDY RECIPES 72

127. Almond Apricot Dips 72
128. Almond Cherry Fudge 72
129. Almond Coconut Candies 73
130. Aloha Brittle 73
131. Angel Food Christmas Candy 74
132. Apple Jelly Candy 74
133. Apricot Balls 75
134. Banana Cream Chocolate Truffles 75
135. Bavarian Mint Fudge 76
136. Ben's English Toffee 76
137. Black 'n' White Pistachio Bark 77
138. Brittle With Mixed Nuts 77
139. Butter Almond Crunch 78
140. Butter Mints 78
141. Butter Pecan Fudge 79
142. Buttery Walnut Toffee 79
143. Candy Bar Fudge 80
144. Candy Cane Fudge 80
145. Candy Cane Truffle Lollipops 81
146. Caramel Cookie Candy 81
147. Caramel Marshmallow Treats 82
148. Caramel Nut Marshmallows 82
149. Caramel Pecan Logs 83
150. Caramel Pecans 83
151. Cashew Candy Crunch 84
152. Cashew Caramel Fudge 84
153. Cherry Almond Bark 85
154. Cherry Swirl Fudge 85
155. Cherry Walnut Fudge 85
156. Chewy Apple Candies 86
157. Chocolate Billionaires 86
158. Chocolate Caramel Cracker Bars 87
159. Chocolate Caramel Turkey Legs 87
160. Chocolate Cashew Clusters 88
161. Chocolate Cashew Crunchies 88
162. Chocolate Cherries 89
163. Chocolate Chews 89
164. Chocolate Chow Mein Clusters 90
165. Chocolate Clusters 90
166. Chocolate Covered Cherries 90
167. Chocolate Crunch Patties 91
168. Chocolate Fudge With Hazelnut 91
169. Chocolate Hazelnut Truffles 92
170. Chocolate Nut Candies 92
171. Chocolate Nut Fudge 93
172. Chocolate Nut Fudge Rolls 93
173. Chocolate Orange Bites 94

174. Chocolate Peanut Brittle 94
175. Chocolate Peanut Butter Candy 95
176. Chocolate Peanut Candy Squares 95
177. Chocolate Peanut Clusters 96
178. Chocolate Pecan Caramels 96
179. Chocolate Pizza Heart 97
180. Chocolate Raisin Truffles 97
181. Chocolate Rum Truffles 98
182. Chocolate Zebra Clusters 98
183. Chocolate Covered Almond Butter Brickle 99
184. Chocolate Covered Pretzels 99
185. Chocolate Dipped Lavender Pine Nut Brittle 100
186. Chocolate Dipped Peanut Nougat 100
187. Chocolate Dipped Pretzel Rods 101
188. Chocolate Peanut Angel Sweets 102
189. Christmas Almond Toffee 102
190. Christmas Candies 103
191. Christmas Crunch Candy 103
192. Christmas Hard Candy 104
193. Cinnamon Almond Brittle 104
194. Cinnamon Rock Candy 105
195. Cinnamon Walnut Brittle 105
196. Coconut Almond Candies 106
197. Coconut Caramels 106
198. Coconut Cashew Brittle 107
199. Coconut Chocolate Creams 107
200. Coconut Drops 108
201. Coconut Joys 108
202. Coconut Marshmallow Squares 109
203. Coconut Peaks 109
204. Coconut Surprise Candy 110
205. Coconut Truffles 110
206. Coconut Yule Trees 111
207. Colorful Snowballs 111
208. Contest Winning Hazelnut Toffee 112
209. Cran Marnier Truffles 112
210. Cranberry Bog Bark 113
211. Cranberry Fudge 113
212. Cranberry Ginger Bark 113
213. Cranberry Gumdrops 114
214. Cream Cheese Candies 114
215. Creamy Peanut Butter Fudge 115
216. Creamy Peppermint Patties 115
217. Crispy Peanut Butter Balls 116
218. Crunchy Chocolate Mint Balls 116
219. Crunchy Cracker Candy 117
220. Crunchy Mint Fudge 117
221. Crunchy Peanut Butter Balls 118
222. Crunchy Peanut Butter Squares 118
223. Dandy Caramel Candies 119
224. Dark Chocolate Raspberry Fudge 119
225. Dipped Peanut Butter Logs 120
226. Double Decker Fudge 120
227. Double Nut English Toffee 121
228. Easy Chocolate Drops 121
229. Easy Chocolate Truffles 121
230. Easy Double Decker Fudge 122
231. Easy Holiday Fudge 123
232. Easy Marshmallow Fudge 123
233. Easy Microwave Caramels 124
234. Easy Microwave Mint Fudge 124
235. Eggnog Fudge 125
236. Family Favorite Cinnamon Candy 125
237. Festive Holiday Fruitcake Bark 126
238. Fruit 'n' Nut Clusters 126
239. Fudge Drops 126
240. Fudge With Candy Bar Bits 127
241. Fudgy Christmas Wreath 127
242. Golden Walnut Caramel Squares 128
243. Goody Goody Gumdrops 128
244. Grandma's Hazelnut Candies 129
245. Green Mint Bark 129
246. Hard Candy Peppermint Twists 130
247. Hazelnut Toffee 131
248. Holiday Divinity 131
249. Holiday Pecan Logs 132
250. Holiday Truffles 132
251. Homemade Gumdrops 133
252. Honey Almond Nougats 133
253. Honey Cream Taffy 134
254. Honey Peanut Squares 135
255. Layered Peanut Butter Chocolate Fudge 135
256. Lime In The Coconut Almond Bark 136
257. Macadamia & Coconut Caramels 136
258. Macadamia Almond Brittle 137
259. Macadamia Fudge 137
260. Macadamia Coconut Candy Clusters 137
261. Maple Pralines 138
262. Maple Walnut Crisps 138
263. Marshmallow Chocolate Covered Cherries 139
264. Marshmallow Puffs 139

#	Title	Page
265.	Marzipan Yule Logs	140
266.	Melting Snowmen	140
267.	Microwave Mint Fudge	141
268.	Milk Chocolate Truffles	141
269.	Minty Chocolate Crackles	142
270.	Minty Snowmen	142
271.	Mocha Cream Truffles	143
272.	Molasses Fudge	143
273.	Mounds Balls	144
274.	No Fuss Truffles	145
275.	Nut Goody Bars	145
276.	Nutty Chocolate Peanut Clusters	145
277.	Nutty Citrus Candy	146
278.	Nutty Sticky Bun Candies	146
279.	Old Fashioned Peppermint Taffy	147
280.	Old Time Butter Crunch Candy	147
281.	Orange Cappuccino Creams	148
282.	Orange Coconut Creams	148
283.	Orange Fantasy Fudge	149
284.	Orange Walnut Candy	149
285.	Orange Almond Chocolate Logs	150
286.	Orange Pistachio Divinity	150
287.	Oreos And Candy Cane Chocolate Bark	151
288.	Peanut Butter Chocolate Cups	151
289.	Peanut Butter Clusters	152
290.	Peanut Butter Pinecones	152
291.	Peanut Butter Snowballs	153
292.	Peanut Butter Swirled Fudge	153
293.	Peanut Buttercream Candy	154
294.	Pecan Brittle	154
295.	Pecan Candy Clusters	155
296.	Pecan Caramel Clusters	155
297.	Pecan Caramels	155
298.	Pecan Chocolate Candies	156
299.	Pecan Cinnamon Fudge	156
300.	Pecan Clusters	157
301.	Pecan Delights	157
302.	Pecan Divinity	158
303.	Penuche Fudge	158
304.	Peppermint Candy	159
305.	Peppermint Fudge	159
306.	Peppermint Fudge Truffles	160
307.	Peppermint Swirl Fudge	160
308.	Pine Nut Divinity	161
309.	Pineapple Fudge	161
310.	Pistachio Coconut Chews	162
311.	Pistachio Cranberry Bark	162
312.	Pulled Molasses Taffy	162
313.	Pumpkin Seed Toffee	163
314.	Puttin' On The Ritz Candy	163
315.	Quick Butterscotch Fudge	164
316.	Quick Coconut Bonbons	164
317.	Raisin Cashew Drops	165
318.	Raspberry Rocky Road Fudge	165
319.	Reindeer Treats	166
320.	Ribbon Fantasy Fudge	166
321.	Rich Peanut Clusters	167
322.	Rich Pistachio Brittle	167
323.	Rocky Road Fudge	168
324.	Rocky Toffee Fudge	168
325.	S'more Drops	169
326.	Salted Peanut Chews	169
327.	Salted Peanut Rolls	169
328.	Saltine Toffee Bark	170
329.	Simple Macadamia Nut Fudge	170
330.	Snowball	171
331.	Sour Cream Walnut Fudge	171
332.	Speedy Oven Fudge	172
333.	Spiced Almond Brittle	172
334.	Spiced Almond Butter Candy	173
335.	Strawberry Parfait Holiday Bark	173
336.	Sugar Cone Spruce Trees	174
337.	Sugarless Licorice Stars	174
338.	Sugarplums	175
339.	Sweetheart Fudge	175
340.	Swirled Peppermint Marshmallows	176
341.	Tempting Truffles	176
342.	Terrific Truffles	177
343.	Three Layer Fudge	177
344.	Three Chocolate Fudge	178
345.	Toasted Coconut Truffles	179
346.	Toffee Peanut Clusters	179
347.	Tootsie Roll Fudge	180
348.	Trail Mix Slices	180
349.	Triple Chocolate Fudge	181
350.	Triple Nut Candy	181
351.	Tropical Nut Bark	182
352.	True Love Truffles	182
353.	Truffle Topiary	183
354.	Truffle Topiary Centerpiece	183
355.	Two Tiered Fudge	184
356.	Walnut Caramel Treats	185
357.	Walnut Caramels	186
358.	White Candy Bark	186

359. White Chocolate Coconut Fudge 187
360. White Chocolate Latte Cups 187
361. White Chocolate Marshmallow Fudge 188
362. White Chocolate Peppermint Fudge 188
363. White Christmas Candy 189
364. White Pecan Fudge 189
365. Wonderful Candies Two Ways 190

INDEX 191
CONCLUSION 194

Chapter 1: Easter Candy Recipes

***

1. Batty Bark

Serving: 1-1/2 dozen. | Prep: 25mins | Cook: 0mins | Ready in:

Ingredients

- 8 ounces milk chocolate, chopped
- 4 ounces semisweet chocolate, chopped
- 1 cup crisp rice cereal
- 1/4 cup unsalted sunflower kernels
- 1/4 cup dried cherries, chopped

Direction

- Let the semisweet chocolate and milk chocolate melt in the microwave, then give it a stir until it is smooth in consistency. Add in the sunflower kernels, cherries and cereal and mix everything together. Line a baking sheet with wax paper then put in the prepared chocolate mixture and spread it out in the shape of a rectangle that is 12x9 inches in size. Keep it in the fridge until the mixture has set.
- Allow the chilled chocolate mixture to rest for 10 minutes at room temperature. Use a 3 1/2-inch bat-shaped cookie cutter to cut out the chocolate mixture. If you want, you may melt the excess trimmings again and cut it as well.

Nutrition Information

- Calories:
- Total Fat:
- Sodium:
- Fiber:
- Total Carbohydrate:
- Cholesterol:
- Protein:

2. Bird Nests

Serving: 2 dozen | Prep: 35mins | Cook: 5mins | Ready in:

Ingredients

- 2 packages (10 to 12 ounces each) white baking chips
- 1 package (10 ounces) pretzel sticks
- 24 yellow chicks Peeps candy
- 1 package (12 ounces) M&M's eggs or other egg-shaped candy

Direction

- Melt baking chips in a big metal bowl above simmering water; mix till smooth. For decorations, put 1/2 cup melted chips aside; keep warm.
- Put pretzel sticks in leftover chips; mix to evenly coat. Drop mixture on waxed paper to 24 mounds; use 2 forks to shape to bird nests.
- In reserved chips, dip bottoms of Peeps; put in nests. Stick the eggs using leftover chips; stand till set.

Nutrition Information

- Calories: 276 calories
- Protein: 4g protein.
- Total Fat: 11g fat (7g saturated fat)
- Sodium: 215mg sodium
- Fiber: 1g fiber)
- Total Carbohydrate: 41g carbohydrate (30g sugars
- Cholesterol: 7mg cholesterol

3. Bird's Nest Treats

Serving: 1 dozen. | Prep: 25mins | Cook: 15mins | Ready in:

Ingredients

- 1/4 cup butter, cubed
- 4-1/2 cups miniature marshmallows
- 1/4 cup creamy peanut butter
- 1/4 cup semisweet chocolate chips
- 4 cups chow mein noodles
- 1 cup jelly beans or candy eggs

Direction

- Melt marshmallows and butter until smooth while stirring occasionally over medium heat in a large saucepan. Add chocolate chips and peanut butter; heat while stirring until smooth, about 2 minutes. Take out of the heat; stir in chow mein noodles until coated well.
- Transfer to 12 mounds on a baking sheet lined with waxed paper. Form each into a nest with fingers; press an indentation in the nest's center. Fill 3-4 candy eggs or jelly beans into each nest. Cool.

Nutrition Information

- Calories: 296 calories
- Sodium: 149mg sodium
- Fiber: 1g fiber
- Total Carbohydrate: 46g carbohydrate (27g sugars
- Cholesterol: 10mg cholesterol
- Protein: 3g protein.
- Total Fat: 12g fat (4g saturated fat)

4. Bird's Nests

Serving: 15 servings. | Prep: 15mins | Cook: 10mins | Ready in:

Ingredients

- 1 package (11-1/2 ounces) milk chocolate chips
- 1 tablespoon shortening
- 1 can (5 ounces) chow mein noodles
- 2/3 cup sweetened shredded coconut
- 45 to 60 jelly beans

Direction

- Melt shortening and chocolate chips in a saucepan on low heat; mix till smooth. Take off from heat; mix in coconut and chow mein noodles till coated well. Divide on wax paper-lined baking sheet to 15 mounds. Form to nests; press an indentation on the middle. In each nest, put 3-4 jellybeans; cool. Keep in airtight container.

Nutrition Information

- Calories: 221 calories
- Sodium: 74mg sodium
- Fiber: 1g fiber)
- Total Carbohydrate: 28g carbohydrate (19g sugars
- Cholesterol: 5mg cholesterol
- Protein: 2g protein.
- Total Fat: 12g fat (6g saturated fat)

5. Bunny Tails

Serving: 48 pieces | Prep: 20mins | Cook: 0mins | Ready in:

Ingredients

- 1 cup white baking chips, melted
- 1 cup sweetened shredded coconut

Direction

- Melt chocolate and make teaspoonful drops of melted chocolate on parchment paper or waxed paper. Use sweetened flaked coconut to sprinkle each chocolate drop and allow to sit till they become dry.

Nutrition Information

- Calories: 29 calories
- Fiber: 0 fiber)
- Total Carbohydrate: 3g carbohydrate (3g sugars
- Cholesterol: 1mg cholesterol
- Protein: 0 protein.
- Total Fat: 2g fat (1g saturated fat)
- Sodium: 8mg sodium

6. Candied Lemon Peel

Serving: 15 | Prep: 10mins | Cook: 1hours | Ready in:

Ingredients

- 3 lemons
- 8 cups cold water, or as needed
- 2 cups white sugar, or as needed

Direction

- Cut lemon to 1/4-in. thick slices; remove fruit pulp. Halve rings so peels become long strips.
- Boil lemon peel and water in a small pan then drain water; with fresh cold water, repeat. Repeat boiling step thrice. Drain; put aside peels.
- Boil 2 cups sugar and 2 cups fresh water, mixing to dissolve sugar; lower heat to low. Mix in citrus peels; simmer till white pith is translucent. Keep peels in syrup to keep soft, refrigerated, or let them dry. In extra sugar, toss dry candied peels then keep at room temperature, airtight.

Nutrition Information

- Calories: 108 calories;
- Total Fat: 0.1
- Sodium: 4
- Total Carbohydrate: 29
- Cholesterol: 0
- Protein: 0.3

7. Candied Pecans

Serving: 10 | Prep: 10mins | Cook: 1hours | Ready in:

Ingredients

- 1 cup white sugar
- 1 teaspoon ground cinnamon
- 1 teaspoon salt
- 1 egg white
- 1 tablespoon water
- 1 pound pecan halves

Direction

- Set your oven to preheat at 250°F (120°C).
- In a bowl, combine cinnamon, salt and sugar.
- Beat the water and egg white in a separate bowl until foamy. Toss the pecans into the egg white mixture and stir in the sugar mixture; mix until the pecans are coated and spread it onto the baking pan.
- Let it bake in the preheated oven for an hour or until the pecans turn entirely brown. Be sure to stir the pecans every 15 minutes during baking time.

Nutrition Information

- Calories: 393 calories;
- Protein: 4.5
- Total Fat: 32.7
- Sodium: 238
- Total Carbohydrate: 26.5
- Cholesterol: 0

8. Candy Easter Eggs

Serving: 9 dozen. | Prep: 30mins | Cook: 0mins | Ready in:

Ingredients

- 1/2 cup butter, softened
- 1/2 cup cold mashed potatoes (prepared without added milk and butter)
- 2 pounds confectioners' sugar
- 1-1/2 cups sweetened shredded coconut
- 1 teaspoon vanilla extract
- 1 pound dark chocolate candy coating, coarsely chopped
- Colored sprinkles

Direction

- Cream butter in a bowl; beat in mashed potatoes. Add confectioners' sugar slowly, beating till smooth. Add vanilla and coconut; mix well. Form to 1-inch ovals; put on baking sheets and refrigerate for 4-6 hours.
- Melt candy coating in a microwave. In coating, dip ovals; let extra drip off. Use sprinkles to decorate. Put on waxed paper; stand till set. Keep in refrigerator in an airtight container.

Nutrition Information

- Calories: 207 calories
- Protein: 0 protein.
- Total Fat: 8g fat (6g saturated fat)
- Sodium: 37mg sodium
- Fiber: 1g fiber)
- Total Carbohydrate: 36g carbohydrate (33g sugars
- Cholesterol: 7mg cholesterol

9. Caramel Cashew Clusters

Serving: 2-1/2 dozen. | Prep: 25mins | Cook: 0mins | Ready in:

Ingredients

- 2 teaspoons butter
- 2 pounds milk chocolate candy coating, coarsely chopped, divided
- 1 cup salted cashew halves
- 28 caramels
- 2 tablespoons heavy whipping cream

Direction

- Line waxed paper on baking sheets and use butter to grease the paper; put aside.
- Melt a pound of candy coating in microwave; mix till smooth. Drop to prepared pans by scant tablespoonfuls. Rest for about 3 minutes, till partially set. Put 6 or 7 cashews on top of each. Rest till fully set.
- Mix cream and caramels in heavy, small saucepan. Cook and mix on low heat till melted; mix till smooth. Pour on top of cashews. In case caramel thickens, rewarm it on low heat. Melt the rest of candy coating; pour on top of caramel. Rest till set.

Nutrition Information

- Calories: 228 calories
- Cholesterol: 2mg cholesterol
- Protein: 2g protein.
- Total Fat: 13g fat (9g saturated fat)
- Sodium: 57mg sodium
- Fiber: 1g fiber)
- Total Carbohydrate: 29g carbohydrate (25g sugars

10. Caramel Pretzel Bites

Serving: 6 dozen. | Prep: 20mins | Cook: 25mins | Ready in:

Ingredients

- 2 teaspoons butter, softened
- 4 cups pretzel sticks

- 2-1/2 cups pecan halves, toasted
- 2-1/4 cups packed brown sugar
- 1 cup butter, cubed
- 1 cup corn syrup
- 1 can (14 ounces) sweetened condensed milk
- 1/8 teaspoon salt
- 1 teaspoon vanilla extract
- 1 package (11-1/2 ounces) milk chocolate chips
- 1 tablespoon plus 1 teaspoon shortening, divided
- 1/3 cup white baking chips

Direction

- Use foil to line a 13x9 in. pan; use softened butter to grease foil. Spread pecans and pretzels on bottom of the prepared pan.
- Mix salt, milk, corn syrup, butter cubes, brown sugar in a large heavy saucepan; cook and stir on medium heat till a candy thermometer reaches 240 degrees (it's the soft ball stage). Get the pan off heat. Put in vanilla and stir. Transfer the mixture onto the pretzel mixture.
- Put a tablespoon of shortening and chocolate chips together and melt in a microwave; stir till the mixture becomes smooth. Spread over the caramel layer. Melt the rest of shortening and white baking chips in the microwave; stir till the mixture becomes smooth. Drizzle over top. Allow to sit till the mixture is set.
- Lift candy out of pan by foil; get rid of foil. Butter a knife and use the knife to chop candy to bite sized pieces.

Nutrition Information

- Calories: 146 calories
- Fiber: 1g fiber)
- Total Carbohydrate: 19g carbohydrate (14g sugars
- Cholesterol: 10mg cholesterol
- Protein: 1g protein.
- Total Fat: 8g fat (3g saturated fat)
- Sodium: 76mg sodium

11. Caramel Pretzel Sticks

Serving: about 3 dozen. | Prep: 02hours00mins | Cook: 35mins | Ready in:

Ingredients

- 2 cups sugar
- 1 cup light corn syrup
- 1 cup butter, cubed
- 1 can (14 ounces) sweetened condensed milk
- 1 package (12 ounces) pretzel rods
- 6 to 12 ounces white candy coating
- 6 to 12 ounces milk chocolate candy coating
- 3/4 cup finely chopped walnuts, optional

Direction

- Mix butter, corn syrup and sugar in a large heavy saucepan; bring the saucepan just to a boil on medium heat, remember to stir constantly. Boil without stirring for 4 minutes. Get the saucepan off heat; pour in milk and stir. Cook on medium low heat, stir while cooking till a candy thermometer reaches 245 degrees (this is the firm ball stage). Keep the saucepan warm.
- Transfer 2 cups of caramel mixture into a glass measuring cup which can hold 2 cups. Dip half of each pretzel into the caramel mixture quickly; let the excess caramel to drip off. Use butter to grease baking sheets well, place pretzels on the buttered baking sheets and allow pretzels to sit till they become firm. (If required, rewarm and replenish the caramel mixture). Melt white candy coating in the microwave; stir till the mixture becomes smooth. Dip the caramel-dipped pretzels halfway into the white coating; place them back to the baking sheets. Melt milk chocolate coating; dip the rest of the pretzels; lay coated pretzels on baking sheets.
- Drizzle milk chocolate coating over white-coated pretzels; drizzle white coating over milk chocolate-coated pretzels. If you like, you

can use walnuts to sprinkle. Keep in airtight containers.

Nutrition Information

- Calories: 132 calories
- Sodium: 224mg sodium
- Fiber: 0 fiber)
- Total Carbohydrate: 21g carbohydrate (14g sugars
- Cholesterol: 5mg cholesterol
- Protein: 1g protein.
- Total Fat: 5g fat (4g saturated fat)

12. Cherry Chocolate Bark

Serving: 18 | Prep: 5mins | Cook: 5mins | Ready in:

Ingredients

- 1 (12 ounce) bag semisweet chocolate chips
- 12 cherry-flavored candy canes, crushed
- 1/3 cup red confectioner's coating (optional)

Direction

- Line aluminum foil on 9x13-in. baking pan.
- Melt chocolate chips in microwave-safe ceramic/glass bowl for 1-3 minutes, varies on microwave, in 30-second intervals, mixing after every melting, till smooth. Don't overheat; chocolate will scorch. Spread melted chocolate quickly and evenly using a spatula in the prepared pan till its bottom is covered. Evenly drizzle the crushed candy on chocolate; lightly pat using clean spatula to help candy settle into chocolate.
- If using, melt red confectioners' coating in microwave-safe ceramic/glass bowl for 1-3 minutes, varies on microwave, in 30-second intervals, mixing after every melting. Put melted coating in resealable plastic bag; snip very small corner of bag off; use to drizzle bark with coating.

- Put pan in fridge/freezer for 30 minutes till hard. Remove from pan; peel foil off. Break to small pieces to serve.

Nutrition Information

- Calories: 180 calories;
- Total Fat: 6.6
- Sodium: 12
- Total Carbohydrate: 31.9
- Cholesterol: < 1
- Protein: 1

13. Chocolate Basket

Serving: 1-1/4 cups. | Prep: 60mins | Cook: 0mins | Ready in:

Ingredients

- Materials needed:
- Thirteen 3-inch pretzel sticks
- Flexible plastic cover to a 16-ounce container (such as sour cream), about 4-1/2 inches diameter x 1/4 inch deep
- Paper towels
- Wire rack
- 1-quart bowl
- Waxed paper
- Chocolate clay:
- 10 ounces dark, milk or white chocolate candy coating, melted
- 1/3 cup light corn syrup

Direction

- Mix corn syrup and candy coating until just blended. Transfer to a sheet of waxed paper to 3/8-in. thickness (about an 8-in. square) and spread.
- Allow to stand without a cover for 2-3 hours at room temperature or until it becomes dry to the touch. Using plastic wrap, wrap tightly;

allow to stand overnight. You can use it right away or store up to 2 weeks.
- To build the Base: 1, Coat pretzels completely with melted chocolate chips or chocolate candy coating. Arrange on a wire rack, refrigerate 10 minutes. Set the rest of the chocolate aside. (You can prepare pretzels one day ahead). Make sure that you use dry and clean plastic cover. Put 2 dampened paper towels in the bottom of the bowl; place cover on the towels (to hold it in place). Put ends of prepared pretzels around the cover's outer edge; placing the other ends against the bowl's side to support the basket sides. Pour or scoop melted chocolate into cover until it reaches 1.8 in. from the top; set the rest of the chocolate aside. Make sure that all pretzel sticks are surrounded with chocolate. Chill for half an hour until chocolate is firm.
- Take out of the bowl. Loosen the edges of plastic carefully; cover; remove. Set base on waxed paper.
- Make 3 ropes about 20 in. long; braid and put aside. Melt the rest of the chocolate again; drop on top of each pretzel. Top with braided ropes; blend the ends to complete the edge. Use melted chocolate to glue pieces of broken pretzels; chill until set.
- Start to Weave, 2. Knead a 1-inch ball of Chocolate Clay until pliable but not soft; roll into 1/4-in.-thick ropes. Start on the pretzel's side, weave rope around pretzels loosely.
- Repeat; overlap with the next rope slightly; press ends together. Keep weaving between pretzels until you reach the top of pretzels; end the last rope on the pretzel's inside.
- Complete the basket, 3. Make 3 ropes about 20 in. long; braid; put aside. Melt the rest of the chocolate again and drop on top of pretzels. Top with braided ropes; finish the edge by blending the ends. Use melted chocolate to glue pieces of broken pretzels; chill until set.

Nutrition Information

- Calories:
- Total Carbohydrate:
- Cholesterol:
- Protein:
- Total Fat:
- Sodium:
- Fiber:

14. Chocolate Cherry Truffles

Serving: 4 dozen. | Prep: 01hours30mins | Cook: 0mins | Ready in:

Ingredients

- 1 cup finely chopped dried cherries
- 1/4 cup cherry brandy
- 11 ounces 53% cacao dark baking chocolate, chopped
- 1/2 cup heavy whipping cream
- 1 teaspoon cherry extract
- COATING:
- 4 ounces milk chocolate, chopped
- 4 ounces dark chocolate, chopped
- Melted dark, milk and white chocolate and pearl dust

Direction

- Soak cherries in brandy, covered, in small bowl for 1 hour till cherries are soft.
- Put dark chocolate in small bowl. Put cream to just a boil in small saucepan. Put on chocolate; whisk till smooth. Mix soaked cherries with liquid and extract in; cool, occasionally mixing, to room temperature. Refrigerate till firm for 1 hour.
- Form to 1-in. balls; put on baking sheets and cover. Refrigerate for minimum 1 hour.
- Melt milk chocolate in microwave; mix till smooth. Dip 1/2 balls in milk chocolate; let excess drip off. Put on waxed paper and let stand till set.
- Melt dark chocolate; mix till smooth. Dip leftover balls in dark chocolate; let excess drip off. Put onto waxed paper; let stand till set.

Drizzle melted chocolate over; decorate as desired with pearl dust. Keep in airtight container in the fridge.

Nutrition Information

- Calories: 80 calories
- Total Fat: 5g fat (3g saturated fat)
- Sodium: 1mg sodium
- Fiber: 1g fiber)
- Total Carbohydrate: 10g carbohydrate (8g sugars
- Cholesterol: 3mg cholesterol
- Protein: 1g protein.

15. Chocolate Easter Eggs

Serving: 2 dozen. | Prep: 25mins | Cook: 0mins | Ready in:

Ingredients

- 1/4 cup butter, softened
- 3/4 cup chunky peanut butter
- 1-1/2 to 2 cups confectioners' sugar, divided
- 1 cup sweetened shredded coconut
- 1/2 cup finely chopped walnuts
- 2 cups (12 ounces) semisweet chocolate chips
- 2 tablespoons shortening

Direction

- Cream peanut butter and butter in a big bowl until fluffy. Put in 1 cup confectioners' sugar slowly then blend well. Mix in nuts and coconut.
- Flip the peanut butter blend onto a lightly dusted surface with some of the leftover confectioners' sugar; knead in enough of the leftover confectioners' sugar until the blend remains the shape when formed. Form into small egg-shaped pieces. Cover then chill for an hour.
- Melt the shortening and chocolate chips in a microwave; mix until smooth. Dip the eggs into the mixture; let excess drip off. Put them onto waxed paper; allow to stand until set. Chill.

Nutrition Information

- Calories: 204 calories
- Sodium: 70mg sodium
- Fiber: 2g fiber)
- Total Carbohydrate: 20g carbohydrate (17g sugars
- Cholesterol: 5mg cholesterol
- Protein: 3g protein.
- Total Fat: 14g fat (6g saturated fat)

16. Chocolate Mascarpone Truffles

Serving: about 4 dozen. | Prep: 45mins | Cook: 5mins | Ready in:

Ingredients

- 12 ounces semisweet chocolate, chopped, divided
- 4 ounces dark chocolate, chopped
- 1/2 cup heavy whipping cream
- 1/2 cup Mascarpone cheese
- 1-3/4 cups pistachios, chopped

Direction

- Mix and cook cheese, cream, dark chocolate and 4-oz. semisweet chocolate in small heavy saucepan on low heat till smooth. Put in small bowl; cover. Refrigerate till firm enough to shape for 3 hours. Form to 1-in. balls; put onto waxed paper-lined baking sheets then chill till firm for 1-2 hours.
- Melt leftover semisweet chocolate in microwave; mix till smooth. Dip balls in chocolate; let excess drip off then roll into pistachios. Put on waxed paper; let it stand till set. Keep in the fridge.

Nutrition Information

- Calories: 103 calories
- Protein: 2g protein.
- Total Fat: 8g fat (4g saturated fat)
- Sodium: 22mg sodium
- Fiber: 1g fiber)
- Total Carbohydrate: 7g carbohydrate (5g sugars
- Cholesterol: 9mg cholesterol

17. Chocolate, Peanut & Pretzel Toffee Crisps

Serving: 2-1/2 pounds. | Prep: 25mins | Cook: 10mins | Ready in:

Ingredients

- 40 saltines
- 3/4 cup butter, cubed
- 3/4 cup packed brown sugar
- 1 teaspoon vanilla extract
- 2 cups (12 ounces) semisweet chocolate chips
- 1 cup cocktail peanuts
- 1 cup broken pretzel sticks
- 3/4 cup M&M's minis

Direction

- Start preheating the oven to 350°. Line foil on a 15x10x1-inch baking pan. Lightly coat foil with oil. Place on the foil with the saltines in a single layer.
- Melt butter in a large heavy saucepan over medium heat. Mix in the brown sugar. Boil; cook while stirring until the sugar dissolves, or about 2-3 mins. Discard from the heat; then stir in the vanilla. Evenly spread over crackers.
- Bake until bubbly, or about 8 to 10 mins. Sprinkle with the chocolate chips immediately. Let the chips soften for 2 mins, spread over the top. Scatter on top with M&M's minis, pretzels and peanuts; settle the toppings into chocolate by shaking the pan. Let it cool.
- Place in the refrigerator, uncovered, until set, or about 60 mins. Break it into pieces. Keep in an airtight container.

Nutrition Information

- Calories:
- Sodium:
- Fiber:
- Total Carbohydrate:
- Cholesterol:
- Protein:
- Total Fat:

18. Chocolate Covered Eggs

Serving: 2 dozen. | Prep: 60mins | Cook: 0mins | Ready in:

Ingredients

- 1/4 cup butter, softened
- 1 jar (7 ounces) marshmallow creme
- 1 teaspoon vanilla extract
- 3 cups plus 1 tablespoon confectioners' sugar, divided
- 3 to 4 drops yellow food coloring
- 2 cups (12 ounces) white baking chips or semisweet chocolate chips
- 2 tablespoons shortening
- Icing of your choice
- Assorted decorating candies

Direction

- Beat vanilla, marshmallow crème and butter till smooth in a big bowl; beat in 3 cups of confectioners' sugar slowly. In a bowl, put 1/4 cup butter mixture, put in yellow food coloring; mix well. Form to 24 small balls; cover. Chill for 30 minutes. In plastic wrap, wrap plain mixture; chill it for 30 minutes.
- Use leftover confectioners' sugar to dust work surface. Divide plain dough to 24 pieces;

around each yellow ball, wrap 1 plain dough piece; roll to egg shape. Put onto wax paper-lined baking sheet; use plastic wrap to cover. Freeze till firm for 15 minutes.
- Melt shortening and chips in a microwave; mix till smooth. In mixture, dip eggs; let excess drip off. Put eggs back on waxed paper; refrigerate till set for 30 minutes. Decorate as desired with decorating candies and icing. Keep in refrigerator in an airtight container.

Nutrition Information

- Calories: 180 calories
- Cholesterol: 5mg cholesterol
- Protein: 1g protein. Diabetic Exchanges: 2 starch
- Total Fat: 7g fat (4g saturated fat)
- Sodium: 22mg sodium
- Fiber: 1g fiber)
- Total Carbohydrate: 31g carbohydrate (27g sugars

19. Chocolate Mallow Peanut Candy

Serving: 5 dozen. | Prep: 10mins | Cook: 0mins | Ready in:

Ingredients

- 1 package (11-1/2 ounces) milk chocolate chips
- 1 package (10 ounces) butterscotch chips
- 1 cup creamy peanut butter
- 1 package (10-1/2 ounces) pastel miniature marshmallows
- 1-3/4 cups salted peanuts
- 1 cup crisp rice cereal

Direction

- Melt peanut butter and chips in a big microwave-safe bowl; mix till smooth. Add cereal, peanuts and marshmallows; stir well.
- Put into a 13x9-inch dish coated in cooking spray; before cutting, refrigerate till firm for 2 hours.

Nutrition Information

- Calories: 121 calories
- Protein: 3g protein. Diabetic Exchanges: 1 starch
- Total Fat: 7g fat (3g saturated fat)
- Sodium: 53mg sodium
- Fiber: 1g fiber)
- Total Carbohydrate: 12g carbohydrate (9g sugars
- Cholesterol: 1mg cholesterol

20. Christmas Candy Bags

Serving: Two bags, 6-1/2 dozen caramels. | Prep: 45mins | Cook: 10mins | Ready in:

Ingredients

- 1 teaspoon plus 1 cup butter, divided
- 2 cups packed brown sugar
- 1 cup light corn syrup
- 1 can (14 ounces) sweetened condensed milk
- 1 teaspoon vanilla extract
- 12 ounces white candy coating, divided
- 2 small paper bags, (6-1/2 X 1-3/4 inches):
- Candy foils or buttered waxed paper for wrapping caramels

Direction

- Caramels: Line aluminum foil on 9-inch square pan; use 1 teaspoon butter to butter foil.
- Put leftover butter, milk, corn syrup and brown sugar together in a heavy saucepan and boil on medium heat, constantly mixing; cook

till it reaches a firm ball stage or candy thermometer reads 248°, constantly mixing. Take off from heat; mix in vanilla.
- Put caramel in prepped pan; cool. Cut to 1-inch squares. Individually wrap caramels in buttered waxed paper/candy foils, twisting ends.
- Bags: Cut 1-inch from top of open end of every paper bag off; put bags aside.
- Break candy coating to chunks; put 4-ounce in microwave-safe bowl. Heat for 45 seconds at 70% powder; mix. Microwave till melted in 10-20-second intervals; mix till smooth.
- Put melted coating into 1 paper bag; to coat inside sides and bottom fully, turn the bag. Spread coating evenly on inside of bag with a pastry brush; use toothpicks to prop bags open.
- Melt 4-ounces extra candy-coating following instruction; repeat coating process with another bag. Refrigerate bags till coating is set for 5-7 minutes; remove toothpicks.
- Melt leftover coating; evenly brush on coating on bags. Refrigerate bags till set for 5-7 minutes more.
- Peel off paper bags; discard. Use caramels to fill candy bags.

Nutrition Information

- Calories: 3656 calories
- Fiber: 0 fiber)
- Total Carbohydrate: 569g carbohydrate (523g sugars
- Cholesterol: 318mg cholesterol
- Protein: 17g protein.
- Total Fat: 158g fat (112g saturated fat)
- Sodium: 1481mg sodium

21. Coconut Almond Candy

Serving: 2 dozen. | Prep: 45mins | Cook: 0mins | Ready in:

Ingredients

- 2 cups sweetened shredded coconut
- 1/2 cup mashed potatoes (with added milk and butter)
- 1/4 teaspoon vanilla extract
- 1/8 teaspoon salt, optional
- 2 cups confectioners' sugar
- 24 unblanched almonds, toasted
- 1 package (11-1/2 ounces) milk chocolate chips
- 1 tablespoon butter

Direction

- Mix salt (if needed), vanilla, potatoes and coconut in a big bowl. Beat in the confectioners' sugar gradually. Refrigerate with the cover for 1 hour, until firm enough to form.
- Form a blend into twenty-four 1-inch ovals using hands dusted with confectioners' sugar. Slightly flatten, and wrap each around 1 almond. Put onto baking sheets lined with waxed paper; freeze for minimum 30 minutes, until firm.
- Melt the butter and chips in a microwave; mix until smooth. Dip the candies in the chocolate blend with a fork; let excess drip off. Bring back to the baking sheets; refrigerate until set. Keep in an airtight container in the refrigerator between layers of waxed paper.

Nutrition Information

- Calories: 167 calories
- Fiber: 1g fiber)
- Total Carbohydrate: 23g carbohydrate (20g sugars
- Cholesterol: 5mg cholesterol
- Protein: 2g protein.
- Total Fat: 8g fat (5g saturated fat)
- Sodium: 61mg sodium

22. Coconut Cream Eggs

Serving: 3 dozen. | Prep: 20mins | Cook: 0mins | Ready in:

Ingredients

- 1 package (8 ounces) cream cheese, softened
- 1 tablespoon butter, softened
- 4 cups confectioners' sugar
- 1 cup sweetened shredded coconut
- 2 cups (12 ounces) semisweet chocolate chips
- 1 tablespoon shortening

Direction

- Beat the butter and cream cheese in a bowl until smooth. Put in coconut and sugar. Refrigerate until easy to manage, about 1-1/2 hours. Mold rounded tablespoonfuls of coconut blend into egg shapes with hands sprinkled with confectioners' sugar. Put onto a baking sheet lined with waxed paper. Freeze until slightly firm, about 2 hours.
- Melt the shortening and chocolate chips. Take a few eggs at a time out of the freezer; dip into chocolate blend until fully coated. Bring back to waxed paper; refrigerate until hardened. Keep in the fridge.

Nutrition Information

- Calories: 137 calories
- Protein: 1g protein.
- Total Fat: 7g fat (4g saturated fat)
- Sodium: 30mg sodium
- Fiber: 1g fiber)
- Total Carbohydrate: 21g carbohydrate (19g sugars
- Cholesterol: 8mg cholesterol

23. Coconut Creme Chocolates

Serving: 2-1/2 dozen. | Prep: 15mins | Cook: 0mins | Ready in:

Ingredients

- 1 jar (7 ounces) marshmallow creme
- 2-2/3 cups sweetened shredded coconut, toasted
- 1 teaspoon vanilla extract
- Dash salt
- 1 milk chocolate candy bar (5 ounces), chopped
- 1-1/2 teaspoons shortening

Direction

- Mix salt, vanilla, coconut and marshmallow crème till blended in a big bowl; refrigerate for not less than 1 hour, with cover.
- Form mixture to 1-inch balls; put on wax paper-lined baking sheet and refrigerate for not less than 3 hours, with cover.
- Melt shortening and chocolate in a microwave; mix till smooth. Plunge coconut balls into chocolate; let excess drip off. Put on waxed paper; stand till set.

Nutrition Information

- Calories: 91 calories
- Total Fat: 5g fat (3g saturated fat)
- Sodium: 36mg sodium
- Fiber: 1g fiber)
- Total Carbohydrate: 12g carbohydrate (10g sugars
- Cholesterol: 1mg cholesterol
- Protein: 1g protein.

24. Coconut Egg Nests

Serving: 1 dozen. | Prep: 20mins | Cook: 0mins | Ready in:

Ingredients

- 6 ounces white candy coating, coarsely chopped
- 6 drops green food coloring
- 1 drop yellow food coloring
- 1 cup sweetened shredded coconut
- 36 jelly beans

Direction

- Melt candy coating microwave bowl, then stir in food coloring until combined. Put in coconut then drop on waxed paper into 12 mounds by tablespoonfuls. Use the end of a wooden spoon handle to make an indentation in the center of each mound. Fill 3 jelly beans into each, then allow to stand until set.

Nutrition Information

- Calories:
- Fiber:
- Total Carbohydrate:
- Cholesterol:
- Protein:
- Total Fat:
- Sodium:

25. Coconut Rocky Road Treats

Serving: about 4-1/2 dozen. | Prep: 35mins | Cook: 0mins | Ready in:

Ingredients

- 1 cup butterscotch chips
- 1 cup semisweet chocolate chips
- 1 package (8 ounces) cream cheese, cubed
- 2 cups miniature marshmallows
- 1/2 cup chopped walnuts
- 2 cups sweetened shredded coconut

Direction

- Line waxed paper on a baking sheet; put aside. Put cream cheese, chocolate chips and butterscotch chips together in a saucepan; mix and cook on low heat till smooth. Take off from heat; mix in nuts and marshmallows. Slightly cool.
- Form to 1-inch balls roll in coconut. Put on prepped baking sheet; refrigerate till firm for 1 hour. Keep in refrigerator in an airtight container.

Nutrition Information

- Calories: 82 calories
- Fiber: 0 fiber)
- Total Carbohydrate: 8g carbohydrate (4g sugars
- Cholesterol: 5mg cholesterol
- Protein: 1g protein. Diabetic Exchanges: 1 fat
- Total Fat: 5g fat (4g saturated fat)
- Sodium: 25mg sodium

26. Coffee Pecan Marshmallows

Serving: 1-1/2 pounds. | Prep: 35mins | Cook: 30mins | Ready in:

Ingredients

- 1 teaspoon butter
- 2 envelopes unflavored gelatin
- 1/2 cup plus 3/4 cup cold water, divided
- 2 cups sugar
- 3/4 cup light corn syrup
- 2 tablespoons instant coffee granules
- 1 cup ground pecans

Direction

- Using foil, line an 8-inch square dish and butter the foil with 1 teaspoon butter; set aside.
- Scatter gelatin on 1/2 cup water in a big metal bowl; put aside. Mix the remaining water, coffee granules, corn syrup and sugar in a big

heavy saucepan. Heat up to a boil, mixing from time to time. Cook, without stirring, until a candy thermometer registers 250° (hard-ball stage).

- Take off from the heat and put into gelatin slowly. Whisk on high speed about 10 minutes until the volume doubles and mixture is thick. Scatter into lined pan. Cover and let cool for 6 hours at room temperature or overnight.
- Scatter cutting board lightly with pecans. Take candy out of pan using foil; flip onto the cutting board. Slice into 1-inch squares; toss in pecans. Put in an airtight container to store in a cool, dry place.

Nutrition Information

- Calories: 45 calories
- Protein: 0 protein. Diabetic Exchanges: 1/2 starch.
- Total Fat: 1g fat (0 saturated fat)
- Sodium: 3mg sodium
- Fiber: 0 fiber)
- Total Carbohydrate: 9g carbohydrate (7g sugars
- Cholesterol: 0 cholesterol

27. Contest Winning Brown Sugar Angel Food Cake

Serving: 16 servings. | Prep: 60mins | Cook: 25mins | Ready in:

Ingredients

- 1-1/2 cups egg whites (about 10)
- 1-3/4 cups packed brown sugar, divided
- 1 cup cake flour
- 1-1/2 teaspoons cream of tartar
- 1-1/2 teaspoons vanilla extract
- 1/2 teaspoon salt
- TOFFEE/TOPPING:
- 1 teaspoon plus 1 cup butter, divided
- 1-1/2 cups chopped pecans
- 1-1/2 cups packed brown sugar
- 1 cup (6 ounces) semisweet chocolate chips
- 1 carton (12 ounces) frozen whipped topping, thawed

Direction

- In a big bowl, put the egg whites and stand for 30 minutes at room temperature. Sift together the flour and 1 cup brown sugar two times; put aside.
- Put oven rack on lowest position; preheat the oven to 350°. Put salt, vanilla and cream of tartar in egg whites; beat at medium speed till soft peaks form. Gradually add leftover brown sugar, approximately 2 tablespoons at a time, beating at high till sugar dissolves and stiff glossy peaks form. Fold in flour mixture slowly, approximately 1/2 cup at time.
- Scoop into 10-inch ungreased tube pan gently; to remove air pockets, use a knife to cut through batter. Bake till light brown and entire top looks dry for 25-30 minutes. Invert pan immediately; fully cool for 1 hour.
- Run a knife around center tube and side of pan; transfer cake onto serving plate.
- Toffee: Line foil on 13x9-inch baking pan; use 1 teaspoon butter to grease foil. Sprinkle pecans in prepped pan; put aside.
- Boil leftover butter and brown sugar in a heavy, small saucepan on medium low heat, constantly mixing; cover. Cook for 2 minutes; mix and cook with a clean spoon till it reaches hard-crack stage or candy thermometer reads 300°. Put into prepped pan immediately. Sprinkle chips over; when melted, spread with knife. Refrigerate till set for 1 hour.
- Use whipped topping to frost cake. Chop 1/2 of toffee finely; press onto cake. If desired, serve with leftover toffee. Keep leftover toffee in airtight container.

Nutrition Information

- Calories: 349 calories
- Total Carbohydrate: 49g carbohydrate (39g sugars

- Cholesterol: 15mg cholesterol
- Protein: 4g protein.
- Total Fat: 15g fat (9g saturated fat)
- Sodium: 167mg sodium
- Fiber: 1g fiber)

28. Cookies & Cream Truffle Balls

Serving: about 3 dozen. | Prep: 30mins | Cook: 0mins | Ready in:

Ingredients

- 1 package (14.3 ounces) Oreo cookies
- 1 package (8 ounces) cream cheese, softened
- 1 package (10 to 12 ounces) white baking chips, melted
- Green jimmies and sprinkles, optional

Direction

- In a food processor, pulse the cookies until fine crumbs shape. Put in the cream cheese; pulse until just mixed. Refrigerate with the cover until firm enough to form.
- Form the blend into 1-inch balls; put onto the waxed paper-lined baking sheets. Freeze with the cover for several hours to overnight.
- Dip the balls into the melted chips; let the excess drip off. Bring back to the pans. Dust instantly with sprinkles and jimmies if desired; allow to stand until set. Store in the covered containers in the fridge.

Nutrition Information

- Calories: 117 calories
- Protein: 1g protein.
- Total Fat: 7g fat (3g saturated fat)
- Sodium: 73mg sodium
- Fiber: 0 fiber)
- Total Carbohydrate: 13g carbohydrate (10g sugars
- Cholesterol: 8mg cholesterol

29. Cranberry Cashew Fudge

Serving: about 1-3/4 pounds (64 pieces). | Prep: 10mins | Cook: 15mins | Ready in:

Ingredients

- 2 teaspoons butter, softened
- 2/3 cup evaporated milk
- 1-2/3 cups sugar
- 1/8 teaspoon salt
- 4 ounces semisweet chocolate, chopped
- 1-1/2 cups miniature marshmallows
- 1/2 cup unsalted cashews, chopped
- 1/2 cup dried cranberries
- 1 teaspoon vanilla extract

Direction

- Use the foil to line the 8-inch square baking plate; use the butter to grease the foil.
- In the big and heavy saucepan, mix the salt, sugar and milk. Let come to a rapid boil on medium heat, whisk continuously. Cook for 5 minutes more, whisk continuously. Take out of the heat.
- Whisk in the marshmallows and chocolate till melted. Whisk in the vanilla, cranberries and cashews. Instantly spread to the prepped pan. Chill till firm or for no less than 2 hours.
- With the foil, lift the fudge from the pan. Take the foil; chop the fudge into 1-inch square pieces. Keep between the layers of the waxed paper in the airtight container.

Nutrition Information

- Calories:
- Fiber:
- Total Carbohydrate:
- Cholesterol:
- Protein:
- Total Fat:

- Sodium:

30. Cranberry Pistachio Truffles

Serving: about 2-1/2 dozen. | Prep: 30mins | Cook: 5mins | Ready in:

Ingredients

- 10 ounces 53% cacao dark baking chocolate, chopped
- 3/4 cup whole-berry cranberry sauce
- 2 tablespoons plus 1-1/2 teaspoons heavy whipping cream
- 2 tablespoons confectioners' sugar
- 2 tablespoons dark baking cocoa
- 1/2 cup finely chopped shelled pistachios

Direction

- Put chocolate in small bowl. Put cream and cranberry sauce to just a boil in small saucepan. Put on chocolate; whisk till smooth. Cool, occasionally mixing, to room temperature. Cover; refrigerate till firm enough to shape for 3 hours.
- Mix cocoa and confectioners' sugar; form truffle mixture to 1-in. balls. Roll into cocoa mixture then pistachios. Keep in airtight container in the fridge.

Nutrition Information

- Calories: 72 calories
- Total Fat: 5g fat (2g saturated fat)
- Sodium: 10mg sodium
- Fiber: 1g fiber)
- Total Carbohydrate: 9g carbohydrate (6g sugars
- Cholesterol: 2mg cholesterol
- Protein: 1g protein.

31. Creamy Chocolate Fudge

Serving: 5 pounds (150 pieces). | Prep: 15mins | Cook: 30mins | Ready in:

Ingredients

- 1 teaspoon plus 1 cup butter, divided
- 4 cups (24 ounces) semisweet chocolate chips
- 1 jar (7 ounces) marshmallow creme
- 4-1/2 cups sugar
- 1 can (12 ounces) evaporated milk
- 2 teaspoons vanilla extract
- 1 cup chopped walnuts, optional

Direction

- Use foil to line a 15x10x1-inch pan; use 1 teaspoon butter to grease the foil. Add the chocolate chips, remaining butter and marshmallow crème into a stand mixer's bowl.
- Mix together the sugar and milk in a large heavy saucepan. Heat it to a rapid boil on medium heat, stir continuously. Cook and stir for about 8 minutes. Add the sugar mixture slowly into the chocolate mixture, beat on medium speed till the fudge starts to hold its shape, for about 3-5 minutes. Beat vanilla into the mix. If you wish, stir walnuts into the mix. Spread into the prepared pan. Refrigerate until firm, with cover, for about 1-2 hours.
- Use foil to lift the fudge out of pan. Take off the foil; slice the fudge into 1-inch squares. Layer the fudge into an airtight container in between waxed paper; refrigerate.
- For freezing: in freezer containers, freeze the fudge, place waxed paper in between each layer. To use, thaw them in the refrigerator before serving.

Nutrition Information

- Calories:
- Cholesterol:
- Protein:
- Total Fat:
- Sodium:

- Fiber:
- Total Carbohydrate:

32. Creamy Coconut Snowballs

Serving: 1-1/2 pounds. | Prep: 40mins | Cook: 0mins | Ready in:

Ingredients

- 1/2 teaspoon plus 1/2 cup butter, softened and divided
- 1-3/4 cups sweetened shredded coconut, divided
- 4 ounces cream cheese, softened
- 3-3/4 cups confectioners' sugar
- 8 ounces white candy coating, chopped
- 2 tablespoons shortening

Direction

- Use foil to line a 9x5-in. loaf pan. Use 1/2 teaspoon butter to grease the foil; put aside. Pulse 3/4 cup coconut in a food processor till it is chopped coarsely. Add the cream cheese and remaining butter into the coconut; pulse until incorporated. Add confectioners' sugar into the mixture slowly; pulse until incorporated. Press the mix into the prepared pan. Refrigerate, covered, for no less than 3 hours.
- Microwave the candy coating and shortening together till melted; stir till smooth. Let it cool down slightly. Lift coconut mixture out of the pan with the foil. Take off the foil gently; slice into 36 pieces. Work with a few pieces at a time, make a ball out of each; refrigerate the remaining pieces.
- Use a toothpick to dip the balls into the melted coating mixture, one by one, and let the excess drip off. Roll them into the remaining coconut; put onto baking sheets lined with waxed paper. Refrigerate till set. For storage, keep refrigerated in an airtight container.

Nutrition Information

- Calories: 144 calories
- Total Fat: 8g fat (5g saturated fat)
- Sodium: 39mg sodium
- Fiber: 0 fiber)
- Total Carbohydrate: 19g carbohydrate (18g sugars
- Cholesterol: 10mg cholesterol
- Protein: 0 protein. Diabetic Exchanges: 1-1/2 fat

33. Creamy Pastel Mints

Serving: about 5 dozen. | Prep: 40mins | Cook: 0mins | Ready in:

Ingredients

- 3 ounces (6 tablespoons) cream cheese
- 1/4 to 1/2 teaspoon peppermint extract
- Red food coloring
- 3 cups confectioners' sugar

Direction

- Allow cream cheese to sit in a bowl at room temperature until slightly softened. Mix in extract until combined. Color the mixture red or pink as you like. Stir in 1/2 confectioners' sugar, little by little.
- Knead in the rest of confectioners' sugar on a work surface until smooth. Split into 3 sections; roll each to 1/4-inch thick. Dusting with additional confectioners' sugar or flour is unnecessary. Use a 1-inch heart shape cookie cutter to cut the candy. Keep in between wax paper layers in a tightly sealed container and store in the fridge.

Nutrition Information

- Calories: 28 calories
- Fiber: 0 fiber)

- Total Carbohydrate: 6g carbohydrate (6g sugars
- Cholesterol: 2mg cholesterol
- Protein: 0 protein.
- Total Fat: 1g fat (0 saturated fat)
- Sodium: 4mg sodium

34. Crunchy Chocolate Eggs

Serving: about 4-1/2 dozen. | Prep: 40mins | Cook: 0mins | Ready in:

Ingredients

- 1 cup packed brown sugar
- 1 cup light corn syrup
- 1 cup peanut butter
- 2 cups cornflakes
- 2 cups crisp rice cereal
- 1/2 cup finely chopped peanuts
- 3-3/4 cups semisweet chocolate chips
- 1-1/2 teaspoons shortening
- Candy sprinkles

Direction

- Combine peanut butter, corn syrup and brown sugar in a heavy saucepan. Cook while stirring over medium heat until they become smooth. Discard from heat; mix in peanuts and cereals.
- Drop onto waxed paper-lined baking sheets by tablespoonfuls when cool enough to handle. Shape into the egg shapes. Place in the refrigerator until firm.
- Melt shortening and chocolate chips in a microwave, then stir until they become smooth. Submerge eggs in the chocolate; let the excess drip off. Arrange on the waxed paper-lined baking sheets. Garnish with the sprinkles. Allow to stand until set.

Nutrition Information

- Calories:

- Total Carbohydrate:
- Cholesterol:
- Protein:
- Total Fat:
- Sodium:
- Fiber:

35. Date Pecan Coconut Candy

Serving: about 6 dozen. | Prep: 60mins | Cook: 0mins | Ready in:

Ingredients

- 1 pound pitted dates, chopped
- 2 cups chopped pecans
- 1 package (16 ounces) miniature marshmallows
- 6 cups sweetened shredded coconut
- 3 packages (12 ounces each) semisweet chocolate chips
- 2 tablespoons shortening

Direction

- Mix together the coconut, pecans, marshmallows and dates in a large bowl. In a food processor or blender, grind the date mixture in batches. Shape the mix into 1-in. balls.
- Melt chocolate chips and shortening in a microwave-safe bowl; stir till smooth. Dip the balls into the chocolate; let the excess drip off. Put the balls onto waxed paper to harden. For storage, keep in an airtight container.

Nutrition Information

- Calories:
- Sodium:
- Fiber:
- Total Carbohydrate:
- Cholesterol:
- Protein:

- Total Fat:

36. Dragonfly Snacks

Serving: 6 servings. | Prep: 30mins | Cook: 0mins | Ready in:

Ingredients

- 8 ounces white candy coating, finely chopped
- 6 Pirouette cookies
- Colored sugar
- 12 pretzels
- 12 large marshmallows

Direction

- Line waxed paper on ungreased baking sheet; put aside. Melt candy coating in microwave; mix till smooth.
- Use candy coating to coat cookies; put on prepped pan. Sprinkle colored sugar over; freeze till firm for 15 minutes.
- Warm leftover candy coating if needed. Dip pretzels in coating; let excess drip off. Force 2 pretzels on each cookie, propping with marshmallows. Sprinkle colored sugar over immediately; stand till set. Remove dragonflies from marshmallows and waxed paper carefully.

Nutrition Information

- Calories: 271 calories
- Fiber: 0 fiber)
- Total Carbohydrate: 37g carbohydrate (29g sugars
- Cholesterol: 1mg cholesterol
- Protein: 1g protein.
- Total Fat: 13g fat (10g saturated fat)
- Sodium: 249mg sodium

37. Easter Egg Candies

Serving: 4 dozen. | Prep: 60mins | Cook: 0mins | Ready in:

Ingredients

- 1/2 cup butter, cubed
- 2 packages (3 ounces each) cook-and-serve vanilla pudding mix
- 1/2 cup milk
- 3-3/4 cups confectioners' sugar
- 1 teaspoon vanilla extract
- 1/2 cup chopped walnuts
- 1 teaspoon maple flavoring
- 1/2 cup sweetened shredded coconut
- 1/2 teaspoon coconut extract
- 2 cups milk chocolate chips
- 2 teaspoons shortening

Direction

- Melt butter in a big saucepan; mix in pudding mixes till blended. Whisk in milk; boil. Mix and cook till thicken for 2 minutes. Take off from heat; mix in vanilla and confectioners' sugar till smooth.
- Divide pudding mixture to 2 bowls. Add maple flavoring and walnuts to the first bowl; mix well. Add coconut extract and coconut to the second bowl; mix well. Cover; refrigerate till firm for 30 minutes. Shape tablespoonfuls pudding mixture to egg shapes; put on wax paper-lined pan. Chill till firm for 30 minutes.
- Melt shortening and milk chocolate chips in microwave-safe bowl; mix till smooth. In chocolate, dip eggs; put on waxed paper till set. Decorate however you want; keep in refrigerator.

Nutrition Information

- Calories: 119 calories
- Protein: 1g protein. Diabetic Exchanges: 1 starch
- Total Fat: 5g fat (3g saturated fat)
- Sodium: 51mg sodium

- Fiber: 0 fiber)
- Total Carbohydrate: 17g carbohydrate (15g sugars
- Cholesterol: 7mg cholesterol

38. Easy Peanut Butter Truffles

Serving: 64 truffles. | Prep: 20mins | Cook: 10mins | Ready in:

Ingredients

- 1 teaspoon plus 1/4 cup butter, divided
- 1/4 cup honey
- 2 cups creamy peanut butter
- 1-1/4 cups confectioners' sugar
- 1 teaspoon vanilla extract
- 1-1/2 cups finely chopped honey-roasted peanuts or miniature semisweet chocolate chips

Direction

- Line foil on 8-inch square pan; use 1 teaspoon butter to grease foil.
- Put leftover butter and honey together in a small saucepan on medium heat; mix and cook till blended; mix in peanut butter till smooth. Take off from heat; whisk in vanilla and confectioners' sugar. Spread in prepped pan; refrigerate till firm, with cover, for 2 hours.
- In shallow bowl, put the peanuts. Lift candy from pan using foil. Remove foil; cut candy to 64 squares. Form squares to balls; roll them in peanuts. Keep in refrigerator in airtight container between waxed paper layers.

Nutrition Information

- Calories: 87 calories
- Sodium: 54mg sodium
- Fiber: 1g fiber)
- Total Carbohydrate: 6g carbohydrate (4g sugars
- Cholesterol: 2mg cholesterol

- Protein: 3g protein.
- Total Fat: 6g fat (1g saturated fat)

39. Eggnog Creams

Serving: 2-1/2 dozen. | Prep: 45mins | Cook: 0mins | Ready in:

Ingredients

- 3-1/2 cups white baking chips, divided
- 1/2 cup butter, softened
- 3 ounces cream cheese, softened
- 2 tablespoons dark rum
- 1/4 teaspoon vanilla extract
- 2 tablespoons shortening
- Ground nutmeg, optional

Direction

- Melt 1 1/2 cups baking chips in microwave; mix till smooth. Cream the cream cheese and butter till smooth in a small bowl. Add vanilla and rum; beat melted chips in. Refrigerate for 1 hour till set, covered.
- Form mixture to 1-in. balls; put on waxed paper-lined baking sheet. Refrigerate till firm and a bit dry to touch for 2 hours.
- Melt leftover baking chips and shortening in microwave; mix till smooth. Dip the balls into mixture; let excess drip off. Put on baking sheet; sprinkle with nutmeg if desired.
- Refrigerate till set for 2 hours. Keep between waxed paper layers in airtight container in the fridge.

Nutrition Information

- Calories: 154 calories
- Total Fat: 11g fat (7g saturated fat)
- Sodium: 51mg sodium
- Fiber: 0 fiber)
- Total Carbohydrate: 12g carbohydrate (12g sugars

- Cholesterol: 15mg cholesterol
- Protein: 1g protein.

40. Favorite Dipped Pretzel Rods

Serving: 2-1/2 dozen. | Prep: 40mins | Cook: 15mins | Ready in:

Ingredients

- 1 package (14 ounces) caramels
- 3 to 4 tablespoons water
- 1-1/3 cups miniature semisweet chocolate chips
- 1 package (10 ounces) peanut butter chips
- 1 cup chopped pecans
- 1 package (12 ounces) pretzel rods

Direction

- Melt caramels in a heavy saucepan with water on low heat. Mix pecans and chips together in a big shallow bowl.
- Add to a 2-cup glass measuring cup with caramel mixture. Dip approximately 1/3 of each pretzel into the caramel mixture (in case mixture turns too thick for dipping, reheat it in the microwave). Let excess caramel drip off, then roll pretzels in the chip mixture. Put these pretzels on waxed paper until they are set. Keep in tightly sealed containers.

Nutrition Information

- Calories: 209 calories
- Protein: 4g protein. Diabetic Exchanges: 2 starch
- Total Fat: 9g fat (3g saturated fat)
- Sodium: 205mg sodium
- Fiber: 2g fiber)
- Total Carbohydrate: 29g carbohydrate (17g sugars
- Cholesterol: 1mg cholesterol

41. German Chocolate Pecan Truffles

Serving: 4 dozen. | Prep: 15mins | Cook: 10mins | Ready in:

Ingredients

- 8 ounces German sweet chocolate, chopped
- 1/2 cup plus 2 tablespoons heavy whipping cream
- 1 tablespoon light corn syrup
- 1 cup sweetened shredded coconut, toasted, divided
- 1 cup finely chopped toasted pecans, divided
- 1/4 teaspoon coconut extract
- 1/8 teaspoon salt

Direction

- Put chocolate in small bowl. Put corn syrup and cream to just a boil in small saucepan. Put on chocolate; let stand, don't mix, for 5 minutes. Whisk chocolate mixture till smooth. Mix salt, extract, 1/4 cup pecans and 1/4 cups coconut in. Cover; refrigerate till firm for minimum of 1 hour.
- Form chocolate mixture to 1-in. balls; roll in leftover pecans and coconut. Keep in airtight container in the fridge.

Nutrition Information

- Calories:
- Protein:
- Total Fat:
- Sodium:
- Fiber:
- Total Carbohydrate:
- Cholesterol:

42. Gianduja

Serving: about 3 pounds. | Prep: 20mins | Cook: 0mins | Ready in:

Ingredients

- 1-1/2 pounds shelled hazelnuts, skins removed
- 3/4 cup canola oil
- 1-1/2 pounds bittersweet chocolate, chopped
- 3 milk chocolate Toblerone candy bars (3.52 ounces each), chopped

Direction

- Use a foil to line an 8-inch square dish. Blend the oil and hazelnuts in a food processor until the mixture forms a paste, covered.
- Melt the bittersweet chocolate in a large saucepan. Add 2 1/4 cups of hazelnut mixture into the saucepan. Pour half of the mixture in a prepared dish. Store the dish inside the refrigerator until the mixture is firm.
- Melt the candy bars and add the remaining hazelnut mixture. Spread the mixture over the bittersweet layer and store inside the refrigerator until firm.
- Reheat remaining bittersweet mixture if necessary and pour it over the candy bar layer. Place it again inside the refrigerator and store until firm. Slice candy bars into 1-inch squares and place it in an airtight container. Keep refrigerated.

Nutrition Information

- Calories: 168 calories
- Sodium: 2mg sodium
- Fiber: 2g fiber)
- Total Carbohydrate: 10g carbohydrate (7g sugars
- Cholesterol: 1mg cholesterol
- Protein: 2g protein.
- Total Fat: 15g fat (4g saturated fat)

43. Gingerbread Caramels

Serving: about 2 pounds. | Prep: 10mins | Cook: 30mins | Ready in:

Ingredients

- 2 teaspoons butter
- 1/2 cup butter, cubed
- 2 cups packed brown sugar
- 1 can (14 ounces) sweetened condensed milk
- 2/3 cup dark molasses
- 1/3 cup dark corn syrup
- 3/4 teaspoon ground ginger
- 3/4 teaspoon ground allspice
- 1/2 teaspoon salt
- 1/4 teaspoon pepper
- 1 teaspoon vanilla extract

Direction

- Using foil, line a 9-inch square baking dish; butter foil with 2 teaspoons butter.
- Mix pepper, salt, allspice, ginger, corn syrup, molasses, milk, brown sugar and cubed butter in a big heavy saucepan. Cook and mix over medium heat until a candy thermometer registers 238° (soft-ball stage).
- Brush down the sides of the pan with a pastry brush dipped in water to get rid of sugar crystals. Cook and mix until thermometer registers 245° (firm-ball stage).
- Take off from heat; mix in vanilla. Put into buttered pan immediately (don't scrape saucepan). Let sit about 4 hours or overnight until firm. Chill for an hour.
- Take candy out of pan using foil; Take off the foil. Slice caramel into 1-inch squares with a buttered knife. Wrap in waxed paper individually; twist ends.
- To Prepare Ahead: Put wrapped caramels in an airtight container to store at room temperature.
- Freeze option: Put wrapped caramels in a freezer container and place in freezer. Defrost at room temperature.

Nutrition Information

- Calories:
- Protein:
- Total Fat:
- Sodium:
- Fiber:
- Total Carbohydrate:
- Cholesterol:

44. Halloween Layered Fudge

Serving: about 2 pounds. | Prep: 15mins | Cook: 0mins | Ready in:

Ingredients

- 1 teaspoon butter
- 2 cups (12 ounces) semisweet chocolate chips
- 1 can (14 ounces) sweetened condensed milk, divided
- 8 ounces white candy coating
- 1/4 teaspoon orange extract
- 1/8 teaspoon orange paste food coloring
- Candy corn, optional

Direction

- Use the foil to line the 8-inch square pan; butter the foil and put aside.
- In the microwave safe bowl, heat 1 cup of the milk and chocolate chips on high setting for half a minute; whisk. Repeat the process till the mixture becomes smooth. Add to the prepped pan. Refrigerate for 10 minutes.
- At the same time, in the microwavable bowl, melt the candy coating along with leftover milk; whisk till smooth. Whisk in the food coloring and extract. Spread on top of the chocolate layer. If you want, scatter with the candy corn.
- Refrigerate till firm or for 60 minutes. With foil, take the fudge out of pan. Chop into 1-inch square pieces.

Nutrition Information

- Calories: 64 calories
- Total Fat: 3g fat (2g saturated fat)
- Sodium: 8mg sodium
- Fiber: 0 fiber)
- Total Carbohydrate: 9g carbohydrate (9g sugars
- Cholesterol: 2mg cholesterol
- Protein: 1g protein. Diabetic Exchanges: 1/2 starch

45. Holiday Marshmallows

Serving: about 3 dozen. | Prep: 35mins | Cook: 10mins | Ready in:

Ingredients

- 2 teaspoons butter
- 1 package (3 ounces) strawberry gelatin
- 1/2 cup water
- 3/4 cup sugar
- 3 tablespoons light corn syrup
- Assorted sprinkles, confectioners' sugar, coarse colored sugar and/or nonpareils

Direction

- Use foil to line an 8-in. square pan and grease the foil lightly using 2 teaspoons butter; put aside.
- Combine gelatin and water in a small saucepan. Cook and stir on medium-low heat until the gelatin dissolves. Add sugar and corn syrup into the mixture; cook and stir till the sugar dissolves (do not boil).
- Transfer the mixture into a large bowl. Chill till it thickens slightly for about 30 minutes. On high speed, beat until mixture is thick and doubles in volume for about 10 minutes.

Spread it into the prepared pan. Refrigerate, covered, for 6 hours or overnight.
- Lift marshmallows out of the pan using foil. Slice into 1-1/4-in. squares or use cutters sprayed lightly with cooking spray to cut into shapes. Roll in garnishes if you wish. For storage, keep in an airtight container in a cool, dry place.

Nutrition Information

- Calories: 31 calories
- Protein: 0 protein. Diabetic Exchanges: 1/2 starch.
- Total Fat: 0 fat (0 saturated fat)
- Sodium: 8mg sodium
- Fiber: 0 fiber)
- Total Carbohydrate: 8g carbohydrate (7g sugars
- Cholesterol: 1mg cholesterol

46. Homemade Chocolate Easter Eggs

Serving: 20 | Prep: 25mins | Cook: 5mins | Ready in:

Ingredients

- 9 ounces 85% dark chocolate, chopped
- 1/4 cup heavy whipping cream
- 3 tablespoons unsalted butter
- 1 tablespoon rum
- 1/4 cup confectioners' sugar, or to taste
- 1/4 cup unsweetened cocoa powder, or as needed
- 1/4 cup coconut flakes, or as needed

Direction

- Put butter, cream and chocolate in top of double boiler above simmering water. Frequently mix, scraping sides down with rubber spatula to prevent scorching, for about 5 minutes till chocolate melts.
- Take off heat; mix rum in then confectioners' sugar. Briefly cool; cover. Cool till firm for about 5 hours in the fridge.
- Form chocolate mixture to oval eggs. Put coconut flakes and cocoa powder to different small bowls. Roll 1/2 chocolate eggs in cocoa powder and other 1/2 into coconut flakes. Put into fridge.

Nutrition Information

- Calories: 111 calories;
- Sodium: 3
- Total Carbohydrate: 10.1
- Cholesterol: 9
- Protein: 1.1
- Total Fat: 7.9

47. Homemade Holiday Marshmallows

Serving: about 9-1/2 dozen. | Prep: 35mins | Cook: 20mins | Ready in:

Ingredients

- 2 teaspoons butter
- 3 envelopes unflavored gelatin
- 1 cup cold water, divided
- 2 cups sugar
- 1 cup light corn syrup
- 1/8 teaspoon salt
- 1 teaspoon clear vanilla extract
- Optional toppings: melted chocolate, hot fudge and/or caramel ice cream topping
- Optional garnishes: baking cocoa, confectioners' sugar, crushed assorted candies, chopped nuts, colored sugars and/or sprinkles

Direction

- Line foil on 13x9-inch. pan; use butter to grease foil. Put aside.

- Sprinkle gelatin on 1/2 cup water in a big metal bowl; put aside. Put leftover water, salt, corn syrup and sugar together in a big heavy saucepan, and boil, occasionally mixing; cook without mixing till it reaches a soft-ball stage or candy thermometer reads 240°.
- Take off from heat; add to gelatin slowly. Beat on high speed for 15 minutes till volume doubles and is thick; beat in vanilla. Spread in prepped pan; cover. Stand for 6 hours – overnight at room temperature.
- Lift marshmallows from pan using foil; cut to 1-inch squares with a pizza cutter/knife coated in cooking spray. If desired, drizzle/dip marshmallows with toppings; as desired, coat with garnishes as you want. Keep in dry, cool place in an airtight container.

Nutrition Information

- Calories: 22 calories
- Total Carbohydrate: 6g carbohydrate (4g sugars
- Cholesterol: 0 cholesterol
- Protein: 0 protein.
- Total Fat: 0 fat (0 saturated fat)
- Sodium: 5mg sodium
- Fiber: 0 fiber)

48. Honey Caramels

Serving: about 1-1/2 pounds. | Prep: 25mins | Cook: 30mins | Ready in:

Ingredients

- 1 teaspoon plus 1/4 cup butter, divided
- 1 cup heavy whipping cream
- 1 cup honey
- 1/2 cup sugar
- 1 cup chopped walnuts
- 1 teaspoon vanilla extract

Direction

- Line foil in an 8-inch square pan then grease foil using a teaspoon of butter; set the pan aside.
- Mix the remaining butter, cream, sugar, and honey in a big heavy saucepan. On medium-low heat, cook and stir until an inserted candy thermometer registers 238 degrees.
- Wash down the sides of the pan to remove the sugar crystals using a pastry brush that is soaked in cold water. While constantly mixing, cook until the candy thermometer registers 255 degrees (hard-ball stage). Mix in vanilla and walnuts; reheat mixture to 255 degrees.
- Take off heat then move to the prepared pan, avoid scraping the saucepan. Let it sit for about 5hrs to overnight until firm.
- Lift the candy out of pan using the foil; get rid of the foil. Slice the candy into one-inch squares then individually wrap with waxed paper. Twist the ends of the paper.

Nutrition Information

- Calories:
- Cholesterol:
- Protein:
- Total Fat:
- Sodium:
- Fiber:
- Total Carbohydrate:

49. Jelly Bean Bark

Serving: 2 pounds. | Prep: 10mins | Cook: 5mins | Ready in:

Ingredients

- 1 tablespoon butter
- 1-1/4 pounds white candy coating, coarsely chopped
- 2 cups small jelly beans

Direction

- Using foil, line a 15x10x1-in. pan; grease foil with butter. Melt candy coating in a microwave; mix until smooth. Lather into lined and greased pan. Put jellybeans over, push down to adhere. Let sit until firm.
- Slice or crack bark into pieces. Put in an airtight container to store.

Nutrition Information

- Calories: 154 calories
- Total Carbohydrate: 27g carbohydrate (23g sugars
- Cholesterol: 1mg cholesterol
- Protein: 0 protein.
- Total Fat: 5g fat (5g saturated fat)
- Sodium: 10mg sodium
- Fiber: 0 fiber)

50. Jelly Bean Brittle

Serving: 2-1/2 pounds. | Prep: 10mins | Cook: 20mins | Ready in:

Ingredients

- 4 tablespoons butter, divided
- 2-1/2 cups small jelly beans
- 3 cups sugar
- 1 cup light corn syrup
- 1/2 cup water
- 1/2 teaspoon salt
- 2 teaspoons baking soda

Direction

- Line foil on 2 15x10x1-inch pans. Melt 1 tablespoon butter; brush on foil. Evenly sprinkle jellybeans over.
- Put water, corn syrup and sugar together in a big heavy saucepan and boil on medium heat, constantly mixing to melt sugar. Wash down pan's sides to remove sugar crystals using pastry brush dipped into water; cook without mixing on medium heat till it reaches a soft-ball stage or candy thermometer reads 240°. Mix in salt and leftover butter; cook, frequently mixing, till it reaches hard-crack stage or thermometer reads 300°.
- Take off from heat. Mix in baking soda; it'll foam. Put on jellybeans immediately; spread using buttered metal spatula. Fully cool.
- Break brittle to pieces; keep in airtight container between waxed paper layers.

Nutrition Information

- Calories: 300 calories
- Total Fat: 2g fat (1g saturated fat)
- Sodium: 229mg sodium
- Fiber: 0 fiber)
- Total Carbohydrate: 72g carbohydrate (65g sugars
- Cholesterol: 6mg cholesterol
- Protein: 0 protein.

51. Kahlua Truffles

Serving: 1-1/2 dozen. | Prep: 10mins | Cook: 10mins | Ready in:

Ingredients

- 1 cup (6 ounces) semisweet chocolate chips
- 1/4 cup butter, cubed
- 1 egg yolk, lightly beaten
- 3 tablespoons Kahlua (coffee liqueur)
- 2 tablespoons cream cheese, softened
- 2/3 cup salted roasted almonds or pistachios, chopped

Direction

- Melt butter and chocolate chips in the top of a metal bowl over simmering water or a double boiler; stir well until smooth.
- Whisk a small amount of the hot mixture into the egg yolk in a small bowl; bring all back to the double boiler and whisk constantly. Over

low heat, cook until the mixture reaches 160° while constantly whisking.
- Remove from the heat; stir in cream cheese and Kahlua until combined. Allow to cool to room temperature, occasionally stirring. Cover and chill until it's easy to shape, for 60 minutes.
- In a small bowl, put in almonds. Form the mixture into 1-in. balls; then roll in almonds. Cover and chill until firm, for about 2 hours. Keep in an airtight container in the fridge.

Nutrition Information

- Calories: 116 calories
- Total Carbohydrate: 9g carbohydrate (7g sugars
- Cholesterol: 19mg cholesterol
- Protein: 2g protein.
- Total Fat: 9g fat (4g saturated fat)
- Sodium: 53mg sodium
- Fiber: 1g fiber)

52. Lemon Bark

Serving: 1-3/4 pounds. | Prep: 5mins | Cook: 5mins | Ready in:

Ingredients

- 2 packages (10 to 12 ounces each) white baking chips
- 1 cup crushed hard lemon candies, divided

Direction

- Line foil on 15x10x1-inch pan; put aside. Melt baking chips in top of double boiler/metal bowl above barely simmering water; mix till smooth. Mix in 2/3 cup of crushed candies; spread in prepped pan. Sprinkle leftover candies over; cool. Refrigerate for 1 hour till set.
- Break to pieces; keep in airtight container.

Nutrition Information

- Calories: 122 calories
- Protein: 1g protein.
- Total Fat: 7g fat (4g saturated fat)
- Sodium: 20mg sodium
- Fiber: 0 fiber)
- Total Carbohydrate: 15g carbohydrate (14g sugars
- Cholesterol: 4mg cholesterol

53. Lemon Fudge

Serving: about 2 pounds. | Prep: 5mins | Cook: 15mins | Ready in:

Ingredients

- 1-1/2 teaspoons plus 6 tablespoons butter, divided
- 2 packages (10 to 12 ounces each) vanilla or white chips
- 2/3 cup sweetened condensed milk
- 2/3 cup marshmallow creme
- 1-1/2 teaspoons lemon extract

Direction

- Use foil to line a 9-inch square pan. Grease the foil using 1-1/2 teaspoons butter; put aside. Melt the remaining butter in a large saucepan over low heat. Add in the chips and milk; cook and stir until chips melt, for 10-12 minutes.
- Stir marshmallow crème and extract into the mix; cook and stir for another 3-4 minutes or till smooth. Transfer into the prepared pan. Chill till set.
- Use foil to lift the fudge out of pan. Throw foil; slice the fudge into squares. Keep in the refrigerator.

Nutrition Information

- Calories: 72 calories
- Sodium: 25mg sodium

- Fiber: 0 fiber)
- Total Carbohydrate: 8g carbohydrate (2g sugars
- Cholesterol: 6mg cholesterol
- Protein: 1g protein. Diabetic Exchanges: 1 fat
- Total Fat: 4g fat (3g saturated fat)

- Calories: 109 calories
- Sodium: 12mg sodium
- Fiber: 0 fiber)
- Total Carbohydrate: 20g carbohydrate (15g sugars
- Cholesterol: 7mg cholesterol
- Protein: 0 protein.
- Total Fat: 3g fat (2g saturated fat)

54. Marbled Orange Fudge

Serving: about 2-1/2 pounds. | Prep: 30mins | Cook: 0mins | Ready in:

Ingredients

- 1-1/2 teaspoons plus 3/4 cup butter, divided
- 3 cups sugar
- 3/4 cup heavy whipping cream
- 1 package white baking chips (10 to 12 ounces)
- 1 jar (7 ounces) marshmallow creme
- 3 teaspoons orange extract
- 12 drops yellow food coloring
- 5 drops red food coloring
- green shoestring licorice, optional

Direction

- Use 1-1/2 teaspoons butter to grease a 13x9-inch baking pan and put aside.
- Mix together remaining butter, cream and sugar in a big heavy saucepan. Over low heat, cook while stirring to dissolve sugar. Boil the mixture and cook while stirring for 4 minutes. Take away from the heat; mix in marshmallow crème and chips until the mixture is smooth.
- Reserve a cup of mixture. Put food coloring and orange extract into the remaining mixture; whisk until combined. Transfer to greased pan. Scoop saved marshmallow mixture by tablespoonfuls and place on top; swirl by cutting through with a knife. Chill while covered till set. Slice into triangular pieces and use licorice to decorate (optional).

Nutrition Information

55. Marshmallow Easter Eggs

Serving: 3 dozen. | Prep: 45mins | Cook: 15mins | Ready in:

Ingredients

- 25 cups all-purpose flour (about 8 pounds)
- 1 large egg
- 2 tablespoons unflavored gelatin
- 1/2 cup cold water
- 2 cups sugar
- 1 cup light corn syrup, divided
- 3/4 cup hot water
- 2 teaspoons vanilla extract
- 1 pound dark chocolate candy coating, melted
- 2 ounces white candy coating, melted

Direction

- In each of the 3 13x9-inch pans, spread 7 cups flour then 4 cups flour in 9-inch square pan. In mild bleach solution, 1-quart warm water to 1 teaspoon chlorine bleach, wash egg carefully; dry. To make an impression, press washed egg halfway in flour; repeat 35 times then put aside.
- Sprinkle gelatin on cold water in a small bowl; put aside. Put hot water, 1/2 cup corn syrup and sugar together in a big saucepan and boil on medium heat, constantly mixing, till it gets soft-ball stage or candy thermometer reads 238°. Take off from heat; mix in leftover corn syrup.
- Put in a big bowl. Put the reserved gelatin, a tablespoon at one time, whipping at high

speed for 10 minutes, until candy has cool down to lukewarm and turn thick. Whip vanilla in.
- In egg depressions, scoop lukewarm gelatin mixture; dust with flour. Stand till set for 3-4 hours.
- Brush extra flour off marshmallow eggs; plunge each into chocolate candy coating. Put on waxed paper, flat side down; stand till set. Put white candy coating into a resealable, heavy-duty plastic bag; cut hole in 1 corner then drizzle on eggs.

Nutrition Information

- Calories: 462 calories
- Total Fat: 5g fat (4g saturated fat)
- Sodium: 15mg sodium
- Fiber: 3g fiber)
- Total Carbohydrate: 94g carbohydrate (26g sugars
- Cholesterol: 6mg cholesterol
- Protein: 10g protein.

56. Mine Run Candy

Serving: 2 pounds. | Prep: 20mins | Cook: 25mins | Ready in:

Ingredients

- 2 teaspoons butter
- 1 cup sugar
- 1 cup dark corn syrup
- 1 tablespoon vinegar
- 1 tablespoon baking soda
- 1 package (11-1/2 ounces) milk chocolate chips
- 1 tablespoon shortening

Direction

- Use foil to line a 13-inch x 9-inch pan and butter the foil; put aside. Mix the vinegar, corn syrup and sugar in a big heavy saucepan.

Cook and mix over medium heat until sugar dissolves. Heat up to a boil. Cook, without stirring, until a candy thermometer registers 300° (hard-crack stage).
- Take off from the heat; mix in baking soda. Put into lined pan immediately. Don't spread candy. Let cool. Take candy out of pan with foil. Remove foil gently; Crack candy into pieces.
- Melt chips with shortening in a microwave; mix until smooth. Plunge candies in the chocolate mixture, let excess drip off. Put on waxed paper; let sit until firm. Put in an airtight container to store.

Nutrition Information

- Calories: 223 calories
- Fiber: 1g fiber)
- Total Carbohydrate: 41g carbohydrate (28g sugars
- Cholesterol: 5mg cholesterol
- Protein: 2g protein.
- Total Fat: 7g fat (3g saturated fat)
- Sodium: 284mg sodium

57. Mini S'mores

Serving: about 4 dozen. | Prep: 50mins | Cook: 5mins | Ready in:

Ingredients

- 2 cups milk chocolate chips
- 1/2 cup heavy whipping cream
- 1 package (14.4 ounces) graham crackers, quartered
- 1 cup marshmallow creme
- 2 cartons (7 ounces each) milk chocolate for dipping
- 4 ounces white candy coating, melted, optional

Direction

- In a small bowl, put chocolate chips. Heat up cream just to a boil in a small saucepan. Put on top of chocolate; mix using a whisk until smooth. Let cool to room temperature about 10 minutes or until mixture has a spreading consistency.
- Smear chocolate mixture on top of half of the graham crackers. Scatter marshmallow creme evenly on top of leftover graham crackers; put over chocolate-covered crackers, pushing to attach.
- Melt dipping chocolate following package instructions. Plunge each s'more into dipping chocolate halfway; let excess drip off. Put on waxed paper-lined baking trays; let sit until dipping chocolate is firm.
- Sprinkle tops with melted white candy coating if needed; let sit until firm. Put in an airtight container to store in the fridge.

Nutrition Information

- Calories: 145 calories
- Sodium: 66mg sodium
- Fiber: 1g fiber)
- Total Carbohydrate: 19g carbohydrate (13g sugars
- Cholesterol: 5mg cholesterol
- Protein: 2g protein.
- Total Fat: 7g fat (4g saturated fat)

58. Nana's Rocky Road Fudge

Serving: about 2-1/2 pounds. | Prep: 15mins | Cook: 5mins | Ready in:

Ingredients

- 1-1/2 teaspoons plus 1 tablespoon butter, divided
- 2 cups (12 ounces) semisweet chocolate chips
- 1 can (14 ounces) sweetened condensed milk
- 2 cups salted peanuts
- 1 package (10-1/2 ounces) miniature marshmallows

Direction

- Use an aluminum foil to line a 13x9-inch baking pan then use 1 1/2 teaspoons of butter to grease the aluminum foil; put it aside.
- Mix the milk, remaining butter and chocolate chips together in a big saucepan. Let the mixture cook over medium heat setting while stirring it until it is smooth in consistency. Remove the pan away from the heat then add in the peanuts and mix well. In a big bowl, put in the marshmallows followed by the prepared chocolate mixture and mix everything together thoroughly. Distribute the marshmallow mixture evenly onto the prepared baking pan and keep it in the fridge until the mixture becomes firm.
- Use the aluminum foil lining to remove the fudge out of the baking pan. Slice the fudge into square shapes that are 1 1/2 inches in size.

Nutrition Information

- Calories: 153 calories
- Total Fat: 8g fat (4g saturated fat)
- Sodium: 39mg sodium
- Fiber: 1g fiber)
- Total Carbohydrate: 20g carbohydrate (16g sugars
- Cholesterol: 4mg cholesterol
- Protein: 3g protein.

59. Neapolitan Fudge

Serving: about 6-1/2 pounds. | Prep: 35mins | Cook: 0mins | Ready in:

Ingredients

- 1-1/2 teaspoons butter
- 1 package (8 ounces) cream cheese, softened
- 3 cups confectioners' sugar

- 16 ounces milk chocolate, melted and cooled
- VANILLA LAYER:
- 1 package (8 ounces) cream cheese, softened
- 3 cups confectioners' sugar
- 16 ounces white baking chocolate, melted and cooled
- 1 tablespoon vanilla extract
- RASPBERRY LAYER:
- 1 package (8 ounces) cream cheese, softened
- 3 cups confectioners' sugar
- 16 ounces white baking chocolate, melted and cooled
- 1 tablespoon raspberry extract
- 8 to 10 drops red food coloring, optional

Direction

- Using foil, line a 13x9-in. pan, use butter to grease foil. Whisk cream cheese in a large bowl until fluffy. Whisk in confectioners' sugar gradually. Whisk in melted milk chocolate. Transfer into lined pan and spread. Keep in the fridge for 10 minutes.
- To prepare vanilla layer, whisk cream cheese until fluffy in large bowl. Whisk in confectioners' sugar gradually. Whisk in vanilla and melted white chocolate. Place and spread on top of chocolate layer. Keep in the fridge for 10 minutes.
- To prepare raspberry layer, whisk cream cheese until fluffy in a large bowl. Whisk in confectioners' sugar gradually. Whisk in raspberry extract and melted white chocolate. Tint with food coloring if preferred. Place over top and spread. Keep in the fridge with a cover for at least 8 hours or overnight.
- Lift fudge out of pan with foil. Get rid of foil; cut fudge into 1-in. squares. Keep squares between layers of waxed paper in an airtight container in the fridge.

Nutrition Information

- Calories: 114 calories
- Sodium: 20mg sodium
- Fiber: 0 fiber)
- Total Carbohydrate: 16g carbohydrate (15g sugars
- Cholesterol: 7mg cholesterol
- Protein: 1g protein.
- Total Fat: 5g fat (3g saturated fat)

60. Nut Fruit Bark

Serving: 1-1/2 pounds. | Prep: 15mins | Cook: 0mins | Ready in:

Ingredients

- 1 pound dark chocolate, coarsely chopped
- 1 teaspoon instant espresso powder
- 1/2 cup dried cherries or blueberries, divided
- 1/2 cup macadamia nuts, chopped and divided
- 1/2 cup chopped cashews, divided
- 1/2 teaspoon coarse sea salt, optional

Direction

- Line a 15x10x1-inch baking pan's sides and bottom with parchment paper; grease the paper and put aside.
- Liquefy chocolate in a metal bowl over hot water or double boiler; mix till smooth. Mix in half of the cherries and nuts and espresso powder. Spread into prepped pan; put leftover cherries and nuts on top; pan will not be full. Scatter salt if preferred. Chill for 15 minutes till firm.
- Shatter into pieces. Keep in an airtight container.

Nutrition Information

- Calories: 147 calories
- Fiber: 2g fiber)
- Total Carbohydrate: 14g carbohydrate (11g sugars
- Cholesterol: 1mg cholesterol
- Protein: 2g protein.

- Total Fat: 10g fat (5g saturated fat)
- Sodium: 26mg sodium

61. Nutty Chocolate Truffles

Serving: 4 dozen. | Prep: 10mins | Cook: 0mins | Ready in:

Ingredients

- 1 package (8 ounces) cream cheese, softened
- 1 cup (6 ounces) semisweet chocolate chips, melted and cooled
- 1 cup crushed vanilla wafers (about 30 wafers)
- 1/4 cup strawberry preserves
- 1-1/4 cups chopped almonds, toasted

Direction

- Beat cream cheese till smooth in big bowl; beat strawberry preserves, wafer crumbs and chocolate in. Cover; refrigerate till easy to handle or for 1 hour minimum.
- Form to 1-in. balls; roll into almonds. Keep in the fridge.

Nutrition Information

- Calories: 68 calories
- Protein: 1g protein. Diabetic Exchanges: 1 fat
- Total Fat: 5g fat (2g saturated fat)
- Sodium: 22mg sodium
- Fiber: 1g fiber)
- Total Carbohydrate: 6g carbohydrate (4g sugars
- Cholesterol: 5mg cholesterol

62. Old Fashioned Lollipops

Serving: 1 dozen. | Prep: 5mins | Cook: 30mins | Ready in:

Ingredients

- 1 cup light corn syrup
- 2/3 cup sugar
- 1-1/2 teaspoons lemon, apple or cherry flavoring
- 1/8 teaspoon yellow, green or red liquid food coloring

Direction

- In hard candy molds, add lollipop sticks or arrange sticks 3-inch apart on greased foil-lined baking sheets; put aside.
- Mix corn syrup and sugar in a heavy saucepan. Heat up to a boil over medium heat, mixing from time to time. Cook for 3 minutes, covered, until sugar crystals are dissolved. Cook over medium-high heat, uncovered, without mixing, until a candy thermometer registers 300° (hard-crack stage).
- Take off from the heat; mix in food coloring and flavoring, maintain a certain distance from mixture as the smell is very strong. Transfer to prepared molds or pour free-form over ends of lollipop sticks on baking sheets right away. Let cool prior to removing.

Nutrition Information

- Calories: 123 calories
- Protein: 0 protein.
- Total Fat: 0 fat (0 saturated fat)
- Sodium: 33mg sodium
- Fiber: 0 fiber)
- Total Carbohydrate: 32g carbohydrate (25g sugars
- Cholesterol: 0 cholesterol

63. Orange Gumdrops

Serving: about 6 dozen. | Prep: 10mins | Cook: 10mins | Ready in:

Ingredients

- 1 teaspoon plus 1 tablespoon butter, softened, divided
- 1 cup sugar
- 1 cup light corn syrup
- 3/4 cup water
- 1 package (1-3/4 ounces) powdered fruit pectin
- 1/2 teaspoon baking soda
- 1-1/2 teaspoons orange extract
- 1 teaspoon grated orange zest
- 4 drops yellow food coloring
- 1 drop red food coloring
- Additional sugar, optional

Direction

- Line foil on sides and bottom of 9x5-inch loaf pan. Use 1 teaspoon butter to grease foil; put aside.
- Use leftover butter to grease sides and bottom of a big heavy saucepan; add corn syrup and sugar. Mix and cook for 9 minutes on medium heat till it boils. Cook on medium high heat, occasionally mixing, till it reaches soft-crack stage, a candy thermometer reads 280°.
- Meanwhile, put baking soda, pectin and water together in another big saucepan, it'll slightly foam; mix and cook for 2 minutes on high heat till it boils. Take off from heat; put aside.
- Take corn syrup mixture off heat when it reaches soft crack stage or 280°. Set pectin mixture back on medium high heat; cook till it starts to simmer. Slowly and carefully scoop corn syrup into pectin mixture in very thin stream, constantly mixing; mix and cook for 1 more minute.
- Take off from heat; mix in food coloring, zest and extract. Put in prepped pan; stand for 2 hours till firm. Cut to squares; if desired, roll in extra sugar.

Nutrition Information

- Calories: 30 calories
- Protein: 0 protein.
- Total Fat: 0 fat (0 saturated fat)
- Sodium: 16mg sodium
- Fiber: 0 fiber)
- Total Carbohydrate: 7g carbohydrate (6g sugars
- Cholesterol: 1mg cholesterol

64. Orange Jelly Candies

Serving: 81 pieces. | Prep: 15mins | Cook: 10mins | Ready in:

Ingredients

- 2 teaspoons butter
- 1 package (1-3/4 ounces) powdered fruit pectin
- 1/2 teaspoon baking soda
- 3/4 cup water
- 1 cup sugar
- 1 cup light corn syrup
- 1/8 teaspoon orange oil
- 5 drops each red and yellow food coloring
- Additional sugar

Direction

- Use 2 teaspoons butter to butter 9-inch square pan; put aside. Mix water, baking soda and pectin in a big saucepan; it'll be foamy. Mix corn syrup and sugar in another saucepan. Boil both mixtures; cook for 4 minutes till sugar mixture reaches a full rolling boil and pectin mixture slightly thins. Put pectin mixture in boiling sugar mixture slowly, constantly mixing; boil, constantly mixing, for 1 minute.
- Take off from heat; mix in food coloring and orange oil. Put in prepped pan immediately; stand for 3 hours till set at room temperature.
- Sprinkle sugar on waxed paper; invert pan onto sugar. Cut candy to 1-inch squares with knife dipped into warm water; roll in extra sugar. Put onto a wire rack; stand at room

temperature, with no cover, overnight. Keep in airtight container.

Nutrition Information

- Calories: 22 calories
- Fiber: 0 fiber)
- Total Carbohydrate: 6g carbohydrate (4g sugars
- Cholesterol: 0 cholesterol
- Protein: 0 protein. Diabetic Exchanges: 1/2 starch.
- Total Fat: 0 fat (0 saturated fat)
- Sodium: 11mg sodium

65. Orange Truffles

Serving: about 4 dozen. | Prep: 20mins | Cook: 0mins | Ready in:

Ingredients

- 3 cups plus 2 tablespoons semisweet chocolate chips, divided
- 2/3 cup heavy whipping cream
- 2 tablespoons butter
- 1 teaspoon orange extract
- 2 tablespoon shortening
- 1/3 cup vanilla or white chips

Direction

- In food processor/blender, process 1 cup and 2 tbsp. chocolate chips till crushed for 30 seconds, covered. Heat butter and cream on high heat in microwave-safe bowl till nearly boiling for 30-90 seconds.
- Put extract and cream mixture slowly on chips in steady stream till smooth as processor/blender runs. Cover; refrigerate till firm for 20-30 minutes. Roll to 1-in. balls. Heat the leftover chocolate chips and shortening on high heat for 45 seconds in a microwave-safe bowl. Stir. Microwave until melted for 10-20 seconds. Mix till smooth. Dip truffles in; transfer to waxed paper to harden.
- Heat vanilla chips for 10 seconds at 70% power in another microwave-safe bowl; mix. Microwave till melted in 5-sec intervals; mix till smooth. Put in pastry/plastic bag. Cut hole in corner of the bag; drizzle on truffles.

Nutrition Information

- Calories: 79 calories
- Total Carbohydrate: 8g carbohydrate (6g sugars
- Cholesterol: 6mg cholesterol
- Protein: 1g protein.
- Total Fat: 6g fat (3g saturated fat)
- Sodium: 8mg sodium
- Fiber: 1g fiber)

66. Pastel Almond Bark

Serving: about 5 dozen. | Prep: 10mins | Cook: 5mins | Ready in:

Ingredients

- 1-1/2 pounds white candy coating, coarsely chopped
- 2 cups pastel miniature marshmallows
- 2 cups Froot Loops
- 1 cup chopped pecans
- 1 cup sweetened shredded coconut

Direction

- Melt candy coating in a microwave-safe bowl; mix until smooth. Mix in the coconut, pecans, cereal and marshmallows.
- On waxed paper, drop the mixture by tablespoonfuls. Allow to cool. Keep at room temperature in an airtight container.

Nutrition Information

- Calories: 91 calories
- Total Carbohydrate: 11g carbohydrate (10g sugars
- Cholesterol: 0 cholesterol
- Protein: 0 protein.
- Total Fat: 5g fat (4g saturated fat)
- Sodium: 10mg sodium
- Fiber: 0 fiber)

67. Peanut Butter Coconut Balls

Serving: about 7 dozen. | Prep: 45mins | Cook: 0mins | Ready in:

Ingredients

- 1 cup butter, softened
- 1 cup crunchy peanut butter
- 2 tablespoons vanilla extract
- 3-1/2 cups confectioners' sugar
- 2 cups graham cracker crumbs
- 2 cups chopped walnuts
- 1-1/3 cups sweetened shredded coconut
- 2-1/2 cups (15 ounces) semisweet chocolate chips
- 4 teaspoons shortening
- Chopped nuts or sprinkles

Direction

- Beat the peanut butter and butter in a big bowl until light and fluffy. Whip in vanilla. Put in confectioners' sugar gradually and stir well. Mix in the coconut, walnuts and cracker crumbs. Roll into 1-inch balls. Put on baking trays; cover and chill for no less than 1 hour.
- Melt shortening with chocolate chips in a microwave; mix until smooth.
- Plunge balls into melted chocolate; let excess drip off. Toss in nuts or sprinkles. Put on waxed paper until harden. Put in an airtight container to store in the fridge.

Nutrition Information

- Calories: 120 calories
- Total Carbohydrate: 12g carbohydrate (9g sugars
- Cholesterol: 6mg cholesterol
- Protein: 2g protein. Diabetic Exchanges: 1 starch
- Total Fat: 8g fat (3g saturated fat)
- Sodium: 55mg sodium
- Fiber: 1g fiber)

68. Peanut Butter Easter Eggs

Serving: 16 | Prep: 15mins | Cook: | Ready in:

Ingredients

- 1 (16 ounce) package confectioners' sugar
- 1 cup creamy peanut butter
- 1/4 cup butter
- 1 tablespoon milk
- 8 (1 ounce) squares semi-sweet chocolate
- 1 tablespoon shortening

Direction

- In a mixing bowl, mix the butter, peanut butter, confectioners' sugar and milk (if necessary, for the moisture) till blended. Form the mixture into two half-pound eggs/form a bunch of smaller eggs. Place the eggs in freezer for 60 minutes.
- Meanwhile, chop the semi-sweet chocolate to small pieces and add in top of the double boiler along with the shortening. Melt on medium heat, whisking often, till smooth. Stick the long-tined fork in top of each peanut butter eggs, dip into the melted chocolate to cover then drain on the waxed paper. Once become set and cooled, decorate the eggs the way you desire.

Nutrition Information

- Calories: 307 calories;

- Total Fat: 16.3
- Sodium: 95
- Total Carbohydrate: 39.1
- Cholesterol: 8
- Protein: 5.1

69. Peanut Butter Eggs

Serving: about 5-1/2 dozen. | Prep: 45mins | Cook: 0mins | Ready in:

Ingredients

- 1 package (8 ounces) cream cheese, softened
- 1/2 cup butter, softened
- 1 jar (17.3 ounces) creamy peanut butter
- 1 teaspoon vanilla extract
- 1 package (2 pounds) confectioners' sugar
- 2 cups sweetened shredded coconut, optional
- 6 cups (36 ounces) semisweet chocolate chips
- 1/3 cup shortening

Direction

- Beat vanilla, peanut butter, butter and cream cheese till smooth in a big bowl; beat in sugar. If desired, mix in coconut. Shape rounded tablespoonfuls to egg shapes; put on waxed paper-lined baking sheets and chill for 30 minutes.
- Melt shortening and chocolate chips in microwave-safe bowl/heavy saucepan; mix till smooth. Dip eggs till coated; put on waxed paper to set.
- Extra decorative eggs: In small plastic bag, put 1/4 cup melted chocolate; cut 1 hole in corner of bag. Pipe chocolate on tops of eggs; keep in refrigerator.

Nutrition Information

- Calories: 204 calories
- Protein: 3g protein.
- Total Fat: 12g fat (5g saturated fat)

- Sodium: 61mg sodium
- Fiber: 1g fiber)
- Total Carbohydrate: 25g carbohydrate (22g sugars
- Cholesterol: 7mg cholesterol

70. Peanut Butter And Marshmallow Chocolate Eggs

Serving: 1-1/2 dozen. | Prep: 35mins | Cook: 0mins | Ready in:

Ingredients

- 6 tablespoons butter, softened
- 1/4 cup creamy peanut butter
- 1/4 cup marshmallow creme
- 1-3/4 cups confectioners' sugar
- 3/4 pound milk chocolate candy coating, coarsely chopped
- 2 teaspoons shortening
- Colored sprinkles, optional

Direction

- Cream marshmallow cream, peanut butter and butter till smooth in a small bowl; beat in confectioners' sugar slowly. Drop on wax paper-lined baking sheet by level tablespoonfuls; shape to egg shapes and freeze for 10 minutes.
- Melt shortening and candy coating in a microwave; mix till smooth. In candy coating, dip eggs; let extra drip off. Put back on baking sheet; if desired, decorate with sprinkles immediately. Stand till set; keep in an airtight container.

Nutrition Information

- Calories: 413 calories
- Cholesterol: 21mg cholesterol
- Protein: 3g protein.
- Total Fat: 23g fat (15g saturated fat)

- Sodium: 113mg sodium
- Fiber: 1g fiber
- Total Carbohydrate: 52g carbohydrate (48g sugars

71. Pineapple Coconut Snowballs

Serving: about 2 dozen. | Prep: 20mins | Cook: 0mins | Ready in:

Ingredients

- 1 package (8 ounces) cream cheese, softened
- 1 can (8 ounces) crushed pineapple, well drained
- 2-1/2 cups sweetened shredded coconut

Direction

- Beat pineapple and cream cheese till combined in a small bowl; cover. Refrigerate it for 30 minutes.
- Roll to 1-inch balls then roll in coconut and refrigerate for 6 hours – overnight.

Nutrition Information

- Calories: 67 calories
- Protein: 2g protein. Diabetic Exchanges: 1 fat
- Total Fat: 5g fat (5g saturated fat)
- Sodium: 55mg sodium
- Fiber: 1g fiber
- Total Carbohydrate: 4g carbohydrate (0 sugars
- Cholesterol: 1mg cholesterol

72. Pretzel Bark Candy

Serving: about 2 pounds. | Prep: 10mins | Cook: 0mins | Ready in:

Ingredients

- 1 pound milk chocolate candy coating, chopped
- 1 pound white candy coating, chopped
- 2 tablespoons creamy peanut butter
- 2 cups coarsely chopped pretzel sticks

Direction

- Use foil to line a 15x10x1-in. pan. In a large microwave-safe bowl, melt peanut butter and candy coatings; mix until smooth. Mix in pretzels.
- Layer evenly into the lined pan. Chill in refrigerator until firm. Crush into pieces.

Nutrition Information

- @type: NutritionInformation

73. Salted Soft Caramels

Serving: 2-1/2 dozen. | Prep: 10mins | Cook: 20mins | Ready in:

Ingredients

- 1/2 cup heavy whipping cream
- 2 tablespoons plus 1-1/2 teaspoons butter
- 1/4 teaspoon kosher salt
- 3/4 cup sugar
- 2 tablespoons water
- 2 tablespoons light corn syrup
- Smoked or kosher salt

Direction

- On a baking sheet, place 30 paper or foil candy cups. Use cooking spray to spritz each cup; put aside. Bring salt, butter, cream to a boil in a small heavy saucepan; keep warm.
- Mix corn syrup, water, sugar in a large heavy saucepan; cook till sugar is dissolved, stirring sometimes. Bring to a boil; cook without stirring for 4 minutes till the mixture becomes golden amber.

- Stir the cream mixture in slowly. Cook and stir on medium heat till a candy thermometer reaches 247 degrees.
- Get the saucepan off heat. Transfer the mixture into the prepared cup liners (remember not to scrape the saucepan). Top with salt. Allow the mixture to sit for 2 hours till firm.

Nutrition Information

- Calories: 45 calories
- Cholesterol: 8mg cholesterol
- Protein: 0 protein.
- Total Fat: 2g fat (2g saturated fat)
- Sodium: 25mg sodium
- Fiber: 0 fiber)
- Total Carbohydrate: 6g carbohydrate (5g sugars

74. Semiformal Evening Truffles

Serving: about 3 dozen. | Prep: 30mins | Cook: 0mins | Ready in:

Ingredients

- 4 cups (24 ounces) semisweet chocolate chips
- 1 package (8 ounces) cream cheese, softened
- 3 tablespoons instant coffee granules
- 2 tablespoons water
- 1 cup sweetened shredded coconut, finely chopped
- 1/2 cup chocolate sprinkles

Direction

- Melt chocolate chips in a big microwave-safe bowl. Add water, coffee granules and cream cheese; beat till smooth. Cover; refrigerate, mixing every 15 minutes, till thicken for 45-60 minutes.
- Form to 3/4-inch balls; roll in sprinkles/coconut. Keep in refrigerator in an airtight container.

Nutrition Information

- Calories: 124 calories
- Total Fat: 8g fat (5g saturated fat)
- Sodium: 25mg sodium
- Fiber: 1g fiber)
- Total Carbohydrate: 14g carbohydrate (11g sugars
- Cholesterol: 6mg cholesterol
- Protein: 1g protein. Diabetic Exchanges: 1-1/2 fat

75. Shamrock Toffee Fudge

Serving: about 2-1/4 pounds. | Prep: 30mins | Cook: 0mins | Ready in:

Ingredients

- 1 can (14 ounces) sweetened condensed milk
- 2 cups vanilla or white chips
- 1 cup milk chocolate chips
- 1 tablespoon butter
- Dash salt
- 3/4 cup chocolate-covered English toffee bits
- 1/8 teaspoon rum extract
- 1 cup vanilla frosting
- Green food coloring

Direction

- Using foil, line a 9-in. square pan and grease the foil; put aside. Mix the chips and milk in a big saucepan. Cook and mix on low heat until chips are melted. Put in the salt and butter; mix until smoothened. Take off from the heat; mix in extract and toffee bits. Put into lined and greased pan. Chill for 2 hours, covered, until set.
- Take fudge out of pan with foil; tear off foil gently. Slice fudge into 1-inch squares. Put the frosting in a small resealable plastic bag; dye with food coloring. Snip a small hole in a corner of bag; pipe a shamrock over each square.

Nutrition Information

- Calories:
- Total Carbohydrate:
- Cholesterol:
- Protein:
- Total Fat:
- Sodium:
- Fiber:

76. Sugary Orange Peel

Serving: 5 cups. | Prep: 15mins | Cook: 02hours40mins | Ready in:

Ingredients

- 4 medium navel oranges
- 2 to 3 cups sugar, divided
- 1 cup water
- 1/2 teaspoon salt
- 1/2 cup semisweet chocolate chips, optional
- 2 teaspoons shortening, optional

Direction

- Score peel from each orange to quarters with a knife; remove peel and white pith attached with fingers. Put peel in a saucepan and submerge in water; boil for 30 minutes, with no cover. Drain; repeat twice.
- Meanwhile, put salt, water and 1 cup sugar together in another saucepan and boil; mix and boil till sugar melts for 2 minutes. Drain peel; put into syrup. Boil; lower heat. Simmer, with no cover, occasionally mixing, till syrup is nearly all absorbed, about 50 to 60 minutes. Carefully watch to avoid scorching. Drain leftover syrup.
- Cool orange peel for 1 hour on foil-lined baking sheet in 1 layer; cut to 1/8-1/4-inch strips. On a 15x10x1-inch ungreased pan, sprinkle leftover sugar. Sprinkle strips on sugar; toss to cover. Stand, occasionally tossing, for 8 hours – overnight.
- Melt shortening and chocolate chips if desired; mix till smooth. Dip 1 end of every orange strip in chocolate; let excess drip off. Stand till set on waxed paper. Keeps for 3 weeks in airtight container.

Nutrition Information

- Calories: 90 calories
- Fiber: 1g fiber)
- Total Carbohydrate: 23g carbohydrate (22g sugars
- Cholesterol: 0 cholesterol
- Protein: 0 protein.
- Total Fat: 0 fat (0 saturated fat)
- Sodium: 59mg sodium

77. Three Chip English Toffee

Serving: about 2-1/2 pounds. | Prep: 15mins | Cook: 30mins | Ready in:

Ingredients

- 1/2 teaspoon plus 2 cups butter, divided
- 2 cups sugar
- 1 cup slivered almonds
- 1 cup milk chocolate chips
- 1 cup chopped walnuts
- 1/2 cup semisweet chocolate chips
- 1/2 cup white baking chips
- 1-1/2 teaspoons shortening

Direction

- Spread a half teaspoon of butter in a 15-in by 10-in by 1-in pan. On medium-low heat, boil the remaining butter and sugar together in a heavy pot while constantly stirring; cover and cook for 2-3 minutes.
- Remove the cover then put in almonds; cook and mix using a clean spoon until golden

brown and an inserted candy thermometer registers 300 degrees or at hard-crack stage.
- Transfer in the buttered pan but avoid scraping the sides of the pot; the top will be buttery. Cool for 1-2 minutes then spread milk chocolate chips on top; set aside for 1-2 minutes then slather the chocolate on top. Spread walnuts then gently press them down using the back of a spoon. Refrigerate for 10 minutes.
- Melt the semisweet chips in the microwave then mix until smooth; dribble on top of the walnuts. Place in the refrigerator for 10 minutes. Melt shortening and vanilla chips; mix until smooth then dribble on top of the walnuts. Cover then place in the refrigerator for 1-2 hours. Break into pieces.

Nutrition Information

- Calories: 397 calories
- Sodium: 197mg sodium
- Fiber: 1g fiber)
- Total Carbohydrate: 32g carbohydrate (26g sugars
- Cholesterol: 52mg cholesterol
- Protein: 4g protein.
- Total Fat: 30g fat (15g saturated fat)

78. Tiger Butter Bark Candy

Serving: about 1-1/4 pounds. | Prep: 10mins | Cook: 5mins | Ready in:

Ingredients

- 1 pound white candy coating, coarsely chopped
- 1/2 cup chunky peanut butter
- 1/2 cup semisweet chocolate chips
- 1/2 teaspoon shortening

Direction

- Use waxed or parchment paper to line a 15x10x1-inch pan. Microwave candy coating and peanut butter until melted and mix to smoothen. Transfer to the lined pan and spread out.
- Microwave shortening and chocolate chips to melt, mix until incorporated. Drizzle over the top, make swirling by running a knife through the mixture.
- Place in the refrigerator till firm. Break the bar into pieces.

Nutrition Information

- Calories: 179 calories
- Total Carbohydrate: 20g carbohydrate (18g sugars
- Cholesterol: 0 cholesterol
- Protein: 2g protein.
- Total Fat: 11g fat (7g saturated fat)
- Sodium: 32mg sodium
- Fiber: 1g fiber)

79. Truffle Cherries

Serving: about 2 dozen. | Prep: 20mins | Cook: 0mins | Ready in:

Ingredients

- 1/3 cup heavy whipping cream
- 2 tablespoons butter
- 2 tablespoons sugar
- 4 ounces semisweet chocolate, chopped
- 1 jar (8 ounces) maraschino cherries with stems, well drained
- COATING:
- 6 ounces semisweet chocolate, chopped
- 2 tablespoons shortening

Direction

- Bring butter, cream and sugar in a small saucepan to a boil, stirring continuously. Take

- off the heat; whisk in chocolate until melted. Chill, covered for a minimum of 4 hours or until easy to handle.
- Pat dry cherries using paper towels to very dry. Form a teaspoonful of chocolate mixture around each cherry, make a ball. Chill, covered, for 2 to 3 hours or until set.
- Microwave shortening and chocolate until melted; stir until smooth. Dip cherries into melted chocolate until coated, dripping off excess. Arrange on waxed paper to firm.

Nutrition Information

- Calories: 57 calories
- Total Fat: 4g fat (2g saturated fat)
- Sodium: 11mg sodium
- Fiber: 0 fiber)
- Total Carbohydrate: 6g carbohydrate (6g sugars
- Cholesterol: 7mg cholesterol
- Protein: 0 protein.

80. Truffle Eggs

Serving: 3 dozen. | Prep: 60mins | Cook: 0mins | Ready in:

Ingredients

- 1/4 cup heavy whipping cream
- 1 tablespoon butter
- 1/2 teaspoon light corn syrup
- 4 ounces semisweet chocolate, chopped
- 2 tablespoons Nutella
- 1 pound white candy coating disks
- 5 to 6 drops blue food coloring
- 1/2 to 1 teaspoon instant coffee granules
- Sweetened shredded coconut, toasted, optional

Direction

- Boil corn syrup, butter and cream in saucepan. Add chocolate; take off heat. Don't mix. Let it stand for 5 minutes. Whisk Nutella in till combined. Put into small bowl; cover. Refrigerate till thickened or for 45-60 minutes, mixing every 15 minutes.
- Form 1 heaping teaspoonful chocolate mixture to egg. Put onto parchment paper-lined baking sheet then repeat with leftover mixture. Refrigerate for 5-10 minutes till firm.
- Meanwhile, melt candy coating in microwave-safe bowl; mix till smooth. Mix food coloring in; dip the eggs in candy coating. Let excess drip off. Put back on baking sheet; sprinkle with coffee granules immediately. Let stand till set. Keep in airtight container in the fridge. If desired, serve eggs above nest of coconut.

Nutrition Information

- Calories: 97 calories
- Total Fat: 6g fat (4g saturated fat)
- Sodium: 4mg sodium
- Fiber: 0 fiber)
- Total Carbohydrate: 11g carbohydrate (11g sugars
- Cholesterol: 3mg cholesterol
- Protein: 0 protein. Diabetic Exchanges: 1 fat

81. White Chocolate Easter Egg Candies

Serving: About 2 dozen (1-1/2 pounds). | Prep: 25mins | Cook: 5mins | Ready in:

Ingredients

- 1 package (10 to 12 ounces) vanilla or white chips
- 3 ounces cream cheese, cubed
- 1 teaspoon water
- 1/2 teaspoon vanilla extract
- Colored sprinkles, colored sugar and/or jimmies

Direction

- Melt chips at 50% powder in microwave-safe bowl. Add vanilla, water and cream cheese; mix till blended. Chill for 1 hour till easy to handle. Shape to 1 1/4-inch eggs quickly; roll in jimmies/colored sugar/sprinkles. Keep in refrigerator in airtight container.

Nutrition Information

- Calories: 76 calories
- Fiber: 0 fiber)
- Total Carbohydrate: 7g carbohydrate (7g sugars
- Cholesterol: 6mg cholesterol
- Protein: 1g protein.
- Total Fat: 5g fat (3g saturated fat)
- Sodium: 22mg sodium

82. White Chocolate Easter Eggs

Serving: about 4 dozen. | Prep: 25mins | Cook: 0mins | Ready in:

Ingredients

- 1/2 cup butter, cubed
- 3 cups confectioners' sugar
- 2/3 cup sweetened condensed milk
- 1 teaspoon vanilla extract
- 2 cups finely chopped pecans
- 1 pound white candy coating, melted
- Gel food coloring, optional

Direction

- Melt butter in a large saucepan. Mix in the vanilla, milk, and confectioners' sugar until smooth. Mix in pecans. Put into a bowl. Refrigerate while covered for 2 hours or until easy to work with. Drop onto the baking sheets that are lined with waxed papers by level tablespoonfuls. Roll into egg shapes. Refrigerate them while covered overnight.
- Dip the eggs into the candy coating. Transfer onto the waxed paper until set. Dip a crumpled, small ball of waxed paper into food coloring to create a speckled look. Press the waxed paper onto a paper plate gently to eliminate any excess food coloring, and then press the color gently onto eggs. Repeat if necessary. Use a paper towel to blot the eggs.

Nutrition Information

- Calories: 144 calories
- Protein: 1g protein.
- Total Fat: 9g fat (4g saturated fat)
- Sodium: 25mg sodium
- Fiber: 0 fiber)
- Total Carbohydrate: 17g carbohydrate (16g sugars
- Cholesterol: 7mg cholesterol

Chapter 2: Halloween Candy Recipes

***

83. Black Widow Bites

Serving: 1 dozen. | Prep: 20mins | Cook: 5mins | Ready in:

Ingredients

- Black shoestring licorice
- 12 grape Jujubes
- 1 cup vanilla or white chips
- 24 red nonpareils
- 12 chocolate wafers

Direction

- Cut licorice to 96 1/2-inch long pieces; poke 1 licorice piece approximately 1/8-inch into candy using a toothpick. Repeat 7 times to create 8 spider legs; repeat with leftover candy and licorice pieces.
- Melt chips in a heavy saucepan/microwave; mix till smooth. Put into a resealable, heavy-duty plastic bag; snip off a small hole from corner of bag. On 1 candy, pipe 2 small dots; put 1 nonpareil immediately on each dot to make eyes. Repeat with leftover candies.
- On each chocolate wafer, pipe a web; pipe melted vanilla chips dot on bottom of spider. Attach to wafer.

Nutrition Information

- Calories:
- Total Carbohydrate:
- Cholesterol:
- Protein:
- Total Fat:
- Sodium:
- Fiber:

84. Bloodshot Eyeballs

Serving: 2 dozen. | Prep: 35mins | Cook: 0mins | Ready in:

Ingredients

- 2 cups confectioners' sugar, divided
- 1/2 cup creamy peanut butter
- 3 tablespoons butter, softened
- 1/2 pound white candy coating, coarsely chopped
- 24 brown Reese's pieces or milk chocolate M&M's
- 1 tablespoon water
- 1/4 to 1/2 teaspoon red food coloring

Direction

- Mix butter, peanut butter and 1 cup confectioners' sugar in a small bowl. Form to 1-inch balls; put on wax paper-lined pan and chill till firm for 30 minutes.
- Melt white candy coating in a microwave; mix till smooth. Plunge the balls in coating; let extra drip off. Put on waxed paper. For pupil, press Reese's candy immediately over each eyeball; stand till set for 30 minutes.
- Mix leftover confectioner's sugar, food coloring and water in a small bowl; put into a resealable, heavy-duty plastic bag. In corner of bag, cut small hole. From pupil, pipe wavy lines downward, making it look like bloodshot eyes; keep in airtight container.

Nutrition Information

- Calories: 139 calories
- Cholesterol: 4mg cholesterol
- Protein: 2g protein.
- Total Fat: 7g fat (4g saturated fat)
- Sodium: 42mg sodium
- Fiber: 0 fiber)
- Total Carbohydrate: 18g carbohydrate (17g sugars

85. Butterscotch Candy

Serving: 40 | Prep: 10mins | Cook: 15mins | Ready in:

Ingredients

- 1/2 cup brown sugar
- 1/4 cup butter
- 1/2 cup white sugar
- 1/2 cup water
- 2 teaspoons vinegar
- 1 pinch salt
- 1/2 teaspoon vanilla extract

Direction

- Liberally brush butter over a 10x15-in. baking pan (with sides).
- In a medium-sized saucepan, mix salt, vinegar, water, white sugar, butter, and brown sugar together over medium heat. Put a cover on and boil it. Uncover and heat until a little syrup will form hard but pliable threads when dropped in cold water, about 270°-290°F (132°C-143°C), do not whisk. Add in vanilla without whisking. Take away from heat and add into the prepared pan. Cool slightly, and then slice into squares and let the candy fully cool.

Nutrition Information

- Calories: 30 calories;
- Cholesterol: 3
- Protein: 0
- Total Fat: 1.2
- Sodium: 9
- Total Carbohydrate: 5.2

86. Caramel Lollipops

Serving: Makes 20 lollipops | Prep: | Cook: | Ready in:

Ingredients

- lollipop molds if desired
- vegetable-oil cooking spray
- 20 lollipop sticks or short (4-inch) wooden skewers
- 2 cups sugar
- 1 cup water
- 2/3 cup light corn syrup
- 1/4 teaspoon orange- or lemon-flavored oil if desired
- mixed jellied candies such as jelly beans or Jujyfruits, or chocolates such as Sno-Caps for decorating

Direction

- Prepare a big bowl of cold water and ice. Use cooking spray to lightly coat 10 lollipop molds and use scissors to cut off pointed ends of skewers if using. Place skewers or lollipop sticks in prepared molds. If not using molds, use a sheet of parchment paper sprayed with cooking spray and 10 skewers and lollipop sticks.
- Place 1/8 teaspoon flavored oil, 1/3 cup corn syrup, 1/2 cup water, and 1 cup sugar in a heavy saucepan over moderate heat and boil while stirring to dissolve sugar. Boil the mixture (do not stir), using a brush dipped in cold water to brush down sugar crystals sticking to side of pan, until the mixture turns pale golden. Keep cooking (do not stir) while swirling pan sometimes until the mixture turns golden in color.
- Take away from the heat and soak the pan's bottom into the ice water to prevent caramel from getting overcooked (the water will splatter and hiss). Pour mixture into 10 molds. (If the mixture hardens too much, put over low heat and heat but do not stir until the consistency becomes spoonable). Decorate quickly with jellied candies if using; or allow lollipops to cool for 5 minutes then decorate with chocolates if using. Alternatively, spoon caramel onto parchment paper to create 10 lollipops. Make similar decorations and press one end of a skewer or lollipop stick onto each candy firmly. Let sit for 30 minutes until entirely cool; take out of the molds or parchment. Following the same steps, make 10 more lollipops. Keep in between wax paper layers in a tightly sealed container and store at cool room temperature for up to 2 weeks.

87. Caramel Pecan Candy

Serving: about 6-1/2 dozen. | Prep: 35mins | Cook: 0mins | Ready in:

Ingredients

- 1/3 cup plus 1/2 cup butter, divided
- 20 Oreo cookies, crushed
- 1 package (14 ounces) caramels
- 3 cups chopped pecans, toasted
- TOPPING:
- 3/4 cup semisweet chocolate chips
- 3 tablespoons butter
- 3 tablespoons heavy whipping cream
- 3 tablespoons light corn syrup
- 3/4 teaspoon vanilla extract

Direction

- Melt 1/3 cup butter in a big saucepan over medium heat; mix in the cookie crumbs. Force into a 9-in. square baking pan, ungreased. Bake for 10 to 12 mins at 325° or until firm. Let cool on a wire rack.
- In the meantime, melt leftover butter and caramels in a small saucepan over low heat. Mix in the pecans. Put on top of crust. Let cool.
- To make the topping, mix the corn syrup, cream, butter and chocolate chips in a small saucepan. Cook and mix over low heat until smooth. Take off from the heat; mix in vanilla. Put on top of caramel layer. Let cool on a wire rack. Chill until chocolate firms up.
- Let candy sit for 5 to 10 mins at room temperature before slicing into 1-in. squares. Put in the fridge to store.

Nutrition Information

- Calories: 94 calories
- Total Fat: 7g fat (3g saturated fat)
- Sodium: 55mg sodium
- Fiber: 1g fiber)
- Total Carbohydrate: 8g carbohydrate (6g sugars
- Cholesterol: 7mg cholesterol
- Protein: 1g protein.

88. Caramel Nut Candy Bars

Serving: 2-1/4 pounds. | Prep: 25mins | Cook: 0mins | Ready in:

Ingredients

- 1-1/2 teaspoons plus 1/4 cup butter, softened, divided
- 2 packages (11-1/2 ounces each) milk chocolate chips
- 1/4 cup shortening
- 1 package (14 ounces) caramels
- 5 teaspoons water
- 1 cup chopped pecans

Direction

- Use foil to line a 13x9-inch pan, then use 1 1/2 teaspoons of butter to grease the foil; put it aside. Let the shortening and milk chocolate chips melt for 1 minute inside the microwave set at 70% power; give it a stir. Let it continue melting in the microwave for extra 10- to 20-second intervals while stirring it until it is smooth in consistency.
- Distribute 1/2 of the prepared milk chocolate mixture evenly into the prepared pan. Keep it in the fridge for 15 minutes or until it becomes firm. Keep the rest of the milk chocolate mixture aside.
- Combine the water, remaining butter and caramels together in a big microwaveable bowl and let it melt; mix well until it is smooth in consistency. Add in the pecans and mix well. Distribute it evenly on top of the milk chocolate layer.
- If need be, reheat the reserved milk chocolate mixture until it is of spread-like consistency. Distribute it evenly on top of the caramel layer. Cover the mixture and keep it in the fridge for 1 hour or until it becomes firm.
- Use the aluminum foil lining to remove the chilled candy from the pan. Carefully peel the foil off the candy then slice the candy into bars that are 1 1/2 x 1 inch in size. Keep it in the fridge.

Nutrition Information

- Calories: 86 calories
- Sodium: 24mg sodium
- Fiber: 0 fiber
- Total Carbohydrate: 9g carbohydrate (8g sugars
- Cholesterol: 4mg cholesterol
- Protein: 1g protein.
- Total Fat: 5g fat (2g saturated fat)

89. Cherry Mice

Serving: 2 dozen. | Prep: 45mins | Cook: 0mins | Ready in:

Ingredients

- 2 cups (12 ounces) semisweet chocolate chips
- 2 teaspoons shortening
- 24 maraschino cherries with stems, well drained
- 24 milk chocolate kisses, unwrapped
- 48 almond slices

Direction

- Melt shortening and chocolate chips in a microwave; mix till smooth. Dip cherry into chocolate mixture, holding each by stem. Put onto waxed paper sheet; stand till set.
- Reheat leftover chocolate; dip cherries once more. Press onto chocolate kiss's bottom. Put almond slices between kiss and cherries for ears; refrigerate till set.

Nutrition Information

- Calories:
- Cholesterol:
- Protein:
- Total Fat:
- Sodium:
- Fiber:
- Total Carbohydrate:

90. Cherry Peanut Butter Balls

Serving: about 2 dozen. | Prep: 30mins | Cook: 0mins | Ready in:

Ingredients

- 1/2 cup butter, softened
- 1 cup peanut butter
- 1 teaspoon vanilla extract
- 2 cups confectioners' sugar
- 24 to 26 maraschino cherries with stems
- Additional confectioners' sugar
- 2 cups (12 ounces) semisweet chocolate chips
- 1/4 cup shortening

Direction

- Beat together the butter and peanut butter in a small bowl till smooth. Beat vanilla into the mixture. Add confectioners' sugar into the mix slowly and combine thoroughly. Refrigerate, covered, for no less than 1 hour.
- Use paper towel to pat dry the cherries. Dust your hands with more confectioners' sugar. Use a rounded tablespoon full of peanut butter mixture to wrap each cherry; shape it into a ball. Occasionally refrigerate the peanut butter mixture while rolling the cherries. Refrigerate, covered, for no less than 1 hour.
- Melt chocolate chips and shortening in a microwave; stir till smooth. Dip the peanut butter balls into the chocolate; let the excess drip off. Put onto waxed paper. Refrigerate for no less than 1 hour or till set.

Nutrition Information

- Calories: 233 calories
- Fiber: 1g fiber)
- Total Carbohydrate: 24g carbohydrate (21g sugars
- Cholesterol: 10mg cholesterol
- Protein: 3g protein.

- Total Fat: 15g fat (6g saturated fat)
- Sodium: 90mg sodium

91. Chocolate Marshmallow Peanut Butter Squares

Serving: 5 dozen | Prep: 15mins | Cook: 5mins | Ready in:

Ingredients

- 1 can (14 ounces) sweetened condensed milk
- 1 package (11 ounces) peanut butter and milk chocolate chips
- 1/2 cup milk chocolate chips
- 1/2 cup creamy peanut butter
- 1 teaspoon vanilla extract
- 1-1/2 cups miniature marshmallows
- 1 cup broken miniature pretzels
- 1 cup Rice Krispies

Direction

- Put the first 5 ingredients in a large heavy saucepan; cook, stirring, over low heat for about 5 minutes or until smooth, and blended. The mixture is expected to be very thick. Put off the heat; mix in remaining ingredients. Spread mixture all over the bottom of an oiled 13x9-inch pan.
- Cover and chill for about 4 hours until firm. Divide into squares. Keep in an airtight container in the fridge.

Nutrition Information

- Calories: 85 calories
- Total Carbohydrate: 12g carbohydrate (8g sugars
- Cholesterol: 3mg cholesterol
- Protein: 1g protein.
- Total Fat: 4g fat (2g saturated fat)
- Sodium: 50mg sodium
- Fiber: 0 fiber)

92. Cinnamon Pumpkin Truffles

Serving: 2 dozen. | Prep: 35mins | Cook: 0mins | Ready in:

Ingredients

- 2 cups white baking chips
- 1/4 cup heavy whipping cream
- 1/4 cup canned pumpkin
- 1 teaspoon ground cinnamon
- 1/4 teaspoon ground ginger
- 1/4 teaspoon ground cloves
- 14 ounces dark chocolate candy coating, coarsely chopped
- 2 tablespoons shortening
- Chocolate and white sprinkles

Direction

- Melt cream and white chips in small microwave-safe bowl; mix till smooth. Add spices and pumpkin; cover. Refrigerate till nearly solid yet still workable for 2 hours.
- Form to 1-in. balls; melt shortening and candy coating in microwave. Mix till smooth. In chocolate mixture, dip truffles; let excess drip off. Roll in sprinkles; put onto waxed paper-lined baking sheets and refrigerate till firm for 1-2 hours.
- Keep in airtight container in the fridge.

Nutrition Information

- Calories: 181 calories
- Total Carbohydrate: 20g carbohydrate (19g sugars
- Cholesterol: 5mg cholesterol
- Protein: 1g protein.
- Total Fat: 11g fat (8g saturated fat)
- Sodium: 14mg sodium
- Fiber: 1g fiber)

93. Crispy Peanut Butter Cocoa Cups

Serving: 21 servings. | Prep: 15mins | Cook: 5mins | Ready in:

Ingredients

- 1 cup sugar
- 1 cup light corn syrup
- 1 cup creamy peanut butter
- 6 cups chocolate-flavored crisp rice cereal

Direction

- Put corn syrup and sugar together in a big saucepan and boil; mix and cook till sugar melts for 1 minute.
- Take off heat; mix in peanut butter. Add the cereal; toss to cover. Drop into foil/paper-lined muffin cups by 1/3 cupfuls; keep in airtight container.

Nutrition Information

- Calories: 198 calories
- Sodium: 142mg sodium
- Fiber: 1g fiber)
- Total Carbohydrate: 34g carbohydrate (19g sugars
- Cholesterol: 0 cholesterol
- Protein: 4g protein.
- Total Fat: 7g fat (1g saturated fat)

94. Dracula Cookies

Serving: 6 cookies. | Prep: 30mins | Cook: 0mins | Ready in:

Ingredients

- 6 hazelnut truffles
- 5 ounces white candy coating, chopped
- 1 green or red Fruit Roll-Up
- 6 Oreo cookies
- 1 can (6.4 ounces) black decorating icing
- 6 slivered almonds, cut in half

Direction

- Put truffles on waxed paper-lined pan. Freeze till chilled or for 10 minutes. Meanwhile, melt candy coating in microwave; mix till smooth. In coating, dip truffles to completely cover; let excess drip off. Put in prepped pan; refrigerate till hardened.
- Cut the fruit roll-up to 2 1/2-in.x1 1/2-in. strips then reheat candy coating if needed. In candy coating, dip truffles once more; let excess drip off. Put 1 onto each cookie. Wrap fruit strip around truffle's base for a cape; let stand till set.
- Pipe mouth, eyes and hair on each with decorating icing and round tip. For fangs, insert almonds. Keep in airtight container.

Nutrition Information

- Calories:
- Sodium:
- Fiber:
- Total Carbohydrate:
- Cholesterol:
- Protein:
- Total Fat:

95. Evil Eye Truffles

Serving: 3 dozen. | Prep: 30mins | Cook: 0mins | Ready in:

Ingredients

- 1 cup chunky peanut butter
- 1/4 cup butter, softened
- 2 cups crisp rice cereal
- 1 cup confectioners' sugar

- 12 ounces white candy coating
- 2 tablespoons shortening
- 36 milk chocolate green M&M's or blue milk chocolate M&M's
- 1 tube red decorating icing
- 1 tube black decorating icing

Direction

- Mix butter and peanut butter in big bowl; mix confectioner's sugar and cereal in till combined well. Shape to 1-in. balls with buttered hands. Melt shortening and candy coating till smooth in microwave. Dip balls in coating; let excess drip off. Put on waxed paper-lined baking sheet. Press M&M in middle of each ball before coating is cool then completely cool.
- Use red icing and small round pastry tip to pipe small wavy lines over balls' sides to look like bloodshot eyes. Use small round pastry tip and black icing frosting to put dot in middle of the M&M for a pupil.

Nutrition Information

- Calories: 135 calories
- Sodium: 79mg sodium
- Fiber: 0 fiber)
- Total Carbohydrate: 14g carbohydrate (11g sugars
- Cholesterol: 4mg cholesterol
- Protein: 2g protein.
- Total Fat: 8g fat (4g saturated fat)

96. Fingers Of Fright

Serving: 10 servings. | Prep: 10mins | Cook: 0mins | Ready in:

Ingredients

- 5 red, black and/or green jelly beans
- 10 circus peanut candies

Direction

- Slice jelly beans into halves lengthways. Press to stick each piece to the end of a circus peanut.

Nutrition Information

- Calories:
- Protein:
- Total Fat:
- Sodium:
- Fiber:
- Total Carbohydrate:
- Cholesterol:

97. Flying Broomstick Cats

Serving: 6 servings. | Prep: 30mins | Cook: 0mins | Ready in:

Ingredients

- Pattern on this page
- 5 ounces milk chocolate candy coating, coarsely chopped, divided
- 6 pretzel dipping sticks
- Yellow sprinkles
- 3/4 cup potato sticks
- 1 tablespoon white baking chips

Direction

- On waxed paper, trace 3 images of cat pattern and put on a baking sheet. Put over top with a separate waxed paper sheet and use tape to secure both to the baking sheet. Do all the steps as above again.
- Melt 2-ounce of candy coating in a small microwavable bowl, then stir until it is smooth. Cut in the corner of a plastic or pastry bag with a small hole, then insert a #3 round pastry tip. Fill melted chocolate into the bag, then pipe on the outlines of 3 cats as well as fill into centers.

- Put on the bottom of each cat with a pretzel stick to make broomstick. Use sprinkles to make collar and eye on each cat. Melt more 2-ounce of candy coating and do the same manner for leftover cats.
- Melt leftover candy coating. Cut in the corner of a plastic or pastry bag with a small hole, then insert a #3 round pastry tip. Fill melted chocolate into the bag, then pipe on one end of each pretzel stick with a little chocolate. Attach the potato sticks to make broom bristles.
- Melt vanilla chips and stir until smooth. Transfer into a pastry bag with a #3 round tip. Pipe the position in which bristles and broomsticks meet each other with lines.

Nutrition Information

- Calories: 164 calories
- Sodium: 46mg sodium
- Fiber: 1g fiber)
- Total Carbohydrate: 21g carbohydrate (15g sugars
- Cholesterol: 0 cholesterol
- Protein: 1g protein.
- Total Fat: 9g fat (7g saturated fat)

98. Four Ingredient Tumbleweeds

Serving: 5 dozen. | Prep: 25mins | Cook: 0mins | Ready in:

Ingredients

- 1 package (11 ounces) butterscotch chips
- 2 tablespoons creamy peanut butter
- 1 jar (12 ounces) dry roasted peanuts
- 1 can (4 ounces) potato sticks

Direction

- Melt peanut butter and butterscotch chips in a microwaveable bowl; mix until smooth. Mix in potato sticks and peanuts.
- Put by tablespoonfuls onto waxed paper-lined trays. Chill until set. Put in an airtight container to store.

Nutrition Information

- Calories: 74 calories
- Sodium: 57mg sodium
- Fiber: 1g fiber)
- Total Carbohydrate: 6g carbohydrate (0 sugars
- Cholesterol: 0 cholesterol
- Protein: 2g protein. Diabetic Exchanges: 1 fat
- Total Fat: 5g fat (2g saturated fat)

99. Gingerbread Truffles

Serving: Makes about 2 dozen | Prep: | Cook: | Ready in:

Ingredients

- 3/4 cup whipping cream
- 10 whole allspice
- 10 whole cloves
- 1 tablespoon mild-flavored (light) molasses
- 1 1/2 teaspoons grated peeled fresh ginger
- 1/2 teaspoon ground cinnamon
- Pinch of salt
- 7 ounces plus 12 ounces bittersweet (not unsweetened) or semisweet chocolate, chopped
- 7 ounces plus 12 ounces high-quality white chocolate (such as Lindt or Perugina), chopped
- 1/2 cup chopped crystallized ginger plus additional for garnish

Direction

- In heavy medium saucepan, bring the first 7 ingredients just to boiling; take out of the heat; allow to steep for an hour.
- In a large metal bowl set over a saucepan of simmering water, mix 7 ounces of each white chocolate and bittersweet chocolate; stir until melted and smooth. Take the bowl out of the

water. Strain cream mixture into chocolate; stir to blend. Stir in half cup chopped crystallized ginger. Chill filling for at least 3 hours until firm.
- Use parchment to line a baking sheet. With 1-inch melon baller, spoon filling and roll between palms to shape into balls. Arrange on parchment. Place truffles in the fridge to chill for a minimum of 2 hours.
- Using parchment, line another sheet. In a medium metal bowl placed over a saucepan of simmering water, arrange 12 ounces bittersweet chocolate; stir until smooth and melted. Take the bowl out of the water. Cool until the inserted thermometer into chocolate reads 115°F. Submerge 1 truffle in chocolate quickly. Lift the truffle out with fork; tap fork against the bowl's side to drip off excess coating. Slide truffle off fork and onto the lined sheet with a knife. Do the same with the rest of the truffles. Chill until set.
- Using parchment, line another baking sheet. In a separate medium metal bowl placed over a saucepan of simmering water, arrange 12 ounces white chocolate; stir until smooth and melted. Take the bowl out of the water. Cool until the inserted thermometer into chocolate reads 100°F. Hold a truffle between your index finger and thumb; coat halfway with white chocolate. Transfer to the lined sheet. Do the same with leftover truffles. If preferred, press small pieces of crystallized ginger atop truffles. Chill for about half an hour until firm. (You can prepare this a week ahead. Keep chilled with a cover.)

Nutrition Information

- Calories: 306
- Fiber: 2 g(8%)
- Total Carbohydrate: 35 g(12%)
- Cholesterol: 16 mg(5%)
- Protein: 3 g(6%)
- Total Fat: 20 g(30%)
- Saturated Fat: 12 g(59%)
- Sodium: 46 mg(2%)

100. Halloween Candy Bark

Serving: 2-3/4 pounds. | Prep: 15mins | Cook: 5mins | Ready in:

Ingredients

- 2 teaspoons butter
- 1-1/2 pounds white candy coating, coarsely chopped
- 2 cups pretzels, coarsely chopped
- 10 Oreo cookies, chopped
- 3/4 cup candy corn
- 3/4 cup dry roasted peanuts
- 1/2 cup milk chocolate M&M's
- 1/2 cup Reese's Pieces

Direction

- Prepare a foil lined 15x10x1-inch baking pan; use butter to grease foil. Microwave candy coating until melted and whisk until smooth. Pour into the greased pan. Scatter with remaining ingredients and press into candy coating. Let sit for 60 minutes.
- Cut or break into pieces. Keep in a tightly closed container.

Nutrition Information

- Calories: 152 calories
- Protein: 1g protein.
- Total Fat: 7g fat (5g saturated fat)
- Sodium: 84mg sodium
- Fiber: 0 fiber)
- Total Carbohydrate: 21g carbohydrate (18g sugars
- Cholesterol: 1mg cholesterol

101. Halloween Chocolate Spiders

Serving: 2 dozen. | Prep: 20mins | Cook: 0mins | Ready in:

Ingredients

- 8 ounces semisweet chocolate, chopped
- 2 cups miniature marshmallows
- Black or red shoestring licorice
- 24 small round candy-coated milk chocolate balls (such as Hersheys or Sixlets)

Direction

- Microwave chocolate at 50% power in a microwaveable bowl for 1.5 minutes, stirring every 30-second. Stir until the chocolate melts and allow to sit for 5 minutes. Mix in marshmallows. Dollop the mixture by tablespoonfuls onto a baking sheet lined with waxed paper. Cut the licorice into pieces of 2 inches; on each mound, press down 8 pieces to make the legs. Press in each 2 chocolate balls to make eyes.
- Chill in the refrigerator for about 20 minutes to firm up.

Nutrition Information

- Calories: 23 calories
- Sodium: 2mg sodium
- Fiber: 0 fiber
- Total Carbohydrate: 5g carbohydrate (3g sugars
- Cholesterol: 0 cholesterol
- Protein: 0 protein.
- Total Fat: 1g fat (0 saturated fat)

102. Homemade Peanut Butter Cups

Serving: 30 | Prep: | Cook: | Ready in:

Ingredients

- 2 cups milk chocolate chips
- 2 tablespoons shortening
- 1/2 cup butter
- 1/2 cup crunchy peanut butter
- 1 cup confectioners' sugar
- 2/3 cup graham cracker crumbs

Direction

- Mix shortening and chocolate chips in 1-quart saucepan. Cook while stirring occasionally over low heat for 3-5 minutes until smooth and melted.
- Loosen top paper cup from stack but not remove from stack to sustain better stability while coating. Coat inside top evenly with about a teaspoon of melted chocolate to about 1/8-inch thickness, using a small pain brush; bring coating almost to top of cup, not over the edge. Do the same with other cups until coat 30 cups; keep them in the fridge.
- Mix peanut butter and margarine or butter in 2-quart saucepan. Cook while stirring occasionally over medium heat for 4-6 minutes until melted. Stir in graham cracker crumbs and confectioners' sugar. Press about half tablespoon filling into each chocolate cup.
- Scoop about half teaspoon melted chocolate over filling; spread to cover. Freeze for about 2 hours until firm, peel paper cups off carefully. Keep in the fridge.

Nutrition Information

- Calories: 140 calories;
- Sodium: 54
- Total Carbohydrate: 13.6
- Cholesterol: 11
- Protein: 2
- Total Fat: 9.5

103. Hosts Of Ghosts

Serving: 26 servings. | Prep: 60mins | Cook: 0mins | Ready in:

Ingredients

- 20 Oreo cookies
- 3 ounces cream cheese, softened
- 6 ounces white candy coating, chopped
- 1 teaspoon shortening

Direction

- Use a covered food processor to blend the cookies until the mixture looks much like coarse crumbs. Slice the cream cheese into 3 portions then put it into the food processor. Cover the food processor and blend the mixture until you get a dough that has a soft texture.
- Shape 2 teaspoons of the prepared dough into a ghost until you form 26 ghost-shaped doughs. Put the ghost-shaped doughs onto a baking sheet that is lined with wax paper.
- Let the shortening and the candy coating melt in the microwave, give it a mix until it is smooth in consistency. Gently coat each of the ghost-shaped doughs with the melted candy coating mixture. Draw eyes onto each coated ghost-shaped dough using a toothpick. Keep it in the fridge afterwards.

Nutrition Information

- Calories: 68 calories
- Total Fat: 4g fat (3g saturated fat)
- Sodium: 33mg sodium
- Fiber: 0 fiber
- Total Carbohydrate: 8g carbohydrate (6g sugars
- Cholesterol: 4mg cholesterol
- Protein: 0 protein. Diabetic Exchanges: 1 fat

104. Licorice Caramels

Serving: 64 | Prep: 10mins | Cook: 30mins | Ready in:

Ingredients

- 1 cup butter
- 2 cups white sugar
- 1 (14 ounce) can sweetened condensed milk
- 1 cup corn syrup
- 1/8 teaspoon salt
- 1 teaspoon anise extract
- black paste food coloring

Direction

- Use foil to line a 9x9 in. dish and butter the foil.
- Put butter in a large saucepan and melt on medium heat. Mix in salt, corn syrup, milk, sugar. Bring to a boil, remember to stir frequently. Keep heating without stirring to 116-120°C (242-248°F) or till a firm but pliable ball forms when you drop a small amount of syrup into cold water. Get the saucepan off heat, put in food coloring, anise and stir. Transfer the mixture into the prepared pan. Allow to cool completely, for several hours.
- To cut, turn the caramel out of pan and remove foil. Butter a knife and use the knife to cut. Use candy wrappers or waxed paper to wrap.

Nutrition Information

- Calories: 84 calories;
- Total Fat: 3.4
- Sodium: 36
- Total Carbohydrate: 13.5
- Cholesterol: 10
- Protein: 0.5

105. Lollipop Ghosts

Serving: 10 lollipops. | Prep: 30mins | Cook: 0mins | Ready in:

Ingredients

- 1-1/2 cups white baking chips
- 1/8 teaspoon coconut extract
- Ghost lollipop/candy molds
- 10 lollipop sticks
- 1/4 cup milk chocolate chips, melted

Direction

- Melt white chips in a microwave; mix until smooth then mix in coconut extract. In the corner of a plastic or pastry bag, make a small hole then attach a #3 round pastry tip; move the melted chips into the bag. Fill ghost molds with the mixture until 3/4 full; insert a lollipop stick into each. Add a small amount of melted chips on top. Place in the freezer for 15mins until firm.
- Take the lollipops out of the molds. Make ghosts' faces with melted milk chocolate chips. Place in the refrigerator until ready to serve.

Nutrition Information

- Calories:
- Protein:
- Total Fat:
- Sodium:
- Fiber:
- Total Carbohydrate:
- Cholesterol:

106. Magic Wands

Serving: 30 | Prep: 30mins | Cook: | Ready in:

Ingredients

- 1 (15 ounce) package pretzel rods
- 1 (16 ounce) container prepared vanilla frosting
- 1/2 cup sprinkles or colored sugar for decoration

Direction

- Dip each pretzel rod not quite halfway in frosting; to coat frosting, roll in sprinkles.

Nutrition Information

- Calories: 134 calories;
- Protein: 1.6
- Total Fat: 3.6
- Sodium: 337
- Total Carbohydrate: 23.7
- Cholesterol: < 1

107. Maple Ginger Fudge

Serving: 1-1/4 pounds. | Prep: 10mins | Cook: 30mins | Ready in:

Ingredients

- 2 teaspoons plus 2 tablespoons butter, divided
- 2 cups sugar
- 2/3 cup heavy whipping cream
- 2 tablespoons light corn syrup
- 1/4 teaspoon ground ginger
- 1/2 teaspoon maple flavoring
- 1/2 cup chopped walnuts

Direction

- Using foil, line a 9x5-in. loaf pan and grease the foil with a teaspoon butter; put aside. Grease the sides of a small heavy saucepan with a teaspoon butter; put in ginger, corn syrup, cream and sugar. Heat up to a boil over medium heat, mixing frequently. Lower the heat; cook until a candy thermometer registers 238° (soft-ball stage), mixing sometimes.

- Take off from the heat. Put in leftover butter and maple flavoring (don't stir). Let cool to 110° for about an hour without mixing. Whip on low speed for 1-2 minutes with a portable mixer or until fudge starts to thicken. Mix in walnuts with a clean, dry wooden spoon for about 5 mins until fudge starts to lose its gloss.
- Spread into lined and greased pan. Chill about half an hour until firm. Lift fudge out of pan with foil. Remove foil; slice fudge into 1-inch squares. Put in an airtight container in the fridge to store.

Nutrition Information

- Calories: 120 calories
- Protein: 1g protein. Diabetic Exchanges: 1 starch
- Total Fat: 5g fat (2g saturated fat)
- Sodium: 13mg sodium
- Fiber: 0 fiber)
- Total Carbohydrate: 18g carbohydrate (17g sugars
- Cholesterol: 12mg cholesterol

108. Marshmallow Ghosts

Serving: about 15 servings. | Prep: 20mins | Cook: 0mins | Ready in:

Ingredients

- 12 ounces white candy coating, coarsely chopped
- 1-1/2 cups miniature marshmallows
- Chocolate decorating gel or assorted candies

Direction

- Melt candy coating in a microwave; mix till smooth. Slightly cool. Mix in marshmallows till coated. Drop on waxed paper by heaping tablespoonfuls; flatten and smooth to ghost shapes.
- For eyes, decorate with candies or gel; fully cool. Keep in an airtight container.

Nutrition Information

- Calories: 137 calories
- Total Carbohydrate: 20g carbohydrate (18g sugars
- Cholesterol: 0 cholesterol
- Protein: 0 protein.
- Total Fat: 6g fat (6g saturated fat)
- Sodium: 2mg sodium
- Fiber: 0 fiber)

109. Marshmallow Witches

Serving: 1 dozen. | Prep: 30mins | Cook: 0mins | Ready in:

Ingredients

- 1/2 cup vanilla frosting, divided
- 36 miniature semisweet chocolate chips
- 12 large marshmallows
- 1 drop each green, red and yellow food coloring, optional
- 1/4 cup sweetened shredded coconut
- 12 chocolate wafers
- 12 miniature peanut butter cups
- 12 milk chocolate kisses

Direction

- Put dab of frosting on bottom of 3 chocolate chips for face of each witch; press 1 for nose and 2 for eyes onto each marshmallow.
- Hair: In small resealable plastic bag, mix 1 drop of water and green food coloring. Add coconut; shake well. Spread a little bit of frosting on sides of marshmallows; press the coconut hair to frosting. In heavy-duty, small resealable plastic bag, put 3 tablespoons frosting; use yellow and red food coloring to tint orange. Put aside.

- Hats: In middle of chocolate wafers, spread some leftover frosting; press peanut butter cups into frosting, upside down. Spread frosting on bottoms of chocolate kisses lightly; put onto peanut butter cups. Cut small hole in corner of plastic/pastry bag; insert small star tip. Use frosting to fill bag; pipe stars around base of every peanut butter cup. Use dab of frosting to secure hat to each witch.

Nutrition Information

- Calories: 121 calories
- Sodium: 69mg sodium
- Fiber: 1g fiber)
- Total Carbohydrate: 18g carbohydrate (11g sugars
- Cholesterol: 2mg cholesterol
- Protein: 2g protein.
- Total Fat: 5g fat (3g saturated fat)

110. Martian Marshmallows

Serving: 3 dozen. | Prep: 20mins | Cook: 10mins | Ready in:

Ingredients

- 12 ounces white candy coating
- 2 teaspoons shortening
- Paste food coloring, optional
- 36 lollipop sticks
- 1 package (10 ounces) large marshmallows (about 36)
- Colored sugar
- Assorted toppings: candy eyes, assorted nonpareils, licorice and sour straws

Direction

- Melt shortening and candy coating in a microwave; mix till smooth. Tint with food coloring if desired.
- In each marshmallow, insert 1 lollipop stick; in melted candy coating, dip marshmallows, turning to coat; let excess drip off then roll in colored sugar. Put a dab of the melted candy coating on assorted toppings; decorate faces as wished. Put onto waxed paper; stand till set.

Nutrition Information

- Calories:
- Protein:
- Total Fat:
- Sodium:
- Fiber:
- Total Carbohydrate:
- Cholesterol:

111. Marzipan Harvest Table Topper

Serving: 1-1/4 cups. | Prep: 60mins | Cook: 0mins | Ready in:

Ingredients

- 7 ounces almond paste
- 1/4 cup light corn syrup
- 1-1/4 cups confectioners' sugar
- Liquid or paste food coloring
- Baking cocoa (optional for acorn coloring)
- Cutting board or other protected work surface
- Cutting board or other protected work surface
- Assorted mini craft baskets and small wooden wagon
- Excelsior
- Cloves
- Leaf-shaped cookie cutters (1 to 2 inches)

Direction

- Marzipan: In a large bowl, break almond paste into crumbles. Knead in corn syrup. Add confectioners' sugar gradually; after each addition, knead well until blended thoroughly. Break off piece of marzipan to preferred size and knead in a little color at a

time to tint with food coloring (add baking cocoa if preferred for brown.)
- Shaping: For each Acorn: Shape a 1/4-1/2-in. slightly oblong ball of brown marzipan.
- About the cap, add more baking cocoa or food coloring to tint a small piece of marzipan until it turns to a slightly darker brown. Shape into a flat circle; press onto top of acorn. For stem, insert brown marzipan or a whole clove into cap. Dot the cap gently with knife point or toothpick for texture.
- For apple: Shape a 3/4-in. ball of red marzipan. Slightly curve slides. Gently pinch bottom to taper. Indent apple's bottom and top with sharp knife or toothpick. For steam, shape a brown marzipan stem or insert a whole clove; press into top indentation.
- For ear of corn: Shape a 1/2-in. ball of yellow marzipan into along cylinder shape about 1-1/2 in. long. Tapper an end slightly to shape the cob's top. Shape small pieces of yellow marzipan into balls for kernels. Press the balls in rows onto cob. Roll ball of green marzipan to 1/8-in. thickness between waxed paper for corn husks. On waxed paper, place on green marzipan's top, create 3 1-3/4-in. long x 1/2-in.-wide elongated leaf shapes. Peel top layer of waxed paper away; cut husks out onto the cob's sides with a knife; overlapping at center front's bottom, then 1 to cover the cob's back, overlap side's edges. Curve top points of every husk out gently.
- For leaves: Knead the same portions of orange, yellow and red marzipan together a few times to make marble effect. Between pieces of waxed paper, roll out to 1/8-in. thickness. Using cookie cutter, cut leaves out. Score veins on the leaves with a sharp knife or toothpick. For stem, form a brown marzipan stem then insert or insert a whole clove. Top with sugar if preferred.
- For pumpkins: Shape orange marzipan into 1/2 in. to 1-1/2 in balls. Slightly depress to make bottom and top flat. Create shallow ridges around sides from center top to bottom with sharp knife or toothpick. For stem, form one of each from brown marzipan stem then insert or insert a whole clove into the center top of each pumpkin.

Nutrition Information

- Calories: 172 calories
- Protein: 2g protein.
- Total Fat: 6g fat (1g saturated fat)
- Sodium: 12mg sodium
- Fiber: 1g fiber)
- Total Carbohydrate: 31g carbohydrate (22g sugars
- Cholesterol: 0 cholesterol

112. Midnight Mice

Serving: 3 dozen. | Prep: 01hours30mins | Cook: 0mins | Ready in:

Ingredients

- 1 cup creamy peanut butter
- 1/4 cup butter, softened
- 1/2 teaspoon vanilla extract
- 1-1/2 cups confectioners' sugar
- 1-1/2 cups crisp rice cereal
- 3/4 cup sliced almonds
- 12 ounces dark chocolate candy coating, chopped
- 1 tablespoon shortening
- 36 pieces black shoestring licorice (2 inches each)
- Assorted candies: Red cake decorator dots, M&M's semisweet miniature baking bits and black sugar

Direction

- Beat together the peanut butter, butter and vanilla in a small bowl till incorporated; beat in confectioners' sugar slowly. Stir cereal into the mixture. Roll the mix into 1-inch balls, taper one end to look much like a mouse. Put

almonds on heads to make ears. Chill in refrigerator until cold.
- Melt together the candy coating and shortening in a large microwave-safe bowl; stir till smooth. Dip the mice into the coating; put onto baking sheets lined with waxed paper. Slide licorice into them right away for tails. Put red dots to make eyes and add M&M's miniature baking bits for noses. Sprinkle using black sugar. Chill in refrigerator until set.

Nutrition Information

- Calories:
- Sodium:
- Fiber:
- Total Carbohydrate:
- Cholesterol:
- Protein:
- Total Fat:

113. Mother Lode Pretzels

Serving: 4-1/2 dozen. | Prep: 35mins | Cook: 0mins | Ready in:

Ingredients

- 1 package (10 ounces) pretzel rods
- 1 package (14 ounces) caramels
- 1 tablespoon evaporated milk
- 1-1/4 cups miniature semisweet chocolate chips
- 1 cup plus 2 tablespoons butterscotch chips
- 2/3 cup milk chocolate toffee bits
- 1/4 cup chopped walnuts, toasted

Direction

- Halve pretzel rods with a sharp knife; put aside. Melt caramels with milk in a big saucepan on low heat. Mix walnuts, toffee bits and chips in a big shallow bowl.
- In 2-cup glass measuring cup, put caramel mixture. Dip cut end of every pretzel piece 2/3 of way into the mixture of caramel; if it gets too thick to dip, reheat in microwave. Let extra caramel drip off; roll pretzels in chip mixture. Put on waxed paper till set; keep in airtight container.

Nutrition Information

- Calories: 114 calories
- Total Carbohydrate: 17g carbohydrate (12g sugars
- Cholesterol: 3mg cholesterol
- Protein: 1g protein. Diabetic Exchanges: 1 starch
- Total Fat: 5g fat (3g saturated fat)
- Sodium: 104mg sodium
- Fiber: 1g fiber)

114. Mounds Of Bugs

Serving: about 1-1/2 dozen. | Prep: 30mins | Cook: 0mins | Ready in:

Ingredients

- 1 package (11.3 ounces) snack-size Mounds candy bars
- 20 pretzels
- 1/4 cup chocolate frosting
- Assorted candies: Nerds, Candy Buttons, Dots and/or sprinkles

Direction

- Poke 3 holes in both of the long sides of every candy bar using a skewer. Break rounded pretzel sections to 1-inch pieces; for legs, insert into holes. Attach candies using frosting.

Nutrition Information

- Calories: 113 calories
- Protein: 0 protein. Diabetic Exchanges: 1 starch

- Total Fat: 6g fat (4g saturated fat)
- Sodium: 157mg sodium
- Fiber: 1g fiber)
- Total Carbohydrate: 15g carbohydrate (10g sugars
- Cholesterol: 0 cholesterol

115. Nutty Caramels

Serving: 1-1/2 pounds. | Prep: 5mins | Cook: 25mins | Ready in:

Ingredients

- 1 teaspoon plus 1/4 cup butter, divided
- 1 cup sugar
- 1 cup light corn syrup
- 1 cup evaporated milk
- 1 cup chopped nuts
- 1 teaspoon vanilla extract
- Melted chocolate, optional

Direction

- Using foil, line a 9-in. square baking pan; grease foil with a teaspoon butter.
- Mix leftover butter, milk, corn syrup and sugar in a big heavy saucepan. Cook and mix over medium heat until a candy thermometer registers 238° (soft-ball stage).
- Brush down the sides of the pan with a pastry brush dipped in water to eliminate sugar crystals. Cook and mix until thermometer registers 248° (firm-ball stage).
- Take off from heat; mix in vanilla and nuts. Put into prepared pan right away (do not scrape saucepan). Let sit until set.
- Lift candy out of pan with foil; tear off foil. Slice caramel into 1-in. squares with a buttered knife. Add a drizzle of chocolate over (optional). Let sit until firm.

Nutrition Information

- Calories: 40 calories
- Cholesterol: 3mg cholesterol
- Protein: 1g protein.
- Total Fat: 2g fat (1g saturated fat)
- Sodium: 14mg sodium
- Fiber: 0 fiber)
- Total Carbohydrate: 6g carbohydrate (5g sugars

116. Peanut Butter Cups

Serving: 12 | Prep: 10mins | Cook: 5mins | Ready in:

Ingredients

- 1 cup semisweet chocolate chips
- 1/4 cup butter
- 1 tablespoon vegetable oil
- 1/4 cup peanut butter

Direction

- Spray a small cup muffin tin with cooking spray. Microwave for 1 to 2 minutes, chocolate with oil and butter in a microwaveable bowl. Stir often until melted. In each muffin cup, add a tablespoon of chocolate mixture.
- Microwave for 30 to 40 seconds peanut butter until melted. In each muffin cup, pour 1 teaspoon of melted peanut butter over the chocolate mixture.
- Refrigerate for 30 minutes until set.

Nutrition Information

- Calories: 143 calories;
- Cholesterol: 10
- Protein: 2
- Total Fat: 11.9
- Sodium: 53
- Total Carbohydrate: 9.9

117. Peanut Butter Pretzel Bites

Serving: 12 | Prep: 15mins | Cook: 2mins |Ready in:

Ingredients

- 48 Original Snack Factory® Pretzel Crisps®
- 1/2 cup peanut butter
- 1 (10 ounce) package vanilla candy melts or chips

Direction

- Place wax paper on a baking sheet. Place 24 pretzel crisps on a sheet facing down.
- Place 1 tsp. of peanut butter on every pretzel crisp. Top the rest of the pretzel crisps facing up and lightly pressing down to create a sandwich.
- Melt melts or chips in a glass or ceramic bowl that's microwave safe in a microwave. Melt at 15 second intervals, mix after every melting. Do this for 1-3 minutes.
- Dip every sandwich with small tongs to the melted candy, or you can use a spoon or fork to drizzle to coat the top. Let the extra coating drip in the bowl. Place the sandwiches on a baking sheet.
- Allow to stand until candy sets. You can place it in the fridge to speed up the process.

Nutrition Information

- Calories: 224 calories;
- Total Fat: 11.6
- Sodium: 216
- Total Carbohydrate: 24.8
- Cholesterol: 0
- Protein: 5

118. Peanut Goody Candies

Serving: 2-3/4 pounds. | Prep: 30mins | Cook: 0mins |Ready in:

Ingredients

- 1-1/2 teaspoons plus 1/2 cup butter, softened, divided
- 1 cup semisweet chocolate chips
- 1 cup butterscotch chips
- 1 cup peanut butter
- 1 cup dry roasted peanuts
- 1/4 cup milk
- 2 tablespoons cook-and-serve vanilla pudding mix
- 3-1/4 cups confectioners' sugar
- 1/2 teaspoon maple flavoring

Direction

- Using foil, line a 13-inch x 9-inch pan and butter the foil with 1-1/2 teaspoons butter; put aside.
- Mix the peanut butter and chips in a microwaveable bowl. Microwave on high, with no cover for 1-2 minutes or until melted; mix until smooth. Smear half of the chocolate mixture into lined pan; chill. Mix peanuts into leftover chocolate mixture; put aside.
- Stir the leftover butter, pudding mix and milk in another microwaveable bowl. Microwave on high, with no cover, for 1-2 minutes or until mixture comes to a boil, mixing once. Combine in maple flavoring and confectioners' sugar slowly.
- Smear on top of chocolate layer. Slather reserved peanut mixture over carefully (may have to rewarm in microwave to spread easily). Chill for 4 hours or until firm.
- Take candy out of pan with foil. Get rid of foil; slice into 1-inch squares. Put in an airtight container to store in the fridge. Take out from the fridge barely prior to serving.

Nutrition Information

- Calories: 73 calories
- Sodium: 39mg sodium
- Fiber: 0 fiber)
- Total Carbohydrate: 8g carbohydrate (7g sugars
- Cholesterol: 3mg cholesterol
- Protein: 1g protein.
- Total Fat: 4g fat (2g saturated fat)

119. Pumpkin Pie Marshmallows

Serving: about 9-1/2 dozen. | Prep: 30mins | Cook: 25mins | Ready in:

Ingredients

- 1/2 cup plus 3/4 cup water, divided
- 1/2 cup pumpkin pie filling
- 4 envelopes unflavored gelatin
- 3 cups sugar
- 1-1/4 cups light corn syrup
- 1/4 teaspoon salt
- 1/2 cup confectioners' sugar
- 1-1/2 teaspoons pumpkin pie spice, optional

Direction

- Line foil on a 13x9-inch pan; coat using cooking spray.
- Mix pie filling and 1/2 cup water in a stand mixer's heatproof bowl; scatter gelatin over to soften.
- Put leftover water, salt, corn syrup and sugar together in a big heavy saucepan and boil, occasionally mixing; cook without mixing on medium heat till it reaches soft-ball stage or candy thermometer reads 240°.
- Take off from heat; drizzle into gelatin gently, beating on high speed; Keep on beating for 10 minutes till doubled in volume and very stiff. Spread in prepped pan; cover. Cool for 6 hours – overnight at room temperature.
- Mix pumpkin pie spice if using, and confectioners' sugar in a small bowl. Lift candy from pan using foil; cut to 1-inch pieces using lightly buttered knife/kitchen scissors. Roll in the confectioners' sugar mixture; keep in cool, dry place in airtight container.
- Make ahead: Keep marshmallows in airtight containers, layered between waxed paper, for 1 week, in refrigerator.
- Freeze: Freeze marshmallows for 1 month in freezer containers.

Nutrition Information

- Calories: 32 calories
- Total Carbohydrate: 8g carbohydrate (6g sugars
- Cholesterol: 0 cholesterol
- Protein: 0 protein.
- Total Fat: 0 fat (0 saturated fat)
- Sodium: 9mg sodium
- Fiber: 0 fiber)

120. Salted Peanut Squares

Serving: 9-3/4 dozen. | Prep: 20mins | Cook: 0mins | Ready in:

Ingredients

- 3-1/2 cups dry roasted peanuts, divided
- 1 package (10 ounces) peanut butter chips
- 2 tablespoons butter
- 1 can (14 ounces) sweetened condensed milk
- 1 jar (7 ounces) marshmallow creme
- 36 miniature Snickers candy bars, chopped

Direction

- Spread 1/2 of peanuts into 13x9-inch greased baking pan. Heat butter and chips for 1 minute at 50% power in a big microwave-safe bowl; mix. Microwave in 20-second intervals till melted; mix till smooth. Mix in sweetened condensed milk and cook on high, with no cover, for 1 minute.

- Mix in candy bars and marshmallow crème; spread in prepped pan. Sprinkle leftover peanuts over. Use plastic wrap to cover; lightly press down.
- Refrigerate till set; cut to 1-inch squares. Keep in an airtight container

Nutrition Information

- Calories: 64 calories
- Protein: 2g protein.
- Total Fat: 3g fat (1g saturated fat)
- Sodium: 47mg sodium
- Fiber: 0 fiber)
- Total Carbohydrate: 7g carbohydrate (5g sugars
- Cholesterol: 2mg cholesterol

121. Scary Eyeballs

Serving: 40 pieces. | Prep: 50mins | Cook: 0mins | Ready in:

Ingredients

- 1-1/2 cups creamy peanut butter
- 1/2 cup butter, softened
- 1 teaspoon vanilla extract
- 3-3/4 cups confectioners' sugar
- 12 ounces white candy coating, chopped
- 1 tablespoon shortening
- 40 milk chocolate M&M's, assorted colors
- Red decorating gel

Direction

- Cream butter and peanut butter till fluffy and light in a small bowl; beat in vanilla. Beat in confectioners' sugar slowly; form to 1-inch balls. Cover; refrigerate for not less than 30 minutes.
- Melt shortening and candy coating in microwave-safe bowl; mix till smooth. In coating, dip peanut butter balls; let extra drip off. Put on waxed paper; put M&Ms on top, plain side up. Stand till set. To make bloodshot eyes, use red gel.

Nutrition Information

- Calories:
- Sodium:
- Fiber:
- Total Carbohydrate:
- Cholesterol:
- Protein:
- Total Fat:

122. Spiced Chocolate Truffles

Serving: about 2 dozen. | Prep: 45mins | Cook: 5mins | Ready in:

Ingredients

- 12 ounces milk chocolate baking bars, divided
- 1/2 cup heavy whipping cream
- 2 tablespoons canned pumpkin
- 1/4 teaspoon ground cinnamon
- 1/4 teaspoon ground ginger
- 1/4 teaspoon ground nutmeg
- Dash ground cloves
- Baking cocoa
- Candy eyeballs, optional

Direction

- Chop 10-oz. chocolate finely; put in small bowl. Heat spices, pumpkin and cream to just a boil in small heavy saucepan. Put on chocolate; let stand for 5 minutes.
- Use a whisk to mix till smooth. Cool it to room temperature; refrigerate for minimum of 4 hours, covered.
- Grate leftover chocolate finely; put in small microwave-safe bowl. Form chocolate mixture to 1-in. balls with hands lightly dusted with baking cocoa. Roll in grated chocolate, it'll be

soft and the truffles may slightly flatten when standing. Melt leftover grated chocolate in microwave if desired to attach eyeballs. Keep in airtight container in the fridge.

Nutrition Information

- Calories: 89 calories
- Cholesterol: 10mg cholesterol
- Protein: 1g protein.
- Total Fat: 6g fat (4g saturated fat)
- Sodium: 7mg sodium
- Fiber: 0 fiber)
- Total Carbohydrate: 9g carbohydrate (8g sugars

123. Spider Nest Candies

Serving: 15 servings. | Prep: 30mins | Cook: 0mins | Ready in:

Ingredients

- 1 package (10 to 12 ounces) white baking chips
- 1 tablespoon shortening
- 1 can (5 ounces) crispy chow mein noodles
- Spider candies and jelly beans

Direction

- Melt shortening and baking chips in a microwave; mix till smooth. Take off from heat; mix in chow mein noodles till coated well.
- Divide to 15 mounds on a waxed paper piece. Form to nets; add jellybeans for eggs and spider candy to each. Stand till set; keep in airtight container.

Nutrition Information

- Calories:
- Fiber:
- Total Carbohydrate:
- Cholesterol:
- Protein:
- Total Fat:
- Sodium:

124. Spiderweb Candy

Serving: 5 candies. | Prep: 20mins | Cook: 0mins | Ready in:

Ingredients

- 1/3 cup semisweet chocolate chips
- 6 ounces white baking chocolate, coarsely chopped
- 1 teaspoon shortening
- 1/3 cup sweetened shredded coconut, coarsely chopped

Direction

- Put the chips in a small microwaveable bowl and let it melt; mix well until it is smooth in consistency. Allow it to cool down a little bit. Place it inside a heavy-duty resealable plastic bag then create a small hole by cutting the corner of the ziplock bag; put it aside.
- Combine the shortening and white chocolate together in a separate small-sized microwaveable bowl and let it melt; mix well until it is smooth in consistency. Add in the coconut and mix well. Line baking sheets with wax paper then put in 2 tablespoonfuls of the white chocolate-coconut mixture and spread it out into a circle that is 4 inches in size. Do the whole process again 4 more times.
- Pipe the reserved melted semi-sweet chocolate in thin concentric circles 1/8 inch away from each other over each of the prepared candy circles. Slowly pull a toothpick starting from the circle in the middle going towards the outer edges of the candy, passing through each of the concentric circles. Wipe the used toothpick until clean. Do the whole process again until you've done a web pattern on each

candy. Keep it in the fridge for 30 minutes or until the candies have set. To store, keep it in an airtight container.

Nutrition Information

- Calories:
- Sodium:
- Fiber:
- Total Carbohydrate:
- Cholesterol:
- Protein:
- Total Fat:

125. Stained Glass Lollipops

Serving: 10-12 candy ornaments. | Prep: 20mins | Cook: 30mins | Ready in:

Ingredients

- 1-1/2 cups sugar
- 3/4 cup water
- 2/3 cup light corn syrup
- 1/2 teaspoon cream of tartar
- 1/2 teaspoon orange oil
- Paste food coloring in colors of your choice
- Fishing line

Direction

- Grease 10 to 12 assorted metal Halloween cookie cutters with butter. Put onto a baking sheet lined with parchment paper and put aside.
- Whisk together cream of tartar, corn syrup, water and sugar in a small heavy saucepan. Put over medium heat; cook while stirring to dissolve sugar. Boil the mixture. Keep cooking (do not stir) until the mixture reaches hard-crack stage, 300 degrees on a candy thermometer.
- Take away from the heat and mix in orange oil. Transfer to big custard cups or ramekins; add food coloring to tint (optional).
- Immediately transfer sugar mixture to greased cookie cutters to 3/16 inch deep. Allow to cool for 60 seconds. Make a hole in top of each candy by poking with a wooden skewer. (Microwave sugar mixture on high in a big custard cup or ramekin for 10 seconds if it becomes hard before transferring to cutters). Just before the candies are set, take out the cutters. String fishing line through holes; tie a knot on each to make a loop. Hang as you like to decorate.

Nutrition Information

- Calories: 152 calories
- Total Carbohydrate: 39g carbohydrate (30g sugars
- Cholesterol: 0 cholesterol
- Protein: 0 protein.
- Total Fat: 0 fat (0 saturated fat)
- Sodium: 11mg sodium
- Fiber: 0 fiber)

126. Trail Mix Clusters

Serving: 4 dozen. | Prep: 20mins | Cook: 5mins | Ready in:

Ingredients

- 2 cups (12 ounces) semisweet chocolate chips
- 1/2 cup unsalted sunflower kernels
- 1/2 cup salted pumpkin seeds or pepitas
- 1/2 cup coarsely chopped cashews
- 1/2 cup coarsely chopped pecans
- 1/4 cup sweetened shredded coconut
- 1/4 cup finely chopped dried apricots
- 1/4 cup dried cranberries
- 1/4 cup dried cherries or blueberries

Direction

- Liquefy chocolate chips in a big microwave-safe bowl; mix till smooth. Mix in the rest of the ingredients.
- Onto baking sheets lined with waxed paper, drop mixture by tablespoonfuls. Chill till firm. Keep in the refrigerator in an airtight container.

Nutrition Information

- Calories: 79 calories
- Total Carbohydrate: 8g carbohydrate (5g sugars
- Cholesterol: 0 cholesterol
- Protein: 2g protein. Diabetic Exchanges: 1 fat
- Total Fat: 6g fat (2g saturated fat)
- Sodium: 26mg sodium
- Fiber: 1g fiber)

Chapter 3: Awesome Holiday Candy Recipes

***

127. Almond Apricot Dips

Serving: 2 dozen. | Prep: 15mins | Cook: 0mins | Ready in:

Ingredients

- 1 package (7 ounces) dried pitted Mediterranean apricots
- 24 whole almonds, toasted
- 4 ounces white candy coating

Direction

- Insert an almond in each apricot. Microwave candy coating to melt; mix until smooth. Plunge each apricot in coating halfway, let excess drip off. Put on a waxed paper-lined baking tray; chill for 15 minutes or until firm. Put in the fridge to store.

Nutrition Information

- Calories: 53 calories
- Sodium: 7mg sodium
- Fiber: 1g fiber)
- Total Carbohydrate: 9g carbohydrate (7g sugars
- Cholesterol: 0 cholesterol
- Protein: 1g protein.
- Total Fat: 2g fat (1g saturated fat)

128. Almond Cherry Fudge

Serving: about 1 pound. | Prep: 20mins | Cook: 0mins | Ready in:

Ingredients

- 2 cups (12 ounces) semisweet chocolate chips
- 1 can (14 ounces) sweetened condensed milk
- 1/2 cup chopped almonds
- 1/2 cup red candied cherries, chopped
- 1 teaspoon almond extract

Direction

- Use foil to line an 8-inch square pan and grease the foil; put aside. Melt together chocolate chips and milk in a microwave on high for about 1 minute; stir. Microwave in extra 10- to 20-second intervals till melted; stir till smooth. Stir the almonds, cherries and extract into the mixture. Spread out into the prepared pan. Cover and refrigerate for about 2 hours or until set.
- Lift the fudge out of the pan with foil. Take off the foil; slice fudge into 1-inch squares. For storage, keep in the refrigerator.

Nutrition Information

- Calories: 55 calories
- Protein: 1g protein.
- Total Fat: 3g fat (1g saturated fat)
- Sodium: 9mg sodium
- Fiber: 0 fiber)
- Total Carbohydrate: 8g carbohydrate (7g sugars
- Cholesterol: 2mg cholesterol

129. Almond Coconut Candies

Serving: 5 dozen. | Prep: 25mins | Cook: 0mins | Ready in:

Ingredients

- 4-1/2 cups confectioners' sugar
- 3 cups sweetened shredded coconut
- 1 cup sweetened condensed milk
- 1/2 cup butter, melted
- 1 teaspoon vanilla extract
- 60 whole unblanched almonds
- FROSTING:
- 1-1/2 cups confectioners' sugar
- 1/2 cup baking cocoa
- 1/2 cup butter, melted
- 3 tablespoons hot coffee

Direction

- Mix the first 5 ingredients together in a large mixing bowl. Form mixture into balls about 1 inch; arrange balls on lightly greased baking sheets. Pat an almond on top of each ball. Refrigerate for 60 minutes.
- Mix frosting ingredients together until no lumps remain; instantly frost over the candies. Refrigerate until frosting is solid. Keep chilled in the fridge.

Nutrition Information

- Calories: 123 calories
- Total Carbohydrate: 18g carbohydrate (16g sugars
- Cholesterol: 10mg cholesterol
- Protein: 1g protein.
- Total Fat: 6g fat (4g saturated fat)
- Sodium: 50mg sodium
- Fiber: 0 fiber)

130. Aloha Brittle

Serving: 1 pound. | Prep: 20mins | Cook: 0mins | Ready in:

Ingredients

- 2 teaspoons butter, divided
- 1/2 cup sweetened shredded coconut
- 1 cup sugar
- 1/2 cup light corn syrup
- 1 jar (3 ounces) macadamia nuts
- 1/2 cup chopped pecans
- 1 teaspoon baking soda
- 1 teaspoon water
- 1 teaspoon vanilla extract

Direction

- Use 1 teaspoon of butter to grease a big baking sheet. Use coconut to sprinkle a 12-inch circle on the prepped pan. Mix corn syrup and sugar in a large heavy saucepan. Cook them over medium heat until a candy thermometer reaches 240° (soft-ball stage), mixing continuously. Mix in the rest of the butter, pecans and macadamia nuts. Stir and cook until the mixture reaches 300° (hard-crack stage)
- Mix vanilla, water and baking soda together. Take the saucepan out from the heat, mix in the baking soda mixture. Pour it on top of the coconut quickly. Let it cool before smashing them into pieces. Put waxed paper between each layer and keep them in an airtight container.

Nutrition Information

- Calories: 164 calories
- Sodium: 119mg sodium
- Fiber: 1g fiber)
- Total Carbohydrate: 23g carbohydrate (19g sugars
- Cholesterol: 1mg cholesterol
- Protein: 1g protein.
- Total Fat: 9g fat (2g saturated fat)

131. Angel Food Christmas Candy

Serving: 1-1/2 pounds. | Prep: 5mins | Cook: 25mins | Ready in:

Ingredients

- 1 cup sugar
- 1 cup dark corn syrup
- 1 tablespoon white vinegar
- 1 tablespoon baking soda
- 1 pound milk chocolate candy coating, melted

Direction

- Mix the vinegar, corn syrup and sugar in a heavy saucepan. Cook over medium heat, constantly mixing until sugar is dissolved. Cook without mixing until reaching 300° (hard-crack stage) on a candy thermometer. Don't overcook.
- Take away from heat then mix in the baking soda quickly. Pour into a 13x9-inch pan coated with butter. Don't spread the candy; the blend won't fill the pan.
- Break into pieces bite-size when cool. Dip into the melted chocolate; put onto waxed paper until chocolate is firm. Keep the candy covered tightly.

Nutrition Information

- Calories: 337 calories
- Sodium: 356mg sodium
- Fiber: 1g fiber)
- Total Carbohydrate: 63g carbohydrate (61g sugars
- Cholesterol: 0 cholesterol
- Protein: 1g protein.
- Total Fat: 11g fat (10g saturated fat)

132. Apple Jelly Candy

Serving: about 6 dozen. | Prep: 20mins | Cook: 20mins | Ready in:

Ingredients

- 2 cups sugar
- 1-3/4 cups unsweetened applesauce
- 2 envelopes unflavored gelatin
- 1 package (3 ounces) lemon gelatin
- 1/2 cup chopped walnuts
- 1 teaspoon vanilla extract
- Superfine, confectioners' and/or granulated sugar

Direction

- Mix together the gelatin, applesauce and sugar in a big saucepan. Allow to stand for a minute, then boil on medium heat, mixing continuously. Let it boil for 15 minutes. Take it out of the heat, then mix in vanilla and walnuts.
- Instantly pour in an 11x7-inch baking dish that's greased. Put cover and let it chill in the fridge overnight. Slice it into 1-inch pieces, then roll it in granulated, confectioners' or superfine sugar. Keep it in an airtight container and put it in the fridge.

Nutrition Information

- Calories: 32 calories

- Sodium: 3mg sodium
- Fiber: 0 fiber)
- Total Carbohydrate: 7g carbohydrate (7g sugars
- Cholesterol: 0 cholesterol
- Protein: 0 protein. Diabetic Exchanges: 1/2 starch.
- Total Fat: 0 fat (0 saturated fat)

133. Apricot Balls

Serving: 12 | Prep: 15mins | Cook: | Ready in:

Ingredients

- 1/2 pound dried apricots
- 1/2 cup brown sugar
- 1/2 cup flaked coconut
- 1/2 (14 ounce) can sweetened condensed milk
- 1 cup flaked coconut for rolling

Direction

- In a food processor, mince the apricots. Put in a bowl and stir with brown sugar. Mix in condensed milk and half cup coconut. Roll into 1-inch balls and toss in coconut. Keep in refrigerator.

Nutrition Information

- Calories: 210 calories;
- Total Fat: 9
- Sodium: 30
- Total Carbohydrate: 32.5
- Cholesterol: 6
- Protein: 2.7

134. Banana Cream Chocolate Truffles

Serving: about 4 dozen. | Prep: 35mins | Cook: 0mins | Ready in:

Ingredients

- 1 package (14.3 ounces) Golden Oreo cookies
- 1 package (8 ounces) cream cheese, softened
- 2 teaspoons banana extract
- 1/3 cup mashed ripe banana
- 1 pound milk chocolate candy coating, melted
- Dried banana chips, coarsely crushed

Direction

- In a food processor, blend cookies into fine crumbs. Beat cream cheese with extract in a mixing bowl until incorporated. Whisk in banana. Mix in cookie crumbs. Cover and freeze, about 2 hours, until solid enough to shape.
- Form mixture into balls about 1 inch. Immerse the balls in candy coating; arrange coated candies on baking sheets lined with waxed paper. Instantly sprinkle top with banana chips.
- Chill for about half an hour until firm. Keep chilled in a covered container in the fridge.

Nutrition Information

- Calories: 110 calories
- Sodium: 45mg sodium
- Fiber: 0 fiber)
- Total Carbohydrate: 13g carbohydrate (9g sugars
- Cholesterol: 5mg cholesterol
- Protein: 1g protein.
- Total Fat: 6g fat (4g saturated fat)

135. Bavarian Mint Fudge

Serving: about 2-1/2 pounds. | Prep: 20mins | Cook: 0mins | Ready in:

Ingredients

- 1-1/2 teaspoons plus 1 tablespoon butter, divided
- 2 cups (12 ounces) semisweet chocolate chips
- 1 package (11-1/2 ounces) milk chocolate chips
- 1 can (14 ounces) sweetened condensed milk
- 1 teaspoon peppermint extract
- 1 teaspoon vanilla extract

Direction

- Use foil to line an 11x7-inch pan and use 1 1/2 teaspoons butter to grease foil; put aside.
- Microwave remaining butter and chocolate chips in a microwaveable bowl until melted; whisk until smooth. Mix in extracts and milk until fully combined. Transfer to the prepped pan. Put in the refrigerator to set.
- Take fudge out of the pan using the foil. Remove foil and slice fudge into 1-in square pieces. Keep refrigerated to store.

Nutrition Information

- Calories: 62 calories
- Cholesterol: 3mg cholesterol
- Protein: 1g protein.
- Total Fat: 3g fat (2g saturated fat)
- Sodium: 13mg sodium
- Fiber: 0 fiber)
- Total Carbohydrate: 8g carbohydrate (8g sugars

136. Ben's English Toffee

Serving: 1-3/4 pounds. | Prep: 20mins | Cook: 30mins | Ready in:

Ingredients

- 2 teaspoons plus 1/2 cup butter, divided
- 1-3/4 cups sugar
- 1/8 teaspoon cream of tartar
- 1 cup heavy whipping cream
- 1 teaspoon rum extract
- 1 cup milk chocolate chips
- 1 cup mixed nuts, chopped and toasted

Direction

- Use 2 teaspoons butter to grease a 15x10x1-in. pan; set aside.
- Mix cream of tartar and sugar in a large heavy saucepan; mix in cream and the leftover butter. Cook and stir on medium heat till a candy thermometer reaches 300 degrees (this is the hard crack stage). Get the saucepan off heat, mix in extract. Transfer the mixture quickly into the prepared pan. Allow the mixture to sit at room temperature till it becomes cool.
- Put chocolate chips into a microwave and melt chips; stir till becomes smooth. Spread over toffee. Use nuts to sprinkle. Let sit for 60 minutes till set. Crack into pieces. Keep in an airtight container.

Nutrition Information

- Calories: 171 calories
- Protein: 2g protein.
- Total Fat: 11g fat (5g saturated fat)
- Sodium: 66mg sodium
- Fiber: 1g fiber)
- Total Carbohydrate: 18g carbohydrate (16g sugars
- Cholesterol: 22mg cholesterol

137. Black 'n' White Pistachio Bark

Serving: 3/4 pound. | Prep: 20mins | Cook: 0mins | Ready in:

Ingredients

- 1 cup (6 ounces) semisweet chocolate chips
- 1/2 cup coarsely chopped pistachios, toasted, divided
- 1/3 cup dried cranberries
- 2/3 cup vanilla or white chips

Direction

- Prepare a baking sheet with foil lining and put aside. Melt chocolate chips in a small microwaveable bowl and whisk to smoothen. Mix in cranberries and a quarter cup of pistachios. Thinly spread a layer onto the bottom of the lined baking sheet.
- Microwave vanilla chips till melted and whisk to smoothen. Scoop the mixture by teaspoonfuls and place onto the chocolate layer.
- Make swirling by running through with a knife. Garnish with the rest of pistachios. Put in the refrigerator to harden. Break to divide into pieces.

Nutrition Information

- Calories: 475 calories
- Total Fat: 29g fat (14g saturated fat)
- Sodium: 95mg sodium
- Fiber: 5g fiber)
- Total Carbohydrate: 56g carbohydrate (32g sugars
- Cholesterol: 6mg cholesterol
- Protein: 7g protein.

138. Brittle With Mixed Nuts

Serving: about 1-3/4 pounds. | Prep: 5mins | Cook: 30mins | Ready in:

Ingredients

- 1-1/2 teaspoons plus 3 tablespoons butter, divided
- 1-1/2 cups sugar
- 1 cup water
- 1 cup light corn syrup
- 1 can (10 ounces) mixed nuts without peanuts
- 1 teaspoon vanilla extract
- 1-1/2 teaspoons baking soda

Direction

- Grease a baking sheet with 1-1/2 teaspoons of butter; put aside. Mix the corn syrup, water and sugar in a big saucepan. Cook over medium heat until a candy thermometer registers 270° (soft-crack stage), mixing from time to time.
- Put in nuts; cook and mix until the mixture gets 300° (hard-crack stage). Take off from the heat; mix in leftover butter and vanilla. Put in baking soda and mix robustly.
- Pour onto greased baking sheet quickly. Using a buttered metal spatula, spread to 1/4-in. thickness. Let cool before cracking into pieces. Put in an airtight container to store.

Nutrition Information

- Calories: 148 calories
- Sodium: 164mg sodium
- Fiber: 1g fiber)
- Total Carbohydrate: 22g carbohydrate (17g sugars
- Cholesterol: 4mg cholesterol
- Protein: 2g protein.
- Total Fat: 7g fat (2g saturated fat)

139. Butter Almond Crunch

Serving: About 1-1/4 pounds. | Prep: 15mins | Cook: 20mins | Ready in:

Ingredients

- 1-1/2 teaspoons plus 1/2 cup butter, divided
- 3/4 cup sweetened shredded coconut
- 1-1/2 cups sugar
- 3 tablespoons water
- 1 tablespoon light corn syrup
- 3/4 cup sliced almonds
- 1/2 cup semisweet chocolate chips

Direction

- Line foil on 13x9-inch pan; use 1 1/2 teaspoon butter to grease foil. Evenly spread coconut in prepped pan; put aside.
- Put corn syrup, water and sugar together in a heavy saucepan and boil on medium heat, occasionally mixing. Add leftover butter; mix and cook till butter melts. Cook without mixing till it reaches a hard-crack stage or candy thermometer reads 300°. Take off from heat; mix in almonds. Put on coconut; cool.
- Melt chocolate chips in a microwave; mix till smooth. Drizzle on candy; cool till firm. Take off from foil; break to pieces. Keep in airtight containers.

Nutrition Information

- Calories: 101 calories
- Fiber: 1g fiber)
- Total Carbohydrate: 13g carbohydrate (12g sugars
- Cholesterol: 8mg cholesterol
- Protein: 1g protein.
- Total Fat: 6g fat (3g saturated fat)
- Sodium: 38mg sodium

140. Butter Mints

Serving: 24 | Prep: 30mins | Cook: 25mins | Ready in:

Ingredients

- 3 cups sugar
- 1 cup water
- 1 cup butter, softened
- 1/4 teaspoon peppermint oil
- 3 drops green food coloring, or as needed

Direction

- Grease a 10x15 inch jellyroll pan with butter, and refrigerate.
- In a heavy saucepan, combine the butter, water, and sugar. Heat until boiling over high heat. Stir from time to time using a wooden spoon. When it begins to boil, lower the heat to medium, and cook for 3 minutes, covered, to wash away the crystals formed on the pan's insides with the steam. Take off the cover, and heat the mixture to 121 to 129°C (250 to 265°F), or until when dropped into cold water, a small amount of syrup forms a rigid ball.
- Take off the heat, and mix in the food coloring and peppermint oil. Due to the strong odor, keep your face away from the steam. Transfer to the chilled pan. Let sit undisturbed for a few minutes.
- To soften, gently fold the hot candy's edges into the center using a rubber spatula. Keep on folding until the candy is cool enough to touch. Grease your fingers with butter, and roll the candy into a ball. Start pulling and stretching. Keep on stretching and pulling for about 5 minutes until the candy is satiny and porous.
- Pull the candy out into a rope of 1/2 inch thick, and use greased scissors to cut into 1/2 inch pieces. Allow the candy to cool thoroughly, then keep in an airtight tin for no less than 24 hours before serving.

Nutrition Information

- Calories: 165 calories;
- Total Fat: 7.7
- Sodium: 54
- Total Carbohydrate: 25
- Cholesterol: 20
- Protein: 0.1

141. Butter Pecan Fudge

Serving: 64 | Prep: 15mins | Cook: 10mins | Ready in:

Ingredients

- 1/2 cup butter
- 1/2 cup brown sugar
- 1/2 cup white sugar
- 1/8 teaspoon salt
- 1/2 cup heavy whipping cream
- 1 teaspoon vanilla extract
- 2 cups confectioners' sugar
- 1 cup chopped pecans

Direction

- Use butter to grease an 8-in. square baking pan.
- Mix salt, white sugar, brown sugar and butter together in a saucepan; add cream. Bring to a boil, stirring till sugar is dissolved and butter is melted. Allow the mixture to boil, stirring often, for 5 minutes
- Get the saucepan off heat; pour in vanilla extract and mix well. Put in confectioners' sugar and stir till the mixture becomes smooth. Fold pecans into fudge.
- Transfer fudge into the prepared pan and cool till it becomes firm, about an hour or two. Chop into 1-inch squares.

Nutrition Information

- Calories: 59 calories;
- Protein: 0.2
- Total Fat: 3.4

- Sodium: 16
- Total Carbohydrate: 7.4
- Cholesterol: 6

142. Buttery Walnut Toffee

Serving: about 1-1/2 pounds. | Prep: 30mins | Cook: 0mins | Ready in:

Ingredients

- 1 tablespoon plus 1 cup butter, softened, divided
- 1 cup whole unblanched almonds, coarsely chopped
- 1 cup sugar
- 1/4 teaspoon salt
- 1/2 teaspoon vanilla extract
- 1 cup milk chocolate chips, melted
- 1/2 cup chopped walnuts

Direction

- Use foil to line an 11x7-inch pan and grease the foil using 1 tablespoon butter. Evenly put the almonds into the pan; put aside.
- Mix together the sugar, salt and remaining butter in a heavy saucepan. Heat to boil, stir continuously. Cook and stir till the mixture turns caramel-colored and reaches a hard-crack stage (a candy thermometer reads 300°). Take off from heat; stir vanilla into the mixture. Pour on top of the almonds right away. Let it cool down through.
- Spread melted chocolate on top of the toffee; sprinkle with walnuts. Let sit till set. Crack into pieces. For storage, keep in an airtight container.

Nutrition Information

- Calories: 381 calories
- Total Fat: 29g fat (13g saturated fat)
- Sodium: 228mg sodium
- Fiber: 2g fiber)

- Total Carbohydrate: 28g carbohydrate (24g sugars
- Cholesterol: 47mg cholesterol
- Protein: 5g protein.

143. Candy Bar Fudge

Serving: 32 | Prep: 20mins | Cook: 10mins | Ready in:

Ingredients

- 1/2 cup butter
- 1/3 cup unsweetened cocoa powder
- 1/4 cup packed brown sugar
- 1/4 cup milk
- 3 1/2 cups confectioners' sugar
- 1 teaspoon vanilla extract
- 30 individually wrapped caramels, unwrapped
- 1 tablespoon water
- 2 cups salted peanuts
- 1/2 cup semisweet chocolate chips
- 1/2 cup milk chocolate chips

Direction

- Grease an 8 x 8-inch square baking pan.
- In a microwave-safe bowl, mix together cocoa powder, brown sugar, milk, and butter. Heat in the microwave until the mixture starts to boil. Add vanilla extract and confectioners' sugar, then stir. Pour mixture into the greased pan.
- In another microwave-safe bowl, combine caramels and water; heat in the microwave until the caramels start to melt. Add peanuts and stir. Pour mixture over the chocolate layer.
- In a small microwave-safe bowl, mix together milk chocolate chips and semisweet chocolate chips; heat in the microwave until melted. Pour into the caramel layer. Refrigerate for 2 hours or until firm before serving.

Nutrition Information

- Calories: 205 calories;
- Sodium: 124
- Total Carbohydrate: 28.4
- Cholesterol: 9
- Protein: 3.2
- Total Fat: 10

144. Candy Cane Fudge

Serving: 64 | Prep: 20mins | Cook: | Ready in:

Ingredients

- 2 (10 ounce) packages vanilla baking chips
- 1 (14 ounce) can sweetened condensed milk
- 1/2 teaspoon peppermint extract
- 1 1/2 cups crushed candy canes
- 1 dash red or green food coloring

Direction

- Use aluminum foil to line an 8x8-in. baking pan; grease foil.
- In a saucepan, mix sweetened condensed milk and vanilla chips over medium heat. Whisk often to nearly melt the chips; take away from the heat and keep stirring till smooth. Once fully melted, mix in candy canes, food coloring and peppermint extract.
- Transfer to the prepped pan and spread over the bottom. Put in the refrigerator for 2 hours before slicing into square pieces.

Nutrition Information

- Calories: 89 calories;
- Total Fat: 2.9
- Sodium: 27
- Total Carbohydrate: 14.1
- Cholesterol: 2
- Protein: 1.1

145. Candy Cane Truffle Lollipops

Serving: 2 dozen. | Prep: 40mins | Cook: 0mins | Ready in:

Ingredients

- 84 miniature candy canes, divided
- 3 cups (18 ounces) semisweet chocolate chips, divided
- 3/4 cup heavy whipping cream
- 1/4 teaspoon peppermint extract
- 1 tablespoon shortening

Direction

- Get rid of hooks from 24 candy canes; set the sticks aside. Crush the leftover candy canes and the hooks.
- In a small bowl put 2 cups of chocolate chips. Put 3/4 cup crushed candy cans in a small saucepan then bring to a boil; cook and stir till the candy are melted. Get the saucepan off heat; put in extract and stir. Pour over chocolate; whisk till the mixture becomes smooth. Cool to room temperature, remember to stir occasionally. Chill in the fridge until the mixture becomes firm.
- Form 24 balls from the chocolate mixture; insert 1 candy cane stick into each truffle. Put shortening and the leftover chocolate chips together in a microwave and melt the mixture, stir till the mixture becomes smooth. Dip truffles into the chocolate liquid; let the excess liquid to drip off. Roll in the rest of squashed candy canes. Place truffles on waxed paper, allow truffles to sit till they are set.

Nutrition Information

- Calories: 209 calories
- Total Carbohydrate: 33g carbohydrate (24g sugars
- Cholesterol: 10mg cholesterol
- Protein: 1g protein.
- Total Fat: 10g fat (6g saturated fat)
- Sodium: 13mg sodium
- Fiber: 1g fiber)

146. Caramel Cookie Candy

Serving: 4 dozen. | Prep: 45mins | Cook: 30mins | Ready in:

Ingredients

- 2 teaspoons plus 2/3 cup butter, softened, divided
- 3/4 cup confectioners' sugar
- 1 large egg
- 1-1/2 teaspoons vanilla extract
- 2 cups all-purpose flour
- 1/2 teaspoon baking powder
- 1/2 teaspoon salt
- CARAMEL LAYER:
- 1 cup sugar
- 1 cup corn syrup
- 1 cup butter, cubed
- 1 can (14 ounces) sweetened condensed milk
- 1 teaspoon vanilla extract
- 2-1/2 pounds dark chocolate candy coating

Direction

- Set oven to preheat at 375°. Use foil to line a 13x9-in. pan and use 2 teaspoons butter to grease the foil; put aside.
- Cream together the confectioners' sugar and remaining butter in a large bowl till fluffy and light. Beat egg and vanilla into the mixture. Mix together the flour, baking powder and salt; add them into the creamed mixture slowly and combine thoroughly. Pat the dough into prepared pan. Bake until lightly browned for about 16-20 minutes. Let it cool down on a wire rack.
- To make the caramel, mix together butter, corn syrup and sugar in a large saucepan. Heat until boiling on medium heat, stir continuously. Gently boil for 4 minutes, do not

stir. Take off from heat; stir milk into the mixture slowly.
- Lower the heat to medium-low and cook until soft-ball stage (a candy thermometer reads 238°), stir continuously. Take off from heat; stir vanilla into the mixture. Transfer into the prepared crust. Refrigerate until caramel is set for about 2 hours.
- Lift the candy out of the pan with foil. Take off the foil gently; slice into 3-1/4x3/4-in. bars. Melt candy coating in a microwave; stir till smooth. Dip the bars into the chocolate; let the excess drip off. Put onto a sheet lined with waxed paper; refrigerate till set. For storage, keep in an airtight container.

Nutrition Information

- Calories: 246 calories
- Sodium: 97mg sodium
- Fiber: 1g fiber)
- Total Carbohydrate: 33g carbohydrate (24g sugars
- Cholesterol: 24mg cholesterol
- Protein: 2g protein.
- Total Fat: 13g fat (9g saturated fat)

147. Caramel Marshmallow Treats

Serving: 5 dozen. | Prep: 30mins | Cook: 0mins | Ready in:

Ingredients

- 1 can (14 ounces) sweetened condensed milk
- 1 package (14 ounces) caramels
- 1 cup butter, cubed
- 1 teaspoon ground cinnamon
- 1/2 teaspoon vanilla extract
- Rice Krispies, coarsely crushed
- 1 package (16 ounces) large marshmallows

Direction

- Use the waxed paper to line the two baking sheets; put aside. In a large saucepan that is set over low heat, cook and stir the butter, caramels, and milk until smooth and melted. Take off from the heat; mix in the vanilla and cinnamon.
- In a shallow bowl, place the Rice Krispies. Use a toothpick to dip each marshmallow into the warm caramel mixture; coat by turning the marshmallow. Press the bottoms into the Rice Krispies; transfer the treats onto the prepared pans. Let them sit until set.

Nutrition Information

- Calories: 98 calories
- Sodium: 55mg sodium
- Fiber: 0 fiber)
- Total Carbohydrate: 15g carbohydrate (12g sugars
- Cholesterol: 11mg cholesterol
- Protein: 1g protein.
- Total Fat: 4g fat (2g saturated fat)

148. Caramel Nut Marshmallows

Serving: 20 servings. | Prep: 20mins | Cook: 0mins | Ready in:

Ingredients

- 1-1/2 cups finely chopped pecans
- 36 caramels
- 2 tablespoons hot water
- 20 large marshmallows

Direction

- Use waxed paper to line a baking sheet; set aside. Put nuts in a shallow dish. Mix water and caramels in a large bowl which can be used in a microwave. Put the bowl without covering into a microwave, microwave on

high till the mixture is melted, about 30-90 seconds, remember to stir 2 times.
- Dip each marshmallow into the melted caramel, then roll caramel marshmallows in pecans. Put marshmallows on the prepared baking sheet. Allow to sit until set.

Nutrition Information

- Calories: 154 calories
- Sodium: 48mg sodium
- Fiber: 1g fiber)
- Total Carbohydrate: 21g carbohydrate (16g sugars
- Cholesterol: 1mg cholesterol
- Protein: 2g protein.
- Total Fat: 8g fat (2g saturated fat)

149. Caramel Pecan Logs

Serving: about 6-1/2 dozen. | Prep: 25mins | Cook: 0mins | Ready in:

Ingredients

- 3 cups confectioners' sugar
- 1 jar (7 ounces) marshmallow creme
- 1 teaspoon vanilla extract
- 1 package (14 ounces) caramels
- 3 tablespoons water
- 1-1/2 cups chopped pecans

Direction

- Mix crème, vanilla and sugar in bowl; knead to smoothen (mixture will become dry). Form to 6 logs, 4-1/2-inch x 1-1/4-inch in size. Refrigerate overnight. Cook and mix water and caramels in the top of a double boiler above boiling water till smooth. Dunk logs in caramel; roll in pecans. Refrigerate for two hours. Slice into 1/3-inch pieces.

Nutrition Information

- Calories: 62 calories
- Fiber: 0 fiber)
- Total Carbohydrate: 11g carbohydrate (9g sugars
- Cholesterol: 0 cholesterol
- Protein: 0 protein.
- Total Fat: 2g fat (0 saturated fat)
- Sodium: 15mg sodium

150. Caramel Pecans

Serving: 4-1/4 pounds. | Prep: 30mins | Cook: 40mins | Ready in:

Ingredients

- 2 teaspoons plus 1 cup butter, divided
- 1-1/4 cups sugar
- 1-1/4 cups packed brown sugar
- 1 cup dark corn syrup
- 2 cups heavy whipping cream, divided
- 2 pounds chopped pecans
- 1 teaspoon vanilla extract

Direction

- Line foil on a pan, 13-inch x 9- inch in size; use 2 teaspoons of butter to grease foil and put aside.
- Mix the rest of the butter, a cup of cream, corn syrup and sugars in a heavy, big saucepan. Cook and mix over moderate heat till sugar dissolves. Boil. Gradually mix in the rest of cream. Cook, without mixing, till a candy thermometer registers 245° or a firm-ball stage.
- Take away from heat; mix in vanilla and pecans. Put into prepped pan, avoid scraping the saucepan). Allow to rest till firm. Remove the candy from pan with foil. Throw the foil; slice candy into an-inch squares. Encase separately in waxed paper; twist ends.

Nutrition Information

- Calories: 107 calories
- Cholesterol: 10mg cholesterol
- Protein: 1g protein. Diabetic Exchanges: 1-1/2 fat
- Total Fat: 9g fat (2g saturated fat)
- Sodium: 19mg sodium
- Fiber: 1g fiber)
- Total Carbohydrate: 8g carbohydrate (5g sugars

151. Cashew Candy Crunch

Serving: 2-1/4 pounds. | Prep: 10mins | Cook: 30mins | Ready in:

Ingredients

- 1 tablespoon plus 1 cup butter, divided
- 2 cups sugar
- 1 cup light corn syrup
- 1 cup water
- 2-1/2 cups unsalted cashew halves
- 1/4 teaspoon baking soda

Direction

- Grease a 15x10x1-in. pan with 1 tablespoon butter; put aside. Mix the water, corn syrup and sugar in a big saucepan. Heat up to a boil, mixing frequently.
- Turn down heat; slice leftover butter into cubes and mix into syrup carefully. Cook and mix until a candy thermometer registers 280° (soft-crack stage). Put in nuts; cook and mix until candy thermometer registers 295°.
- Take off from the heat; mix in baking soda. Add into greased pan immediately. Cool; crack into pieces. Put in an airtight container to store.

Nutrition Information

- Calories: 171 calories
- Sodium: 54mg sodium

- Fiber: 0 fiber)
- Total Carbohydrate: 21g carbohydrate (14g sugars
- Cholesterol: 14mg cholesterol
- Protein: 2g protein.
- Total Fat: 10g fat (4g saturated fat)

152. Cashew Caramel Fudge

Serving: about 3 pounds. | Prep: 25mins | Cook: 0mins | Ready in:

Ingredients

- 2 teaspoons plus 1/2 cup butter, softened, divided
- 1 can (5 ounces) evaporated milk
- 2-1/2 cups sugar
- 2 cups (12 ounces) semisweet chocolate chips
- 1 jar (7 ounces) marshmallow creme
- 24 caramels, quartered
- 3/4 cup salted cashew halves
- 1 teaspoon vanilla extract

Direction

- Using foil, line a 9-inch square pan; spread 2 teaspoons butter on the foil. Put aside.
- Mix the leftover butter, sugar and milk in a big heavy saucepan. Cook over medium heat and mix till sugar is melted. Bring to a rapid boil; allow to boil for 5 minutes, mixing continuously. Take off heat; mix in marshmallow creme and chocolate chips till melted. Fold the vanilla, cashews and caramels in.
- In prepped pan, pour the mixture. Cool down. Lift fudge out of pan using foil. Get rid of foil; into 1-inch squares, slice the fudge. Keep in an airtight container.

Nutrition Information

- Calories: 85 calories

- Fiber: 0 fiber)
- Total Carbohydrate: 14g carbohydrate (12g sugars
- Cholesterol: 4mg cholesterol
- Protein: 1g protein.
- Total Fat: 4g fat (2g saturated fat)
- Sodium: 33mg sodium

153. Cherry Almond Bark

Serving: about 1 pound. | Prep: 25mins | Cook: 0mins | Ready in:

Ingredients

- 1 pound white candy coating, coarsely chopped
- 3/4 cup chopped candied cherries
- 1/2 cup unblanched whole almonds

Direction

- Melt coating in a microwave-safe bowl, stir until smooth. Add almonds and cherries. Spread the mixture on top of a baking sheet lined with foil. Chill in refrigerator until firm. Smash into pieces.

Nutrition Information

- Calories: 201 calories
- Total Fat: 10g fat (7g saturated fat)
- Sodium: 7mg sodium
- Fiber: 0 fiber)
- Total Carbohydrate: 27g carbohydrate (25g sugars
- Cholesterol: 0 cholesterol
- Protein: 1g protein.

154. Cherry Swirl Fudge

Serving: 5 dozen. | Prep: 15mins | Cook: 0mins | Ready in:

Ingredients

- 1-1/2 teaspoons butter
- 1 package (10 to 12 ounces) white baking chips
- 1 can (16 ounces) or 2 cups vanilla frosting
- 1 teaspoon cherry or almond extract
- 4 drops red liquid food coloring

Direction

- Use foil to line an 8-inch square pan; grease the foil with butter. Melt chips in a microwave-safe bowl; stir it till smooth. Beat frosting and extract into the mix till smooth. Transfer into the prepared pan.
- Sparsely add drops of food coloring onto the fudge; use a knife to cut through fudge to swirl. Cover and refrigerate until firm, for about 4 hours, before cutting into squares.

Nutrition Information

- Calories: 60 calories
- Fiber: 0 fiber)
- Total Carbohydrate: 8g carbohydrate (5g sugars
- Cholesterol: 1mg cholesterol
- Protein: 0 protein.
- Total Fat: 3g fat (1g saturated fat)
- Sodium: 21mg sodium

155. Cherry Walnut Fudge

Serving: 3 pounds. | Prep: 20mins | Cook: 0mins | Ready in:

Ingredients

- 3 tablespoons butter, divided
- 2 cups (12 ounces) dark chocolate chips

- 2 cups (12 ounces) semisweet chocolate chips
- 1 jar (7 ounces) marshmallow creme
- 4-1/2 cups sugar
- 1 can (12 ounces) evaporated milk
- 2 cups chopped walnuts
- 2 cups dried cherries
- 1 teaspoon vanilla extract
- 1/2 teaspoon almond extract

Direction

- Use the foil to line the 13x9-inch pan; use 1 tablespoon of the butter to butter foil and put aside. Put marshmallow crème and chocolate chips into the big bowl; put aside.
- In the big sauce pan, boil the leftover butter, milk and sugar on medium heat, whisk frequently. Lower the heat; let simmer, with no cover, for 6 minutes, whisk once in a while. Gradually add on top of the chocolate mixture; whisk till smooth. Whisk in extracts, cherries and walnuts.
- Add to the prepped pan. Allow it to rest at the room temperature till cool. With foil, lift the fudge out of the pan. Lightly peel off the foil; chop the fudge into 1-inch square pieces. Keep in the airtight container in fridge.

Nutrition Information

- Calories: 97 calories
- Sodium: 7mg sodium
- Fiber: 0 fiber)
- Total Carbohydrate: 16g carbohydrate (14g sugars
- Cholesterol: 2mg cholesterol
- Protein: 1g protein. Diabetic Exchanges: 1 starch
- Total Fat: 4g fat (2g saturated fat)

156. Chewy Apple Candies

Serving: about 7 dozen. | Prep: 10mins | Cook: 20mins | Ready in:

Ingredients

- 1-1/4 cups raspberry or cinnamon applesauce, divided
- 2 envelopes unflavored gelatin
- 2 cups sugar
- 2 teaspoons vanilla extract
- 1 cup coarsely chopped walnuts
- 1/2 cup confectioners' sugar

Direction

- Mix gelatin and half cup applesauce in a big bowl; put aside to soften. Heat up sugar and leftover applesauce to a boil in a 2 quarts saucepan. Put in gelatin mixture; bring back to boiling. Boil for 15 minutes, mixing continuously. Take off from the heat; mix in nuts and vanilla.
- Put into a buttered 8-inch square pan. Cover and refrigerate overnight. Slice into 1-1/2-inch x 1/2-inch pieces; toss in confectioners' sugar. Chill for a few hours. Put in an airtight container to store in the fridge.

Nutrition Information

- Calories: 68 calories
- Cholesterol: 0 cholesterol
- Protein: 1g protein.
- Total Fat: 2g fat (0 saturated fat)
- Sodium: 1mg sodium
- Fiber: 0 fiber)
- Total Carbohydrate: 13g carbohydrate (12g sugars

157. Chocolate Billionaires

Serving: about 2 pounds. | Prep: 45mins | Cook: 0mins | Ready in:

Ingredients

- 1 package (14 ounces) caramels
- 3 tablespoons water

- 1-1/2 cups chopped pecans
- 1 cup crisp rice cereal
- 3 cups milk chocolate chips
- 1-1/2 teaspoons shortening

Direction

- Using waxed paper, line 2 baking sheets; grease the paper; put aside. Mix water and caramels in a large heavy saucepan; cook while stirring until smooth over low heat. Stir in cereal and pecans until coated. Drop onto prepared pans by teaspoonfuls. Keep in the fridge until firm or for 10 minutes.
- In the meantime, melt shortening and chocolate chips in a microwave; stir until smooth. Coat candy with chocolates on all sides; drip off excess. Transfer on lined pans. Keep in the fridge until set. Keep in an airtight container.

Nutrition Information

- Calories: 172 calories
- Fiber: 1g fiber)
- Total Carbohydrate: 20g carbohydrate (17g sugars
- Cholesterol: 4mg cholesterol
- Protein: 2g protein.
- Total Fat: 10g fat (4g saturated fat)
- Sodium: 51mg sodium

158. Chocolate Caramel Cracker Bars

Serving: 27 bars. | Prep: 15mins | Cook: 10mins | Ready in:

Ingredients

- 1 teaspoon plus 3/4 cup butter, cubed
- 45 Club crackers (2-1/2x1 inch)
- 1 can (14 ounces) sweetened condensed milk
- 1/2 cup packed brown sugar
- 3 tablespoons light corn syrup
- 1 cup (6 ounces) semisweet chocolate chips

Direction

- Line foil on 9-in. square baking pan; use 1 tsp. butter to grease foil. Put 1 layer crackers in pan.
- Boil leftover butter, corn syrup, brown sugar and milk in big saucepan on medium heat, occasionally mixing. Lower heat to keep low boil; mix and cook for 7 minutes. Take off heat. Spread 1/3 mixture evenly on crackers. Repeat caramel and cracker layers two times.
- Sprinkle chocolate chips immediately on caramel; let stand till glossy for 3-5 minutes. Spread on top; cover. Refrigerate till chocolate is set for 2 hours. Lift layers from pan using foil; cut to 3x1-in. bars.

Nutrition Information

- Calories: 176 calories
- Protein: 2g protein.
- Total Fat: 10g fat (6g saturated fat)
- Sodium: 126mg sodium
- Fiber: 0 fiber)
- Total Carbohydrate: 22g carbohydrate (18g sugars
- Cholesterol: 19mg cholesterol

159. Chocolate Caramel Turkey Legs

Serving: 20 servings. | Prep: 20mins | Cook: 0mins | Ready in:

Ingredients

- 40 caramels
- 20 honey wheat braided pretzel twists
- 3 ounces milk chocolate, melted

Direction

- Melt caramels on high in the microwave for 10 to 15 seconds until softened. Make it look like turkey leg by molding 2 softened caramels around the lower half of each braided pretzel. Plunge in melted chocolate; let the excess drip off. Put on waxed paper; let sit until firm. Put in an airtight container 1-2 weeks to store.

Nutrition Information

- Calories: 112 calories
- Protein: 1g protein.
- Total Fat: 3g fat (1g saturated fat)
- Sodium: 102mg sodium
- Fiber: 0 fiber)
- Total Carbohydrate: 21g carbohydrate (16g sugars
- Cholesterol: 2mg cholesterol

160. Chocolate Cashew Clusters

Serving: 3 pounds. | Prep: 20mins | Cook: 10mins | Ready in:

Ingredients

- 16 ounces white baking chocolate, chopped
- 7 ounces milk chocolate, chopped
- 7 ounces bittersweet chocolate, chopped
- 4 cups salted cashews
- 3/4 cup milk chocolate English toffee bits

Direction

- On low heat, cook and stir the chocolates in a large heavy saucepan until melted. Take off from heat; stir cashews and toffee bits into the mixture. Drop by tablespoonfuls onto waxed paper. Refrigerate till set for about 10-15 minutes. For storage, keep in an airtight container.

Nutrition Information

- Calories: 101 calories
- Cholesterol: 2mg cholesterol
- Protein: 2g protein.
- Total Fat: 7g fat (3g saturated fat)
- Sodium: 60mg sodium
- Fiber: 0 fiber)
- Total Carbohydrate: 8g carbohydrate (6g sugars

161. Chocolate Cashew Crunchies

Serving: 6-7 dozen. | Prep: 25mins | Cook: 0mins | Ready in:

Ingredients

- 2 cups (12 ounces) chocolate chips
- 2 cups (12 ounces) butterscotch chips
- 1 package (12 ounces) chow mein noodles
- 1-1/2 cups cashew pieces

Direction

- Microwave butterscotch chips and chocolate on high for 1-1/2 minutes or until melted. Mix to blend well. Put in cashews and chow mein noodles. Put by teaspoonfuls onto waxed paper to cool. Put in airtight containers to store in the fridge.

Nutrition Information

- Calories: 171 calories
- Sodium: 77mg sodium
- Fiber: 1g fiber)
- Total Carbohydrate: 19g carbohydrate (12g sugars
- Cholesterol: 1mg cholesterol
- Protein: 2g protein.
- Total Fat: 11g fat (5g saturated fat)

162. Chocolate Cherries

Serving: 5 dozen. | Prep: 30mins | Cook: 0mins | Ready in:

Ingredients

- 60 maraschino cherries with stems
- 2 cups confectioners' sugar
- 3 tablespoons butter, softened
- 3 tablespoons light corn syrup
- 1/4 teaspoon salt
- 2 cups (12 ounces) semisweet chocolate chips
- 2 tablespoons shortening

Direction

- Using paper towels, pat the cherries dry. Put aside. Combine salt, corn syrup, butter and sugar in a small bowl, then mix well. Knead until they become smooth. Place in the refrigerator, covered, for about 60 mins.
- Shape into 1/2-in. balls, then flatten into 2-inch circle. Cover each circle around 1 cherry and roll lightly in hands. Arrange the cherries on waxed paper-lined baking sheets, stems up. Loosely cover, then place in the refrigerator for 60 mins.
- In a heavy saucepan or microwave, melt shortening and chocolate chips. Stir until they become smooth. Holding onto stem, submerge each cherry into the chocolate; let excess drip off. Place on the waxed paper; allow to stand until set. Place in the refrigerator until hardened. Preserve in a covered container. Place in the refrigerator for about 1 to 2 weeks. Then enjoy!

Nutrition Information

- Calories: 64 calories
- Protein: 0 protein.
- Total Fat: 3g fat (1g saturated fat)
- Sodium: 18mg sodium
- Fiber: 0 fiber)
- Total Carbohydrate: 11g carbohydrate (10g sugars
- Cholesterol: 2mg cholesterol

163. Chocolate Chews

Serving: 18 | Prep: | Cook: | Ready in:

Ingredients

- 1 cup semisweet chocolate chips
- 1/2 cup butter, softened
- 1/2 cup white sugar
- 1/2 cup packed brown sugar
- 2 eggs
- 1/2 teaspoon vanilla extract
- 2 cups all-purpose flour
- 1/2 teaspoon baking powder
- 1/2 teaspoon baking soda

Direction

- Over very low heat, melt the chocolate chips in a heavy saucepan. Stir to melt evenly.
- Cream sugars and butter together until light. Beat in one egg at a time. Stir in vanilla and melted chocolate.
- Whisk baking soda, baking powder and flour in a bowl. Slowly add to the butter mixture. Thoroughly blend. Form into 1-inch balls; arrange on greased cookie sheet.
- Bake for 12-14 minutes at 350°F (180°C). Let sit for 1-2 minutes on cookie sheet; transfer to a rack to cool.

Nutrition Information

- Calories: 194 calories;
- Sodium: 96
- Total Carbohydrate: 28.1
- Cholesterol: 34
- Protein: 2.6
- Total Fat: 8.6

164. Chocolate Chow Mein Clusters

Serving: 8 clusters. | Prep: 15mins | Cook: 0mins | Ready in:

Ingredients

- 1/2 cup semisweet chocolate chips
- 1/2 cup butterscotch chips
- 1/2 cup chow mein noodles
- 1/2 cup salted peanuts

Direction

- Melt chocolate and butterscotch chips in a microwave. Stir until they become smooth. Mix in peanuts and chow mein noodles till well coated.
- Drop onto the waxed paper-lined baking sheet by rounded tablespoonfuls. Place in the refrigerator until set, about 120 mins.

Nutrition Information

- Calories: 199 calories
- Fiber: 2g fiber)
- Total Carbohydrate: 20g carbohydrate (16g sugars
- Cholesterol: 1mg cholesterol
- Protein: 4g protein.
- Total Fat: 13g fat (7g saturated fat)
- Sodium: 64mg sodium

165. Chocolate Clusters

Serving: 12 | Prep: | Cook: | Ready in:

Ingredients

- 1 cup semisweet chocolate chips
- 1 cup butterscotch chips
- 1 cup peanuts
- 1 cup chow mein noodles

Direction

- Put the butterscotch chips and chocolate chips in a saucepan and let it melt over low heat setting. Remove the pan away from the heat and put in the chow mein noodles and peanuts right away. Mix everything together until well-coated. Drop the mixture onto a cookie sheet that is lined with wax paper; allow it to rest until the mixture has set then keep it in the fridge. Serve afterwards.

Nutrition Information

- Calories: 239 calories;
- Cholesterol: 0
- Protein: 3.8
- Total Fat: 15.4
- Sodium: 34
- Total Carbohydrate: 22.7

166. Chocolate Covered Cherries

Serving: 50 | Prep: | Cook: | Ready in:

Ingredients

- 8 tablespoons melted butter
- 6 tablespoons corn syrup
- 1 (14 ounce) can sweetened condensed milk
- 1 teaspoon vanilla extract
- 3 pounds confectioners' sugar
- 3 (10 ounce) jars maraschino cherries, drained
- 2 cups semisweet chocolate chips
- 1/2 tablespoon shortening

Direction

- In a large mixing bowl, mix together sugar, vanilla, sweetened condensed milk, corn syrup and butter. Knead the dough; then shape it

into walnut-sized balls with a cherry in the centre. Chill in the freezer.
- In a double boiler, melt shortening and chocolate chips together. Dip the cooled balls in the chocolate, allow to cool down on parchment paper.

Nutrition Information

- Calories: 209 calories;
- Sodium: 24
- Total Carbohydrate: 42.4
- Cholesterol: 8
- Protein: 1.2
- Total Fat: 4.7

167. Chocolate Crunch Patties

Serving: about 4 dozen. | Prep: 15mins | Cook: 0mins | Ready in:

Ingredients

- 2 cups (12 ounces) butterscotch chips
- 1 cup (6 ounces) milk chocolate chips
- 1-1/2 cups dry roasted peanuts
- 1 cup crushed thick ripple-cut potato chips

Direction

- Combine chocolate chips and butterscotch in a medium microwaveable bowl. Microwave for 1 to 3 minutes on 50% power, stirring every minute, until softened. Mix until smooth. Put in potato chips and peanuts; stir well. Drop mixture onto waxed paper-lined baking sheets by teaspoonfuls. Allow to firm.

Nutrition Information

- Calories: 209 calories
- Cholesterol: 3mg cholesterol
- Protein: 4g protein.
- Total Fat: 13g fat (7g saturated fat)
- Sodium: 108mg sodium
- Fiber: 1g fiber)
- Total Carbohydrate: 20g carbohydrate (16g sugars

168. Chocolate Fudge With Hazelnut

Serving: about 2-1/2 pounds (64 pieces). | Prep: 10mins | Cook: 10mins | Ready in:

Ingredients

- 1 teaspoon butter
- 1/2 cup butter, cubed
- 2 cups packed brown sugar
- 1/2 cup whole milk
- 1 cup Nutella
- 1 teaspoon vanilla extract
- 3 cups confectioners' sugar
- 1/2 cup chopped hazelnuts, optional

Direction

- Use a foil to line an 8-in. square pan; use 1 teaspoon of butter to grease the foil.
- In a large saucepan, combine milk, brown sugar, and cubed butter. Heat until it fully boils over medium heat while stirring constantly. Cook for 2 minutes, stirring regularly. Take off from the heat.
- Mix in vanilla and Nutella; put into a large bowl. Add in the confectioners' sugar; at medium speed, beat the mixture for 2 minutes or until smooth. Spread into the prepared pan right away. If you wish, sprinkle hazelnuts on top. Cover and refrigerate for 1 hour or until firm.

Nutrition Information

- Calories:
- Sodium:
- Fiber:

- Total Carbohydrate:
- Cholesterol:
- Protein:
- Total Fat:

169. Chocolate Hazelnut Truffles

Serving: Makes about 80 truffles | Prep: | Cook: |Ready in:

Ingredients

- Unsweetened cocoa powder for dusting
- 1 cup hazelnuts, toasted , loose skins rubbed off with a kitchen towel, and cooled
- 3/4 cup all-purpose flour
- 1/2 cup sugar
- 1/2 teaspoon salt
- 1/2 stick (1/4 cup) unsalted butter
- 6 oz fine-quality bittersweet chocolate (not unsweetened), finely chopped
- 2 large whole eggs
- 2 large egg yolks
- 1 cup heavy cream
- 1/8 teaspoon salt
- 12 oz fine-quality bittersweet chocolate (not unsweetened), finely chopped
- Special equipment: a small metal offset spatula

Direction

- Preparation: For hazelnut base: Prepare the oven by preheating to 350°F. Grease with butter the sides and bottom of an 8-inch square metal baking pan, then sprinkle with cocoa powder, getting rid of excess.
- Nicely grind nuts, flour, salt and sugar in a food processor
- In a 2-qt. saucepan, dissolve butter then separate from heat. Mix in chocolate until smooth. Stir in eggs, 1 at a time, stirring until smooth. Whisk in nut flour until just blended.
- Place batter in baking pan and equally spread and bake in the preheated oven for 15-20 minutes placing it at the center until top turns dry and firm and a tester poked into middle comes out with crumbs adhering. Let it fully cool for at least 2 hours in pan on rack.
- For ganache: In a bowl, lightly whisk egg yolks. Make cream with salt just to a boil in a small heavy saucepan, then mix half of it to yolks in a slow stream, stirring constantly. Stir yolk mixture into remaining cream and cook over low heat, stirring, until slightly thickened and an instant-read thermometer reads 170°F (keep from boiling).
- Separate from heat and stir in chocolate, stirring until smooth. Place ganache over hazelnut base in pan, using an offset spatula to smooth the top, and chill for at least 5 hours, covered, until solid.
- Use a warmed thin knife to slice into squares, cleaning off knife after every slice, and take from pan while still cold.
- Serve truffles at room temperature or cold.
- Cooks' notes: You can chill the truffles for up to 7 days.
- Froze in pan, tightly covered with foil, for 1 month.

170. Chocolate Nut Candies

Serving: 12-1/2 dozen. | Prep: 15mins | Cook: 10mins | Ready in:

Ingredients

- 3 cups (18 ounces) semisweet chocolate chips
- 2 cups creamy peanut butter
- 1 cup butter, cubed
- 1/2 cup evaporated milk
- 1/4 cup instant vanilla pudding mix
- 1 teaspoon vanilla extract
- 2 pounds confectioners' sugar
- 3 cups salted peanuts

Direction

- Melt peanut butter and chocolate chips over low heat in a heavy saucepan, whisking frequently. Transfer half of mixture to a buttered 15x10x1-inch pan, then chill. Put the rest of the chocolate mixture aside.
- Bring pudding mix, milk and butter in a separate saucepan to a boil; boil for 1 minute, whisking constantly. Put off the heat; transfer to a large mixing bowl; add vanilla. Slowly mix in sugar. Spread over the layer of chocolate in the pan; put into the fridge to chill.
- Put peanuts into the reserved chocolate mixture; spread over filling. Put into the fridge to chill. Divide into 1x1 1/2-inch bars.

Nutrition Information

- Calories:
- Protein:
- Total Fat:
- Sodium:
- Fiber:
- Total Carbohydrate:
- Cholesterol:

171. Chocolate Nut Fudge

Serving: 36 | Prep: 15mins | Cook: 10mins | Ready in:

Ingredients

- 1 (12 ounce) bag semisweet chocolate chips
- 1/2 cup sour cream
- 3/4 cup confectioners' sugar
- 1/4 teaspoon salt
- 2 cups finely crushed vanilla wafer crumbs
- 1/2 cup broken walnuts

Direction

- Line aluminum foil in an 8-in by 8-in baking pan.
- On low heat, melt chocolate chips for 10 minutes in a big heavy pan until smooth and melted, constantly mix to prevent scorching. Mix salt, confectioners' sugar, and sour cream into the chocolate; stir in vanilla wafer crumbs and broken walnut pieces. Slather the fudge in the foil-lined pan. Chill until firm then slice into squares.

Nutrition Information

- Calories: 119 calories;
- Cholesterol: 1
- Protein: 1.2
- Total Fat: 6.5
- Sodium: 50
- Total Carbohydrate: 15.9

172. Chocolate Nut Fudge Rolls

Serving: about 2-1/4 pounds. | Prep: 30mins | Cook: 25mins | Ready in:

Ingredients

- 2 tablespoons butter
- 1 ounce unsweetened chocolate
- 3 cups sugar
- 1 cup whole milk
- 1/4 cup honey
- 1/8 teaspoon salt
- 1 teaspoon white vinegar
- 1 teaspoon vanilla extract
- 2 cups (12 ounces) semisweet chocolate chips
- 1 tablespoon shortening
- 3 cups chopped walnuts

Direction

- Put chocolate and butter in a large heavy saucepan and melt on low heat. Put in salt, honey, milk and sugar. Bring to a boil on medium heat; remember to stir sometimes. To

cover, put a lid on and keep boiling for 2 more minutes. Remove the lid and cook without stirring till a candy thermometer reaches 240 degrees (this is the soft ball stage). Get the saucepan off heat; add vinegar and stir.
- Allow the mixture to cool to 110 degrees. Put in vanilla; beat vigorously for 8 to 10 minutes till the mixture becomes thick there is no gloss remaining. Butter a baking sheet and transfer the thickened mixture on to the baking sheet. Allow the mixture to sit till it is cool enough to handle. Knead for 2 to 3 minutes. Use the kneaded mixture to make 4x1-1/2 in. rolls. Use waxed paper to line baking sheets and lay rolls on the prepared baking sheets; chill the rolls for 3 to 4 hours.
- Put chocolate chips and shortening together and melt in the microwave; stir till the mixture becomes smooth. Dip rolls in chocolate; let the excess chocolate to drip off. Roll in nuts. Lay roll on the waxed paper-lined baking sheets and chill till they become firm. Divide into 1/4 in. slices.

Nutrition Information

- Calories: 394 calories
- Sodium: 39mg sodium
- Fiber: 2g fiber)
- Total Carbohydrate: 53g carbohydrate (47g sugars
- Cholesterol: 5mg cholesterol
- Protein: 6g protein.
- Total Fat: 21g fat (6g saturated fat)

173. Chocolate Orange Bites

Serving: about 4 dozen. | Prep: 35mins | Cook: 0mins | Ready in:

Ingredients

- 1 package (9 ounces) chocolate wafers, crushed
- Sugar substitute equivalent to 1/2 cup sugar
- 1/4 cup reduced-fat butter, melted
- 1/4 cup thawed orange juice concentrate
- 1 teaspoon grated orange zest
- 1/2 cup confectioners' sugar
- Baking cocoa and/or additional confectioners' sugar

Direction

- In a small bowl, mix together the first five ingredients. Roll it into 3/4-in. balls; then roll the balls in confectioners' sugar. Refrigerate, covered, for at least 2 hours.
- Sprinkle them lightly with cocoa and/or confectioners' sugar before serving. Keep refrigerated in an airtight container.

Nutrition Information

- Calories: 35 calories
- Protein: 0 protein. Diabetic Exchanges: 1/2 starch.
- Total Fat: 1g fat (1g saturated fat)
- Sodium: 37mg sodium
- Fiber: 0 fiber)
- Total Carbohydrate: 6g carbohydrate (2g sugars
- Cholesterol: 2mg cholesterol

174. Chocolate Peanut Brittle

Serving: about 1-1/4 pounds. | Prep: 5mins | Cook: 15mins | Ready in:

Ingredients

- 1 cup sugar
- 1/4 cup light corn syrup
- 2 cups salted peanuts
- 1 teaspoon butter
- 1/4 cup baking cocoa
- 1 teaspoon baking soda
- 1 teaspoon vanilla extract

Direction

- Grease a metal spatula and a 15x10x1 in. pan. Set aside.
- Mix corn syrup and sugar in a microwave safe bowl (size 2 qt.). Microwave without a cover on high for 4 minutes; stir. Cook for 3 minutes more. Add butter, peanuts and stir. Microwave a half to a minute or till the mixture gets a light amber color (be careful as the mixture will be pretty hot).
- Mix in vanilla, baking soda, cocoa quickly till everything is combined. Transfer the mixture into the prepared pan immediately; use the prepared metal spatula to spread. Cool before cracking into pieces. Keep in an airtight container to store.

Nutrition Information

- Calories: 139 calories
- Total Carbohydrate: 16g carbohydrate (12g sugars
- Cholesterol: 1mg cholesterol
- Protein: 4g protein. Diabetic Exchanges: 1-1/2 fat
- Total Fat: 7g fat (1g saturated fat)
- Sodium: 132mg sodium
- Fiber: 2g fiber)

175. Chocolate Peanut Butter Candy

Serving: about 2-1/2 pounds. | Prep: 10mins | Cook: 0mins | Ready in:

Ingredients

- 1 pound white candy coating, coarsely chopped
- 1-1/2 cups creamy peanut butter
- 2 cups (12 ounces) semisweet chocolate chips

Direction

- Melt candy coating in a big microwaveable bowl; mix until smooth. Mix in peanut butter; spread onto a waxed paper-lined baking tray thinly.
- Melt chocolate chips in the other microwaveable bowl; mix until smooth. Sprinkle on top of candy-coating mixture; run a knife through mixture to swirl the chocolate. Refrigerate until set.
- Crack into pieces. Put in an airtight container to store in the fridge.

Nutrition Information

- Calories: 316 calories
- Cholesterol: 0 cholesterol
- Protein: 5g protein.
- Total Fat: 21g fat (11g saturated fat)
- Sodium: 84mg sodium
- Fiber: 2g fiber)
- Total Carbohydrate: 31g carbohydrate (27g sugars

176. Chocolate Peanut Candy Squares

Serving: 12 dozen. | Prep: 20mins | Cook: 0mins | Ready in:

Ingredients

- 1 tablespoon plus 1 cup butter, divided
- 1 package (12 ounces) semisweet chocolate chips
- 1 package (10 to 11 ounces) butterscotch chips
- 1 jar (18 ounces) peanut butter
- 1 can (16 ounces) salted peanuts
- 1 can (14 ounces) sweetened condensed milk
- 1 package (3 ounces) cook-and-serve vanilla pudding mix
- 1 teaspoon maple flavoring
- 1 package (2 pounds) confectioners' sugar

Direction

- Butter a 15x10x1-inch pan with 1 tablespoon butter; put aside. Cook and mix peanut butter and chips in a saucepan over low heat, until chips melts and turn smooth. Scatter half into buttered pan; chill. Put peanuts into the leftover mixture; put aside.
- Mix the leftover butter, pudding mix and milk in a saucepan; cook and mix until mixture heats up to a boil. Cook and mix for a minute. Take off from the heat; mix in maple flavoring. Whip pudding mixture and confectioners' sugar in a bowl until smooth. Spread over bottom layer carefully. Spread with saved peanut mixture gently. Refrigerate for no less than a day. Slice into 1-inch squares. Chill in airtight containers.

Nutrition Information

- Calories:
- Total Fat:
- Sodium:
- Fiber:
- Total Carbohydrate:
- Cholesterol:
- Protein:

177. Chocolate Peanut Clusters

Serving: 10 dozen. | Prep: 10mins | Cook: 5mins | Ready in:

Ingredients

- 2 pounds white candy coating, coarsely chopped
- 1 package (12 ounces) semisweet chocolate chips
- 1 package (11-1/2 ounces) milk chocolate chips
- 5 cups salted dry roasted peanuts

Direction

- In a heavy saucepan, cook while stirring chips and candy coating over low heat until smooth and melted. Let cool for 10 mins. Then mix in peanuts.
- Drop on the waxed paper-lined baking sheets by rounded tablespoonfuls. Place in the refrigerator for 45 mins or until firm.

Nutrition Information

- Calories: 206 calories
- Protein: 4g protein.
- Total Fat: 14g fat (7g saturated fat)
- Sodium: 103mg sodium
- Fiber: 1g fiber)
- Total Carbohydrate: 20g carbohydrate (17g sugars
- Cholesterol: 1mg cholesterol

178. Chocolate Pecan Caramels

Serving: about 2-1/2 pounds (about 6-3/4 dozen). | Prep: 20mins | Cook: 15mins | Ready in:

Ingredients

- 1 tablespoon plus 1 cup butter, softened, divided
- 1-1/2 cups coarsely chopped pecans, toasted
- 1 cup (6 ounces) semisweet chocolate chips
- 2 cups packed brown sugar
- 1 cup light corn syrup
- 1/4 cup water
- 1 can (14 ounces) sweetened condensed milk
- 2 teaspoons vanilla extract

Direction

- Use a foil to line a 13x9-in. pan; use 1 tablespoon of butter to grease the foil. Sprinkle chocolate chips and pecans on top; put aside.
- In a heavy saucepan that is set over medium heat, melt the rest of the butter. Add the water,

corn syrup, and brown sugar. Cook and stir until the mixture boils. Stir in milk. Cook, stirring continuously until it reaches into a firm-ball stage (a candy thermometer reads 248°).
- Take off from the heat and add in the vanilla. Transfer into the prepared pan (without scraping the saucepan). Allow it to cool thoroughly before slicing.

Nutrition Information

- Calories: 190 calories
- Total Carbohydrate: 26g carbohydrate (23g sugars
- Cholesterol: 16mg cholesterol
- Protein: 1g protein.
- Total Fat: 10g fat (5g saturated fat)
- Sodium: 76mg sodium
- Fiber: 1g fiber)

179. Chocolate Pizza Heart

Serving: 1-3/4 pounds. | Prep: 15mins | Cook: 0mins | Ready in:

Ingredients

- 1-1/2 cups milk chocolate chips
- 1 cup butterscotch chips
- 3/4 cup miniature marshmallows
- 3/4 cup chopped salted peanuts
- 3/4 cup crushed potato chips
- 2 tablespoons sweetened shredded coconut
- 7 maraschino cherries, halved
- 1/4 cup milk chocolate M&M's
- 2 tablespoons vanilla or white chips
- 1/2 teaspoon shortening

Direction

- Draw a 10-inch heart with a pencil on a waxed paper. Put the paper on a baking sheet, pencil mark down; put aside.
- Melt the butterscotch chips and chocolate in a big microwave-safe bowl; mix until smooth. Mix in potato chips, peanuts and marshmallows. Instantly distribute into the heart shape in the prepared pan. Dust with coconut; top with M&M's and cherries.
- Melt the shortening and vanilla chips in a microwave; mix until smooth. Pour on top. Refrigerate for 1-1/2 hours, until firm. Discard the waxed paper. Allow to stand at room temperature for 10 minutes prior to cutting.

Nutrition Information

- Calories: 291 calories
- Cholesterol: 5mg cholesterol
- Protein: 5g protein.
- Total Fat: 17g fat (9g saturated fat)
- Sodium: 82mg sodium
- Fiber: 1g fiber)
- Total Carbohydrate: 31g carbohydrate (15g sugars

180. Chocolate Raisin Truffles

Serving: 2-1/2 dozen. | Prep: 15mins | Cook: 5mins | Ready in:

Ingredients

- 1 cup milk chocolate chips
- 1/4 cup light corn syrup
- 2 tablespoons confectioners' sugar
- 1-1/2 teaspoons vanilla extract
- 1-1/2 cups raisins
- Nonpareils, sprinkles and/or ground nuts

Direction

- Melt chips in microwave-safe bowl. Mix vanilla, confectioners' sugar and corn syrup in till smooth. Mix raisins in till coated evenly.
- By teaspoonfuls, drop on waxed paper-lined baking sheet then roll truffles in nuts/sprinkles/nonpareils.

Nutrition Information

- Calories: 61 calories
- Protein: 1g protein.
- Total Fat: 2g fat (1g saturated fat)
- Sodium: 9mg sodium
- Fiber: 0 fiber)
- Total Carbohydrate: 12g carbohydrate (10g sugars
- Cholesterol: 1mg cholesterol

181.   Chocolate Rum Truffles

Serving: 3 dozen. | Prep: 25mins | Cook: 0mins | Ready in:

Ingredients

- 14 ounces semisweet chocolate, divided
- 1 cup heavy whipping cream
- 1/3 cup butter, softened
- 1 teaspoon rum extract
- 1/2 cup finely chopped pecans or walnuts, toasted

Direction

- Chop 12-oz. chocolate coarsely; put aside. Heat cream on low heat in saucepan till bubbles appear around pan's sides. Take off heat; add chopped chocolate, mixing till smooth and melted.
- Cool it to room temperature; mix extract and butter in. Tightly cover; refrigerate till firm or for 6 hours.
- Grate leftover chocolate; put in shallow dish. Add nuts; put aside. Form tablespoonfuls chilled chocolate mixture to balls. Put onto waxed paper-lined baking sheets. Refrigerate till easy to handle if truffles are soft. In chocolate-nut mixture, roll truffles. Keep in airtight container in the fridge.

Nutrition Information

- Calories: 54 calories
- Sodium: 20mg sodium
- Fiber: 0 fiber)
- Total Carbohydrate: 1g carbohydrate (1g sugars
- Cholesterol: 14mg cholesterol
- Protein: 0 protein.
- Total Fat: 6g fat (3g saturated fat)

182.   Chocolate Zebra Clusters

Serving: 2-1/2 dozen. | Prep: 30mins | Cook: 0mins | Ready in:

Ingredients

- 2 cups (12 ounces) semisweet chocolate chips
- 12 ounces white candy coating, coarsely chopped, divided
- 1-1/4 cups salted peanuts
- 1-1/4 cups crisp rice cereal
- 2-1/4 cups miniature marshmallows
- 1 teaspoon shortening

Direction

- Using waxed paper, line 2 baking sheets; put aside. Melt 7 oz. white candy coating and chips at 70% power in a microwave; stir until smooth. Stir in cereal and peanuts. Slightly cool; fold in marshmallows. Drop onto lined baking sheets by rounded tablespoonfuls.
- Melt the rest of the candy coating and shortening in microwave; stir until smooth. Place in a plastic bag or pastry; create a small hole in the corner of the bag. Drizzle over clusters. Keep in the fridge for 5 minutes or until set. Keep in an airtight container.

Nutrition Information

- Calories: 166 calories

- Total Carbohydrate: 20g carbohydrate (17g sugars)
- Cholesterol: 0 cholesterol
- Protein: 2g protein.
- Total Fat: 10g fat (5g saturated fat)
- Sodium: 40mg sodium
- Fiber: 1g fiber)

183. Chocolate Covered Almond Butter Brickle

Serving: about 1-3/4 pounds. | Prep: 10mins | Cook: 20mins | Ready in:

Ingredients

- 1-1/2 teaspoons plus 2 tablespoons unsalted butter, divided
- 1 cup crunchy almond butter
- 1/2 teaspoon baking soda
- 1 teaspoon plus 2 tablespoons water, divided
- 3/4 cup sugar
- 3/4 cup light corn syrup
- 1 teaspoon almond extract
- 1 cup 60% cacao bittersweet chocolate baking chips
- 1/3 cup chopped almonds, toasted
- 3/4 cup sweetened shredded coconut

Direction

- Use 1 1/2 teaspoons butter to grease a 15x10x1-inch pan. In a microwaveable bowl, put almond butter; cover and heat at 50% power until soft for 30 to 60 seconds, mixing once. Mix together 1 teaspoon water and baking soda in a small bowl until dissolved. Put aside baking soda mixture and almond butter.
- Mix together 2 tablespoons water, corn syrup and sugar in a big heavy saucepan. Put on medium heat and boil while stirring frequently. Dip a pastry brush in water and brush down the pan's sides to get rid of sugar crystals. Cook for 10 minutes while stirring frequently until mixture reaches soft-ball stage, about 240 degrees. Put in remaining butter; cook while stirring constantly for another 5 minutes until mixture achieves hard-crack stage, about 300 degrees.
- Put off the heat, mix in dissolved baking soda, almond extract and softened almond butter. (Mixture will have foams). Quickly transfer to the greased pan. Spread out to 1/4-inch thick.
- Scatter chocolate chips on top; allow to sit until chocolate starts to melt. Evenly spread out and scatter coconut and almonds on top, lightly press into chocolate to stick. Wait until slightly cool. Put in the refrigerator until chocolate sets, about an hour.
- Break into pieces. Store in a tightly sealed container with waxed paper between layers.

Nutrition Information

- Calories:
- Fiber:
- Total Carbohydrate:
- Cholesterol:
- Protein:
- Total Fat:
- Sodium:

184. Chocolate Covered Pretzels

Serving: 20 pretzels. | Prep: 55mins | Cook: 5mins | Ready in:

Ingredients

- 12 ounces milk chocolate candy coating disks
- 20 large sourdough pretzels, divided
- Colored sprinkles
- 12 ounces white candy coating disks

Direction

- Melt milk chocolate in a microwave; mix till smooth. Into chocolate, dip 10 pretzels, let the excess drip off. Transfer to waxed paper. Use sprinkles to decorate half of the pretzels. Refrigerate until set, or for 10 minutes.
- Melt white chocolate; mix till smooth. Dip the rest of the pretzels in white chocolate, let the excess drip off. Put onto waxed paper. Use sprinkles to decorate half of the pretzels. Chill until set, or for 10 minutes.
- Drizzle milk chocolate over the plain white-coated pretzels. Drizzle white chocolate over the pretzels coated with plain milk chocolate. Chill until set, or for 10 minutes. Keep in an airtight container.

Nutrition Information

- Calories: 207 calories
- Sodium: 143mg sodium
- Fiber: 0 fiber)
- Total Carbohydrate: 28g carbohydrate (23g sugars
- Cholesterol: 1mg cholesterol
- Protein: 1g protein.
- Total Fat: 10g fat (9g saturated fat)

185. Chocolate Dipped Lavender Pine Nut Brittle

Serving: 3 pounds. | Prep: 15mins | Cook: 25mins | Ready in:

Ingredients

- 1 tablespoon butter, melted
- 3 cups sugar
- 1 cup light corn syrup
- 1/2 cup water
- 4-1/2 cups pine nuts
- 1/4 cup butter, softened
- 2 teaspoons baking soda
- 2 teaspoons vanilla extract
- 1 teaspoon dried lavender flowers
- 1/2 teaspoon salt
- 1 pound dark chocolate candy coating, coarsely chopped

Direction

- Use melted butter to grease two 15x10x1-inch pans; put aside.
- Mix together the sugar, corn syrup and water in a large saucepan. Cook, do not stir, on medium heat until it reaches a thread stage (a candy thermometer reads 230°). Add pine nuts into the mix carefully; cook and stir constantly until it reaches a hard-crack stage (mixture reaches 300°).
- Take off from heat; stir the salt, baking soda, vanilla, lavender and softened butter into the mixture. Transfer into the prepared pans right away. Spread it out into the thickness of 1/4-inch. Let it cool down before breaking into pieces.
- Melt the chocolate coating in a microwave; stir till smooth. Into the melted chocolate, dip each candy piece halfway; let the excess drip off. Put onto waxed paper and let sit until set. For storage, keep in an airtight container.

Nutrition Information

- Calories: 390 calories
- Total Carbohydrate: 49g carbohydrate (38g sugars
- Cholesterol: 6mg cholesterol
- Protein: 7g protein.
- Total Fat: 21g fat (7g saturated fat)
- Sodium: 191mg sodium
- Fiber: 1g fiber)

186. Chocolate Dipped Peanut Nougat

Serving: about 4-1/2 pounds (about 150 pieces). | Prep: 40mins | Cook: 20mins | Ready in:

Ingredients

- 1 tablespoon butter
- 1 jar (16 ounces) dry roasted peanuts
- 3 jars (7 ounces each) marshmallow creme
- 2-1/4 cups sugar
- 2-1/4 cups corn syrup
- 6 tablespoons butter, cubed
- 1-1/2 teaspoons vanilla extract
- 1/4 teaspoon salt
- 1 to 1-1/2 pounds dark or milk chocolate candy coating, melted

Direction

- Use foil to line a 15x10x1 in. pan, let the ends of foil extend over sides of pan by an inch; use a tablespoon of butter to grease foil. Use peanuts to sprinkle evenly into pan.
- Put marshmallow crème in a large heatproof bowl. Mix corn syrup and sugar in a large heavy saucepan. Bring to a boil on medium heat and stir constantly to dissolve sugar. Dip a pastry brush in water then use the brush to wash down sides of pan to remove sugar crystals. Cook without stirring for 10 minutes till a candy thermometer reaches 280 degrees (this is the soft crack stage).
- Get the saucepan off heat; allow it to cool for 2 minutes. Transfer the sugar mixture over marshmallow crème (remember not to scrape the saucepan). Mix in salt, vanilla, cubes of butter. Pour the mixture over peanuts in pan immediately, remember to spread evenly. Let sit for 3 hours in minimum or till set.
- Lift candy out of pan by foil. Remove foil gently. Grease a knife and use the knife to cut candy into 1x1 in. squares.
- Dip candy into melted candy coating; let the excess coating to drip off. Line baking sheets by waxed paper then place candy on baking sheets; chill in the fridge till candy is set. Place between waxed paper layers and store in airtight containers.

Nutrition Information

- Calories:
- Protein:
- Total Fat:
- Sodium:
- Fiber:
- Total Carbohydrate:
- Cholesterol:

187. Chocolate Dipped Pretzel Rods

Serving: about 4-1/2 dozen. | Prep: 25mins | Cook: 10mins | Ready in:

Ingredients

- 3 cups chopped toasted almonds
- 2 packages (14 ounces each) caramels, unwrapped
- 2 tablespoons water
- 2 packages (10 ounces each) pretzel rods
- 2 packages (10 to 12 ounces each) white baking chips
- 2 packages (10 to 12 ounces each) dark chocolate chips
- Assorted sprinkles, optional

Direction

- Arrange almonds in a shallow dish. Microwave water and caramels in a large measuring cups on high power, stirring after each 60 seconds, until caramels are melted.
- Immerse 3/4 of each pretzel into melted caramel, dripping off excess. (Rewarm caramel in the microwave if the mixture looks too thick for dipping). Roll coated pretzels in almonds. Arrange on waxed paper until firm.
- Melt white baking chips in a microwave; whisk until no lumps remain. Immerse 1/2 of the caramel-coated pretzels in the melted white baking chips, dripping off the excess. Garnish with sprinkles if desired; place back onto the waxed paper until firm. Repeat the

steps with the rest of pretzels and chocolate chips.
- Wrap pretzels in cellophane gift bags and tie with ribbon; or store in airtight container

Nutrition Information

- Calories: 245 calories
- Sodium: 278mg sodium
- Fiber: 2g fiber)
- Total Carbohydrate: 34g carbohydrate (22g sugars
- Cholesterol: 3mg cholesterol
- Protein: 5g protein.
- Total Fat: 12g fat (5g saturated fat)

188. Chocolate Peanut Angel Sweets

Serving: 2 dozen. | Prep: 30mins | Cook: 0mins | Ready in:

Ingredients

- 1-1/2 cups miniature marshmallows
- 6 tablespoons butter, cubed
- 2 cups (12 ounces) semisweet chocolate chips
- 1/4 cup confectioners' sugar
- 1 cup dry roasted peanuts
- 1-3/4 cups sweetened shredded coconut, coarsely chopped

Direction

- In a large microwave-safe bowl, melt together butter and marshmallows; mix until blended. Mix in chocolate chips until they melt. Mix in confectioners' sugar till smooth. Fold in the peanuts.
- Roll the mixture into 1-in. balls; then roll the balls in coconut. Put onto pans lined with waxed paper. Chill in refrigerator for about 15 minutes until firm. Keep in an airtight container.

Nutrition Information

- Calories: 176 calories
- Total Fat: 12g fat (7g saturated fat)
- Sodium: 90mg sodium
- Fiber: 2g fiber)
- Total Carbohydrate: 17g carbohydrate (13g sugars
- Cholesterol: 8mg cholesterol
- Protein: 2g protein.

189. Christmas Almond Toffee

Serving: about 1-1/2 pounds. | Prep: 50mins | Cook: 0mins | Ready in:

Ingredients

- 1 tablespoon plus 2 cups butter, divided
- 2 cups sugar
- 1 cup slivered almonds
- 1/4 cup water
- 1 teaspoon salt
- 1 teaspoon vanilla extract
- 1 package (11-1/2 ounces) milk chocolate chips, divided
- 1/2 cup finely chopped almonds

Direction

- Use 1 tablespoon butter to grease a 15x10x1-in. pan; put aside. Melt the remaining butter in a large heavy saucepan. Add sugar, slivered almonds, water and salt into the butter; cook and stir on medium heat until approaching hard-crack stage (a candy thermometer reads 295°). Take off from heat; stir vanilla into the mixture.
- Transfer into the prepared pan quickly. Let sit until cooled at room temperature for about 1 hour.
- Melt 1 cup chocolate chips in a microwave; spread atop the toffee. Refrigerate till set for

about 45 minutes. Flip onto a large ungreased baking sheet. Melt the rest of the chips; spread atop the toffee. Sprinkle chopped almonds on top. Let sit for 1 hour. Crack into bite-sized pieces. For storage, keep in an airtight container.

Nutrition Information

- Calories: 325 calories
- Sodium: 218mg sodium
- Fiber: 1g fiber)
- Total Carbohydrate: 28g carbohydrate (26g sugars
- Cholesterol: 46mg cholesterol
- Protein: 3g protein.
- Total Fat: 24g fat (13g saturated fat)

190. Christmas Candies

Serving: about 2-1/2 dozen. | Prep: 20mins | Cook: 0mins | Ready in:

Ingredients

- 3 tablespoons baking cocoa
- 1 can (14 ounces) sweetened condensed milk
- 2 tablespoons butter
- Finely chopped pistachios

Direction

- Boil the butter, milk and cocoa in a small heavy saucepan and mix it continuously. Lower the heat to low and let it cook while stirring, until it becomes thick.
- Move to a small bowl. Put cover and let it chill in the fridge. Roll it to 1-inch balls, then roll it in the pistachios. Keep it in the fridge.

Nutrition Information

- Calories: 51 calories
- Cholesterol: 7mg cholesterol
- Protein: 1g protein.
- Total Fat: 2g fat (1g saturated fat)
- Sodium: 25mg sodium
- Fiber: 0 fiber)
- Total Carbohydrate: 7g carbohydrate (7g sugars

191. Christmas Crunch Candy

Serving: about 1-1/2 pounds. | Prep: 10mins | Cook: 25mins | Ready in:

Ingredients

- 1 teaspoon butter, softened
- 2 cups sugar
- 2/3 cup light corn syrup
- 1/2 cup water
- 3 tablespoons butter, cubed
- 2 cups Rice Krispies
- 1 cup salted cashews
- 1-1/2 teaspoons baking soda
- 1 teaspoon vanilla extract

Direction

- Line a baking pan 15x10x1-inch in size with foil. With a teaspoon butter, grease foil.
- Mix water, corn syrup and sugar in a big heavy saucepan; boil over medium heat, mixing continuously.
- Cook over medium heat and mix till a candy thermometer registers 240° (a soft-ball stage). Mix in butter; cook but avoid mixing till mixture reaches 300° (a hard-crack stage), using a pastry brush dipped in water to brush down sides of pan as necessary.
- Take off heat. Mix in vanilla, baking soda, cashews and cereal. Immediately put in prepped pan. With a buttered metal spatula, scatter mixture to 1/4-inch thickness. Cool down fully; shatter into pieces.
- To make ahead: Keep candy in an airtight container up to a month.

Nutrition Information

- Calories:
- Total Carbohydrate:
- Cholesterol:
- Protein:
- Total Fat:
- Sodium:
- Fiber:

192. Christmas Hard Candy

Serving: about 2 pounds. | Prep: 5mins | Cook: 60mins | Ready in:

Ingredients

- 3-1/2 cups sugar
- 1 cup light corn syrup
- 1 cup water
- 1/4 to 1/2 teaspoon cinnamon or peppermint oil
- 1 teaspoon red or green food coloring

Direction

- In a large heavy saucepan, combine water, corn syrup, and sugar. Cook on medium-high heat until it reaches into a hard-crack stage (candy thermometer reads 300°) while stirring occasionally. Take off from the heat; mix in food coloring and oil; due to the strong odor, keep your face away from mixture.
- Transfer onto an oiled baking sheet immediately. Let it cool; smash into pieces. Keep in airtight containers.

Nutrition Information

- Calories: 114 calories
- Protein: 0 protein.
- Total Fat: 0 fat (0 saturated fat)
- Sodium: 13mg sodium
- Fiber: 0 fiber)
- Total Carbohydrate: 30g carbohydrate (26g sugars
- Cholesterol: 0 cholesterol

193. Cinnamon Almond Brittle

Serving: about 2 pounds. | Prep: 15mins | Cook: 20mins | Ready in:

Ingredients

- 1 teaspoon plus 3 tablespoons butter, cubed
- 2 cups sugar
- 3/4 cup light corn syrup
- 1/4 cup water
- 3 cups slivered almonds, toasted
- 2 teaspoons ground cinnamon
- 1/2 teaspoon salt
- 1-1/2 teaspoons baking soda
- 1 teaspoon vanilla extract

Direction

- Set the oven at 200° and start preheating. Use 1 teaspoon of butter to grease two baking sheets; place in the oven to warm.
- Mix water, corn syrup and sugar together in a large heavy saucepan. Boil the mixture, stirring constantly till the sugar is dissolved. Wash down the sides of the pan with a pastry brush dipped in water, to discard any sugar crystals. Cook over medium heat, no stirring, till a candy thermometer registers 240° (soft-ball stage). Mix in the remaining butter, salt, cinnamon and almonds; cook while stirring frequently till the thermometer registers 300° (hard-crack stage), brushing the sides of the pan as necessary.
- Take away from the heat; mix in vanilla and baking soda. Transfer into the prepared pans immediately, spreading to 1/4-in. thickness. Allow to cool completely.
- Break the brittle into pieces. Place in an airtight container, between layers of waxed paper, for storage.

Nutrition Information

- Calories: 142 calories
- Sodium: 111mg sodium
- Fiber: 1g fiber)
- Total Carbohydrate: 21g carbohydrate (19g sugars
- Cholesterol: 3mg cholesterol
- Protein: 2g protein.
- Total Fat: 6g fat (1g saturated fat)

194. Cinnamon Rock Candy

Serving: about 2 pounds. | Prep: 20mins | Cook: 25mins | Ready in:

Ingredients

- 1 cup water
- 3-3/4 cups sugar
- 1-1/4 cups light corn syrup
- 1 teaspoon red liquid food coloring
- 1 teaspoon cinnamon oil
- 1/3 cup confectioners' sugar

Direction

- Line foil on 15x10x1-inch pan; butter foil. Put aside. Put food coloring, corn syrup, sugar and water together in a big heavy saucepan and boil on medium heat, occasionally mixing; cover. Cook to melt sugar crystals for 3 minutes.
- Uncover; cook without mixing on medium high heat for 25 minutes till it is at hard-crack stage or candy thermometer reads 300°. Take off from heat; mix in cinnamon oil. Keep face away from mixture; oil is very strong. Put onto prepped pan immediately; fully cool for 45 minutes.
- Use edge of metal mallet to break candy to pieces; sprinkle confectioners' sugar on both sides of candy. Keep in airtight container.

Nutrition Information

- Calories: 132 calories
- Sodium: 16mg sodium
- Fiber: 0 fiber)
- Total Carbohydrate: 34g carbohydrate (30g sugars
- Cholesterol: 0 cholesterol
- Protein: 0 protein.
- Total Fat: 0 fat (0 saturated fat)

195. Cinnamon Walnut Brittle

Serving: 3/4 pound. | Prep: 20mins | Cook: 0mins | Ready in:

Ingredients

- 1 cup sugar
- 1/2 cup light corn syrup
- 1 cup chopped walnuts
- 1 teaspoon butter
- 1/2 teaspoon ground cinnamon
- 1 teaspoon baking soda
- 1 teaspoon vanilla extract

Direction

- Grease a baking tray with butter; put aside. Mix corn syrup and sugar in a 2 quarts microwaveable bowl. Microwave on high for 3 minutes, with no cover; mix. Cook on high for 2-1/2 minutes more, with no cover. Mix in the cinnamon, butter and walnuts.
- Microwave on high for 2 minutes more, with no cover, until mixture turns into a pale amber color (it will be very hot).
- Mix in vanilla and baking soda immediately until light and foamy. Put onto prepared pan quickly; scatter out with a metal spatula. Let cool; crack into pieces.

Nutrition Information

- Calories: 57 calories

- Total Carbohydrate: 9g carbohydrate (8g sugars
- Cholesterol: 0 cholesterol
- Protein: 1g protein.
- Total Fat: 2g fat (0 saturated fat)
- Sodium: 42mg sodium
- Fiber: 0 fiber)

196. Coconut Almond Candies

Serving: 3-1/2 dozen. | Prep: 01hours15mins | Cook: 0mins |Ready in:

Ingredients

- 2 cups sweetened shredded coconut, chopped
- 3 tablespoons sweetened condensed milk
- 3 tablespoons confectioners' sugar
- 2 teaspoons butter, softened
- 1 package (12 ounces) semisweet chocolate chips, divided
- 8 ounces white candy coating
- 1 tablespoon shortening
- 1 package (2-1/4 ounces) unblanched almonds

Direction

- Whip the butter, confectioners' sugar, milk and coconut in a big bowl until blended (mixture will be sticky); put aside.
- Melt shortening, candy coating and chocolate chips in a microwaveable bowl; mix until smooth. Scoop about half teaspoon chocolate mixture into 42 paper-lined mini muffin tins.
- Roll half teaspoonfuls of coconut mixture into balls; push into chocolate gently. Put an almond on top of each. Scoop a teaspoon chocolate mixture on top of each. Let sit until firm. Put in an airtight container to store.

Nutrition Information

- Calories:
- Protein:

- Total Fat:
- Sodium:
- Fiber:
- Total Carbohydrate:
- Cholesterol:

197. Coconut Caramels

Serving: 4 pounds. | Prep: 15mins | Cook: 45mins | Ready in:

Ingredients

- 1 tablespoon butter
- 3 cups sweetened shredded coconut, divided
- 1-1/2 cups coarsely chopped salted roasted almonds, divided
- 3 cups sugar
- 1 can (13.66 ounces) coconut milk
- 1-1/2 cups light corn syrup
- 3/4 cup butter, cubed
- 1/3 cup heavy whipping cream
- 3 teaspoons vanilla extract
- 1 teaspoon ground ginger
- 1/2 teaspoon salt

Direction

- Use a foil to line a 13x9-in. pan; use 1 tablespoon of butter to grease the foil. Layer 3/4 cup of almonds and 1 cup of coconut on top; put aside.
- In a Dutch oven, combine cream, cubed butter, corn syrup, coconut milk, and sugar. Over medium heat, cook and stir the mixture until it reaches into a soft-ball stage (candy thermometer must read 238°), for about 40 minutes.
- Dip a pastry brush in water and use it to wash down the pan's sides to remove the sugar crystals. Cook and stir the mixture until it reaches into a firm-ball stage (thermometer must read 244°), for about another 5 minutes.
- Remove it from the heat and mix in the remaining almonds, ginger, vanilla, salt, and 1

cup of coconut. Pour it into the prepared pan immediately (don't scrape the saucepan). Sprinkle the remaining coconut on top. Let it sit until firm, for about 5 hours or overnight.
- Lift the candy out of the pan using the foil; take off the foil. Cut the caramel into 1-in. squares using a buttered knife. Wrap each in waxed paper; twist the ends.

Nutrition Information

- Calories:
- Protein:
- Total Fat:
- Sodium:
- Fiber:
- Total Carbohydrate:
- Cholesterol:

198. Coconut Cashew Brittle

Serving: about 3 pounds. | Prep: 25mins | Cook: 10mins | Ready in:

Ingredients

- 2 tablespons plus 1 cup butter, divided
- 2 cups cashew halves
- 2 cups sweetened shredded coconut
- 2 cups sugar
- 1 cup light corn syrup
- 1/2 cup plus 1 teaspoon water, divided
- 2 teaspoons vanilla extract
- 1-1/2 teaspoons baking soda

Direction

- Spread a tablespoon butter on each of two pans with 15x10x1-inch in size; reserve.
- On a third 15x10x1-in. baking pan, mix together coconut and cashews. Bake at 350° till golden brown, about 8 to 10 minutes, mixing from time to time.
- Mix together the half cup water, corn syrup and sugar in a big heavy saucepan. Cook over medium heat and mix till mixture boils. Put in leftover butter; cook and mix till butter is melted. Keep cooking till a candy thermometer registers 300° a hard-crack stage, avoid mixing.
- Meantime, mix together the leftover water, baking soda and vanilla. Take saucepan away from heat; put in coconut and cashews. Put in baking soda mixture; mix till frothy and light. Immediately pour onto prepped baking sheets. Scatter to a-quarter-inch thickness using a buttered metal spatula. Allow to cool prior to shatter into pieces. Keep in an airtight container.

Nutrition Information

- Calories: 290 calories
- Protein: 3g protein.
- Total Fat: 17g fat (8g saturated fat)
- Sodium: 277mg sodium
- Fiber: 1g fiber
- Total Carbohydrate: 34g carbohydrate (27g sugars
- Cholesterol: 20mg cholesterol

199. Coconut Chocolate Creams

Serving: about 3 dozen. | Prep: 20mins | Cook: 0mins | Ready in:

Ingredients

- 2-1/2 cups sweetened shredded coconut
- 1 cup (6 ounces) semisweet chocolate chips
- 1/2 cup evaporated milk
- 2-1/2 cups confectioners' sugar
- 1/3 cup chopped pecans
- 1/3 cup chopped maraschino cherries

Direction

- Put coconut in a blender; put a lid on and pulse till they are chopped finely. Add milk and chocolate chips in a microwave safe bowl and melt them; stir till the mixture becomes smooth. Add cherries, pecans, 1-1/4 cups coconut, confectioners' sugar and stir. Put a lid on and chill in the fridge for 2 hours or till the mixture become firm. Set the rest of the coconut aside.
- Using the chocolate mixture to make one inch ball; roll in the reserved coconut. Use waxed paper to line baking sheets and place the balls on these prepared baking sheets. Chill in the fridge for 2 hours or till the balls become firm. Put the balls in airtight container and store in the fridge.

Nutrition Information

- Calories: 205 calories
- Cholesterol: 2mg cholesterol
- Protein: 1g protein.
- Total Fat: 9g fat (6g saturated fat)
- Sodium: 44mg sodium
- Fiber: 1g fiber)
- Total Carbohydrate: 31g carbohydrate (27g sugars

200. Coconut Drops

Serving: 1-1/4 pounds. | Prep: 15mins | Cook: 0mins | Ready in:

Ingredients

- 1 package (14 ounces) sweetened shredded coconut
- 6 drops red food coloring
- 6 drops green food coloring
- 1 pound white candy coating, coarsely chopped

Direction

- Split the coconut among 2 bowls. Put green food coloring on one bowl then red food coloring to another; toss to coat the coconut.
- On low heat, melt the candy coating in a heavy saucepan; drop the coating by tablespoonfuls on waxed paper. While still warm, scatter green coconut on half of each drop then the pink coconut on the other half; gently press down. Place in the refrigerator until firm.

Nutrition Information

- Calories: 220 calories
- Sodium: 52mg sodium
- Fiber: 1g fiber)
- Total Carbohydrate: 26g carbohydrate (22g sugars
- Cholesterol: 0 cholesterol
- Protein: 1g protein.
- Total Fat: 13g fat (12g saturated fat)

201. Coconut Joys

Serving: 1-1/2 dozen. | Prep: 20mins | Cook: 0mins | Ready in:

Ingredients

- 1-1/2 cups sweetened shredded coconut
- 1 cup confectioners' sugar
- 1/4 cup butter, melted
- 1 ounce milk chocolate, melted
- 2 tablespoons chopped pecans

Direction

- Combine butter with confectioners' sugar and coconut in a large bowl. Shape mixture into balls about 1 inch.
- Create an indentation in the middle of each ball using the end of a wooden spoon handle. Fill the indentation with chocolate. Scatter top with pecans. Arrange on a baking sheet lined with waxed paper. Refrigerate until chocolate is hardened. Keep chilled in the fridge.

Nutrition Information

- Calories: 101 calories
- Sodium: 38mg sodium
- Fiber: 0 fiber)
- Total Carbohydrate: 11g carbohydrate (10g sugars
- Cholesterol: 7mg cholesterol
- Protein: 0 protein. Diabetic Exchanges: 1 starch
- Total Fat: 6g fat (4g saturated fat)

202. Coconut Marshmallow Squares

Serving: 3 dozen (about 1-1/2 pounds. | Prep: 15mins | Cook: 25mins | Ready in:

Ingredients

- 2 envelopes unflavored gelatin
- 1-1/4 cups cold water, divided
- 2 cups sugar
- 2 egg whites, lightly beaten
- 1 teaspoon vanilla extract
- 2-1/2 cups sweetened shredded coconut, chopped
- 2 to 3 drops red or yellow food coloring, optional

Direction

- Sprinkle gelatin on 1/2 cup cold water in a heavy-duty mixer's big bowl; put aside. Put leftover water and sugar together in a heavy saucepan; mix and cook on low heat till sugar melts; cook on medium heat till it reaches a soft-ball stage or candy thermometer reads 234°, mixing from time to time. Take off from heat; put on gelatin slowly, constantly beating. Add egg whites immediately; to be sure mixture is not less than 160°, use candy thermometer. Beat for 15-20 minutes; beat in vanilla. Put into 9-inch greased square pan; cool till firm enough to cut to squares, for 3 hours.
- Mix food coloring (optional) and coconut in a shallow bowl; roll the marshmallow squares into coconut. Keep in the fridge in airtight container.

Nutrition Information

- Calories:
- Fiber:
- Total Carbohydrate:
- Cholesterol:
- Protein:
- Total Fat:
- Sodium:

203. Coconut Peaks

Serving: about 3 dozen. | Prep: 20mins | Cook: 10mins | Ready in:

Ingredients

- 1/4 cup butter
- 3 cups sweetened shredded coconut
- 2 cups confectioners' sugar
- 1/4 cup half-and-half cream
- 1 cup (6 ounces) semisweet chocolate chips
- 2 teaspoons shortening

Direction

- Use waxed paper to line a baking sheet; put aside. Cook butter in a big saucepan over medium-low heat for 5 minutes until turning golden brown. Take away from heat; mix in cream, sugar, and coconut.
- Drop onto the prepared cookie sheet with rounded teaspoonfuls. Chill for 25 minutes until easy to use.
- Roll the mixture into balls, and then form each into a cone. Put back onto the cookie sheet, chill for 15 minutes.

- In the meantime, melt shortening and chocolate chips in a microwave, whisk until smooth. Dip into the chocolate with the end of the cones, let the excess drip off. Put back onto the waxed paper to harden. Put in an airtight container to store in the fridge.

Nutrition Information

- Calories: 205 calories
- Protein: 1g protein.
- Total Fat: 12g fat (8g saturated fat)
- Sodium: 69mg sodium
- Fiber: 1g fiber)
- Total Carbohydrate: 27g carbohydrate (23g sugars
- Cholesterol: 8mg cholesterol

204. Coconut Surprise Candy

Serving: about 4 dozen. | Prep: 15mins | Cook: 0mins | Ready in:

Ingredients

- 2-1/2 cups sweetened shredded coconut
- 2-1/2 cups confectioners' sugar
- 1/3 cup mashed potatoes (prepared without milk and butter)
- 1 cup (6 ounces) semisweet chocolate chips
- 1 tablespoon shortening
- Chopped walnuts, optional

Direction

- Combine mashed potatoes, sugar, and coconut in a large bowl; stir well. Shape mixture into 1-inch balls; arrange on baking sheets lined with waxed paper. Melt shortening and chocolate chips in a double boiler or microwave; whisk until no lumps remain. Dunk balls into chocolate, then coat with walnuts if desired. Place balls back into the waxed paper and wait until chocolate is firm.

Nutrition Information

- Calories: 137 calories
- Protein: 1g protein.
- Total Fat: 6g fat (4g saturated fat)
- Sodium: 27mg sodium
- Fiber: 1g fiber)
- Total Carbohydrate: 22g carbohydrate (19g sugars
- Cholesterol: 0 cholesterol

205. Coconut Truffles

Serving: 36 | Prep: 10mins | Cook: | Ready in:

Ingredients

- 2 (16 ounce) boxes confectioners' sugar
- 1 (14 ounce) can sweetened condensed milk
- 1 cup butter
- 2 1/2 cups chopped walnuts
- 1 (14 ounce) package shredded coconut
- 1 (24 ounce) bag chocolate chips

Direction

- Line waxed paper on baking sheet.
- Mix butter, sweetened condensed milk and sugar in bowl. Mix coconut and walnuts into dough; use plastic wrap to cover bowl. Freeze for minimum of 1 hour till dough is firm.
- Shape dough to 1-in. balls; put on prepped baking sheet. Freeze for minimum of 30 minutes till firm.
- In double boiler/bowl above pan of simmering water, melt chocolate chips, frequently mixing till smooth.
- Dip balls in melted chocolate till coated; cool on prepped baking sheet till chocolate hardens.

Nutrition Information

- Calories: 369 calories;
- Total Fat: 20

- Sodium: 84
- Total Carbohydrate: 49.3
- Cholesterol: 17
- Protein: 3.3

206. Coconut Yule Trees

Serving: 2 dozen. | Prep: 15mins | Cook: 0mins | Ready in:

Ingredients

- 3 cups sweetened shredded coconut
- 2 cups confectioners' sugar
- 1/4 cup butter, softened
- 1/4 cup half-and-half cream
- 1 teaspoon almond extract
- 2 to 4 ounces dark chocolate candy coating
- Vanilla frosting, green sugar and assorted sprinkles

Direction

- Mix the first 5 ingredients in a large bowl. Drop by tablespoonfuls onto a baking sheet lined with waxed paper; keep in the fridge for an hour with a cover. Form into trees; transfer back to baking sheet.
- Melt chocolate coating in a microwave; stir until smooth. Scoop over or dip trunks of trees; let any excess drip off. Arrange on waxed paper; allow to rest until set. Garnish trees as preferred with sprinkles, green sugar and frosting.

Nutrition Information

- Calories: 130 calories
- Total Fat: 7g fat (6g saturated fat)
- Sodium: 51mg sodium
- Fiber: 1g fiber)
- Total Carbohydrate: 17g carbohydrate (15g sugars
- Cholesterol: 6mg cholesterol
- Protein: 0 protein.

207. Colorful Snowballs

Serving: 16 popcorn balls. | Prep: 10mins | Cook: 5mins | Ready in:

Ingredients

- 1 quart popped popcorn
- 2 cups crisp rice cereal
- 20 large marshmallows
- 1/4 cup butter, cubed
- 1 cup red and green milk chocolate M&M's

Direction

- Mix cereal and popcorn in a big greased bowl. Stir butter and marshmallows in a big saucepan over low heat. Cook and mix until marshmallows melts and mixture turn smooth. Put on top of popcorn mixture. Put in M&M's; mix until blended.
- Roll 1/3 cupfuls into balls with lightly buttered hands when cool enough to handle. Put on waxed paper-lined baking trays. Let cool.

Nutrition Information

- Calories: 144 calories
- Fiber: 1g fiber)
- Total Carbohydrate: 21g carbohydrate (14g sugars
- Cholesterol: 9mg cholesterol
- Protein: 1g protein.
- Total Fat: 6g fat (4g saturated fat)
- Sodium: 97mg sodium

208. Contest Winning Hazelnut Toffee

Serving: about 1-3/4 pounds. | Prep: 15mins | Cook: 30mins | Ready in:

Ingredients

- 2 teaspoons plus 1 cup butter, divided
- 1 cup sugar
- 3 tablespoons water
- 1 tablespoon light corn syrup
- 1/3 cup chopped hazelnuts
- TOPPING:
- 2 cups (12 ounces each) semisweet chocolate chips
- 1/2 cup finely chopped hazelnuts

Direction

- Use foil to line a 13x9-inch pan; use cooking spray to coat the foil and reserve. Use 2 teaspoons butter to grease the sides of large heavy saucepan. Chunk remaining butter; put in pan. Mix in the corn syrup, water and sugar. Whisk and cook until mixture is golden brown and a candy thermometer registers 300°F (hard crack stage).
- Separate from heat; mix in hazelnuts. Place into prepare pan without scraping; equally spread. Allow to stand for about 1 hour at room temperature until cool.
- Liquify chocolate chips in a microwave; whisk until smooth. Equally spread over toffee. Dust with hazelnuts, cautiously pressing down. Allow to stand for 1 hour. Split into bite-size pieces. Refrigerate.

Nutrition Information

- Calories: 197 calories
- Protein: 1g protein.
- Total Fat: 15g fat (8g saturated fat)
- Sodium: 83mg sodium
- Fiber: 1g fiber)
- Total Carbohydrate: 19g carbohydrate (17g sugars
- Cholesterol: 21mg cholesterol

209. Cran Marnier Truffles

Serving: 5 dozen. | Prep: 35mins | Cook: 10mins | Ready in:

Ingredients

- 1-1/2 cups sugar
- 1 can (5 ounces) evaporated milk
- 1/2 cup butter, cubed
- 8 ounces 53% cacao dark baking chocolate, chopped
- 2 cups miniature marshmallows
- 1 tablespoon Grand Marnier
- 2 teaspoons grated orange zest
- 1/2 cup dried cranberries, chopped
- 12 ounces semisweet chocolate, chopped
- 2 tablespoons shortening
- Baking cocoa, optional

Direction

- Boil butter, milk and sugar in heavy saucepan on medium heat; cook, constantly mixing, till its soft-ball stage and candy thermometer reads 234°.
- Take off heat; mix dark chocolate in till melted. Mix orange zest, Grand Marnier and marshmallows in till blended. Mix cranberries in; put in bowl. Refrigerate for 1 1/2 hours till easy to handle.
- Form to 1-in. balls; put onto waxed paper-lined baking sheets. Refrigerate for 1 hour till firm, covered.
- Melt shortening and semisweet chocolate in microwave; mix till smooth. In chocolate, dip truffles; let excess drip off. Put on lined baking sheets; refrigerate till set. If desired, you could instead roll undipped truffles into cocoa; keep in airtight container in the fridge.

Nutrition Information

- Calories: 96 calories
- Sodium: 14mg sodium
- Fiber: 1g fiber)
- Total Carbohydrate: 13g carbohydrate (11g sugars
- Cholesterol: 5mg cholesterol
- Protein: 1g protein.
- Total Fat: 5g fat (3g saturated fat)

210. Cranberry Bog Bark

Serving: 2 pounds. | Prep: 15mins | Cook: 0mins | Ready in:

Ingredients

- 1 cup dried cranberries
- 1-1/2 pounds white chocolate or candy coating, coarsely chopped
- 2 cups broken walnuts

Direction

- Steam dried cranberries, covered in a vegetable steamer for 2 to 3 minutes. Transfer to a paper towel; drain and let cool.
- Microwave the chocolate to melt. Take out of the heat and mix in walnuts and steamed dried cranberries. Transfer to a baking sheet lined with foil and even out. Put in the refrigerator to harden, or about half an hour. Break into pieces of 2 inches.

Nutrition Information

- Calories: 350 calories
- Sodium: 39mg sodium
- Fiber: 1g fiber)
- Total Carbohydrate: 34g carbohydrate (31g sugars
- Cholesterol: 6mg cholesterol
- Protein: 6g protein.
- Total Fat: 22g fat (8g saturated fat)

211. Cranberry Fudge

Serving: 16 | Prep: | Cook: | Ready in:

Ingredients

- 1 (12 ounce) package fresh or frozen cranberries
- 1/2 cup light corn syrup
- 2 cups semisweet chocolate chips
- 1/2 cup confectioners' sugar
- 1/4 cup evaporated milk
- 1 teaspoon vanilla extract

Direction

- Line plastic wrap on the bottom and sides of an 8x8-inch pan. Put aside.
- Bring corn syrup and cranberries in a medium saucepan to a boil. Boil on high until liquid is reduced to three tablespoons, stirring occasionally, about 5-7 minutes. Take away from the heat.
- Add the chocolate chips immediately, stirring until they are completely melted. Put in the vanilla extract, evaporated milk, and confectioner's sugar, vigorously stirring until the mixture is glossy and thick. Transfer into the pan. Chill, covered, until firm.

Nutrition Information

- Calories: 229 calories;
- Total Fat: 8.8
- Sodium: 11
- Total Carbohydrate: 35.8
- Cholesterol: 1
- Protein: 2.5

212. Cranberry Ginger Bark

Serving: about 1-1/2 pounds. | Prep: 25mins | Cook: 0mins | Ready in:

Ingredients

- 18 ounces white baking chocolate, chopped
- 2/3 cup dried cranberries
- 2/3 cup crystallized ginger, chopped
- 2/3 cup lightly salted cashews
- 2 ounces dark chocolate chips

Direction

- Microwave white chocolate until melted and mix until smooth. Mix together cashews, ginger, and cranberries. Reserve two-thirds cup of mixture. Mix into melted chocolate the rest of cranberry mixture.
- Pour over a baking sheet lined with wax paper. Garnish with saved cranberry mixture.
- Let sit for 30 minutes in the refrigerator to harden.
- Microwave dark chocolate chips to melt, mix to smoothen. Glaze onto candy. Put into the refrigerator to harden. Break apart the bar to divide. Keep in a tightly closed container to store.

Nutrition Information

- Calories: 172 calories
- Sodium: 31mg sodium
- Fiber: 0 fiber
- Total Carbohydrate: 21g carbohydrate (16g sugars
- Cholesterol: 4mg cholesterol
- Protein: 2g protein.
- Total Fat: 9g fat (5g saturated fat)

213. Cranberry Gumdrops

Serving: about 5 dozen. | Prep: 20mins | Cook: 10mins | Ready in:

Ingredients

- 2 envelopes unflavored gelatin
- 1/2 cup cold water
- 1 can (16 ounce) jellied cranberry sauce
- 2 cups sugar, divided
- 3 packages (3 ounces each) raspberry gelatin
- Additional sugar, optional

Direction

- Scatter unflavored gelatin on top of water in a saucepan; let sit for 2 minutes to soften. Put in cranberry sauce and a cup of sugar; cook on low heat about 10 minutes until sugar dissolves and sauce melts. Mix until smooth.
- Take off from the heat and put in raspberry gelatin; mix about 3 minutes until completely dissolved. Put into an 8-inch square dish sprayed with cooking spray. Cover and let sit for 12 hours at room temperature or up to overnight (do not chill).
- Slice into 1-inch squares; toss in leftover sugar. Put on baking trays; let sit 3 hours at room temperature. Flip pieces over and let sit 3 more hours. Toss in more sugar if preferred. Put in an airtight container to store at room temperature.

Nutrition Information

- Calories: 85 calories
- Total Fat: 0 fat (0 saturated fat)
- Sodium: 11mg sodium
- Fiber: 0 fiber
- Total Carbohydrate: 21g carbohydrate (19g sugars
- Cholesterol: 0 cholesterol
- Protein: 1g protein.

214. Cream Cheese Candies

Serving: 72 | Prep: 20mins | Cook: | Ready in:

Ingredients

- 1 (3 ounce) package cream cheese, softened
- 1/4 teaspoon peppermint extract

- 3 cups confectioners' sugar

Direction

- In the small-sized mixing bowl, whip the cream cheese with the peppermint extract. Whip in 1/2 of confectioners' sugar till smooth. Knead in the rest of the confectioners' sugar till incorporated completely. Form the dough into half-inch balls, add onto the baking sheets, flatten using the fork, and let rest for 60 minutes to harden. Keep it stored in the airtight containers in the fridge.

Nutrition Information

- Calories: 24 calories;
- Cholesterol: 1
- Protein: 0.1
- Total Fat: 0.4
- Sodium: 4
- Total Carbohydrate: 5

215. Creamy Peanut Butter Fudge

Serving: 24 | Prep: 10mins | Cook: 10mins | Ready in:

Ingredients

- 4 cups white sugar
- 1 cup light brown sugar
- 1/2 cup butter
- 1 (12 fluid ounce) can evaporated milk
- 1 (7 ounce) jar marshmallow creme
- 1 (16 ounce) jar peanut butter
- 1 teaspoon vanilla extract

Direction

- Coat a 13"x9" baking dish with grease.
- Mix together evaporated milk, butter, brown sugar and sugar in a medium saucepan on moderate heat. Bring the mixture to a boil while stirring constantly, then boil about 7 minutes. Take away from the heat and stir in marshmallow crème until melted and well blended. Stir in vanilla and peanut butter until smooth, then spread in prepped pan. Allow to cool prior to cutting into squares.

Nutrition Information

- Calories: 357 calories;
- Total Fat: 14.6
- Sodium: 140
- Total Carbohydrate: 54.1
- Cholesterol: 15
- Protein: 5.9

216. Creamy Peppermint Patties

Serving: about 8 dozen. | Prep: 40mins | Cook: 0mins | Ready in:

Ingredients

- 1 package (8 ounces) cream cheese, softened
- 1 teaspoon peppermint extract
- 9 cups confectioners' sugar
- 1-1/2 cups milk chocolate chips
- 1-1/2 cups semisweet chocolate chips
- 3 tablespoons shortening

Direction

- Beat extract and cream cheese until smooth. Slowly pour in confectioners' sugar and beat thoroughly.
- Form into balls of an inch. Put on baking sheets lined with waxed paper. Press down to form flat patties with diameters of 1-1/2 to 1-3/4 inches. Refrigerate while covered for an hour till chilled.
- Microwave shortening and chips until melted; whisk until smooth. Wait until slightly cool. Plunge patties in melted chocolate; letting

excess drip off; put on waxed paper till set. Keep refrigerated to store.

Nutrition Information

- Calories: 275 calories
- Sodium: 33mg sodium
- Fiber: 0 fiber)
- Total Carbohydrate: 51g carbohydrate (48g sugars
- Cholesterol: 12mg cholesterol
- Protein: 1g protein.
- Total Fat: 8g fat (4g saturated fat)

217. Crispy Peanut Butter Balls

Serving: 12 | Prep: 15mins | Cook: |Ready in:

Ingredients

- ½ cup natural peanut butter, almond butter or sunflower seed butter
- ¾ cup crispy rice cereal
- 1 teaspoon pure maple syrup
- ½ cup dark chocolate chips, melted (see Tip)

Direction

- Line wax or parchment paper onto a baking sheet. In a medium bowl, mix maple syrup, peanut butter, and cereal. Fold mixture into 12 balls by using about two teaspoons for each. Transfer onto the prepared baking sheet. Chill the balls for about 15 minutes until firm.
- Fold the balls in the melted chocolate. Place back into the freezer for about 15 minutes until chocolate is set.

Nutrition Information

- Calories: 112 calories;
- Sodium: 45
- Sugar: 5

- Total Fat: 7
- Saturated Fat: 2
- Fiber: 1
- Cholesterol: 0
- Total Carbohydrate: 8
- Protein: 3

218. Crunchy Chocolate Mint Balls

Serving: 4-1/2 dozen. | Prep: 45mins | Cook: 5mins | Ready in:

Ingredients

- 1 package (10 ounces) mint chocolate chips
- 1/4 cup butter, softened
- 1 can (14 ounces) sweetened condensed milk
- 1-1/4 cups chocolate wafer crumbs (about 22 wafers)
- White jimmies

Direction

- Melt butter and chips in double boiler/metal bowl above hot water; mix till smooth. Mix milk in; add wafer crumbs. Stir to coat. Refrigerate till easy to handle for 1 hour.
- Roll to 1-in. balls then roll into jimmies. Put on 15x10x1-in. waxed paper-lined baking pan; freeze till firm. Put into resealable plastic freezer bag; can be frozen for maximum 1 month.
- Using frozen balls: thaw it at room temperature.

Nutrition Information

- Calories: 70 calories
- Cholesterol: 5mg cholesterol
- Protein: 1g protein.
- Total Fat: 3g fat (2g saturated fat)
- Sodium: 33mg sodium
- Fiber: 0 fiber)

- Total Carbohydrate: 10g carbohydrate (8g sugars
- Protein: 2g protein.
- Total Fat: 15g fat (8g saturated fat)

219. Crunchy Cracker Candy

Serving: 2-1/2 pounds. | Prep: 20mins | Cook: 5mins | Ready in:

Ingredients

- 3 cups butter-flavored cracker sticks, halved
- 3/4 cup butter, cubed
- 3/4 cup packed brown sugar
- 1 package (11-1/2 ounces) milk chocolate chips
- 2 tablespoons shortening
- 1 cup chopped pecans, optional
- 1 cup English toffee bits or almond brickle chips, optional

Direction

- Put cracker sticks in a greased 15x10x1-in. baking pan; put aside. Over medium heat, heat up brown sugar and butter to a boil in a big saucepan, mixing frequently. Cook and mix for 3-4 minutes or until sugar dissolves. Pour on top of crackers; mix to coat.
- Bake for 5 minutes at 350°, mixing once. In the meantime, melt shortening and chips in a microwave; mix until smooth. Sprinkle over cracker sticks; toss until coated.
- Scatter with toffee bits and pecans (optional); toss to coat. Spread onto baking sheets lined with waxed paper. Let cool until firm; break apart. Put in an airtight container to store.

Nutrition Information

- Calories: 231 calories
- Sodium: 176mg sodium
- Fiber: 1g fiber)
- Total Carbohydrate: 24g carbohydrate (17g sugars
- Cholesterol: 22mg cholesterol

220. Crunchy Mint Fudge

Serving: 2-1/2 pounds. | Prep: 5mins | Cook: 5mins | Ready in:

Ingredients

- 1 teaspoon butter
- 1 can (14 ounces) sweetened condensed milk
- 2 cups (12 ounces) semisweet chocolate chips
- 1 cup Andes creme de menthe baking chips
- 1-1/2 cups coarsely crushed candy canes, divided
- 1 teaspoon vanilla extract

Direction

- Use foil to line a 9 in. square baking pan. Use butter to grease foil; put aside.
- Put chips and milk in a large microwave safe bowl and mix. Put the bowl in the microwave without a cover and microwave on high for 60 seconds; stir. Cook for half a minute to a minute more, stirring every 30 seconds, or till chips are melted. Mix in vanilla and 1 and a quarter cup of candy canes.
- Pour the mixture into the prepared pan. Use the remaining candy canes to sprinkle; gently press down. Cover and chill in the fridge for 2 hours or till firm. Use foil to lift fudge out of pan. Remove the foil gently, chop fudge into an inch square. Keep in an airtight container to store.

Nutrition Information

- Calories:
- Protein:
- Total Fat:
- Sodium:
- Fiber:
- Total Carbohydrate:

- Cholesterol:

221. Crunchy Peanut Butter Balls

Serving: 2-1/2 dozen. | Prep: 30mins | Cook: 0mins | Ready in:

Ingredients

- 1 cup peanut butter
- 1 jar (7 ounces) marshmallow creme
- 1-1/2 cups crisp rice cereal
- 1-1/2 cups (9 ounces) semisweet chocolate chips
- 4 teaspoons shortening

Direction

- Mix together marshmallow crème and peanut butter in a big bowl, then put in cereal and stir until well-coated.
- Melt shortening and chocolate chips in a microwave, mix until smooth. Roll cereal mixture into 1 inch balls. Dip into the chocolate and let excess drip off. Arrange on a pan lined with waxed paper, then chill until set.

Nutrition Information

- Calories: 123 calories
- Cholesterol: 0 cholesterol
- Protein: 3g protein.
- Total Fat: 7g fat (3g saturated fat)
- Sodium: 59mg sodium
- Fiber: 1g fiber)
- Total Carbohydrate: 14g carbohydrate (10g sugars

222. Crunchy Peanut Butter Squares

Serving: about 4 pounds. | Prep: 30mins | Cook: 5mins | Ready in:

Ingredients

- 1 teaspoon butter
- 5 cups cornflakes
- 1 package (10 ounces) peanut butter chips
- 1 cup light corn syrup
- 1/2 cup sugar
- 1/2 cup packed brown sugar
- 1-3/4 cups creamy peanut butter, warmed
- 1 cup dry-roasted peanuts
- 9 milk chocolate candy bars (1.55 ounces each)

Direction

- Use foil to line a 13-inch x 9-inch baking pan and grease the foil using 1 teaspoon butter; put aside. Add cornflakes into a large bowl; put aside. Melt the peanut butter chips in a microwave; stir till smooth. Spread out into the prepared pan.
- Mix together the corn syrup, sugar and brown sugar in a small saucepan. Heat until boiling on medium heat, stir continuously. Take off from heat. Stir peanut butter into the mixture till smooth. Stir peanuts into the mixture.
- Pour on top of the cornflakes right away; fold to incorporate. Spread on top of the peanut butter chips.
- Place chocolate bars on top. Bake until chocolate melts, at 350° for 2-4 minutes; and spread evenly. Chill until firm, for 30 minutes at the most. Lift the candy out of the pan with foil. Throw the foil; slice into 1-in. squares. For storage, keep in an airtight container.

Nutrition Information

- Calories: 77 calories
- Fiber: 1g fiber)
- Total Carbohydrate: 9g carbohydrate (5g sugars

- Cholesterol: 0 cholesterol
- Protein: 2g protein.
- Total Fat: 4g fat (1g saturated fat)
- Sodium: 57mg sodium

- Sodium: 28mg sodium
- Fiber: 0 fiber)
- Total Carbohydrate: 8g carbohydrate (6g sugars

223. Dandy Caramel Candies

Serving: about 9 dozen. | Prep: 30mins | Cook: 0mins | Ready in:

Ingredients

- 1-1/2 teaspoons plus 1 cup butter, divided
- 1 cup sugar
- 1 cup packed brown sugar
- 1 cup dark corn syrup
- 2 cups heavy whipping cream
- 3-3/4 cups chopped pecans (about 1 pound)
- 1 teaspoon vanilla extract
- Dark or milk chocolate candy coating, melted

Direction

- Butter 1-1/2 teaspoons of butter over a pan, about 13 inches x 9 inches. Put aside. Combine cream, butter, corn syrup and sugars in a heavy saucepan.
- Boil, stirring constantly, over medium-high heat. Over medium heat, cook until a candy thermometer registers 248° (firm-ball stage). Discard from heat; mix in vanilla and pecans. Spread into the prepared pan quickly. Let cool.
- Cut into 1-inch squares. Transfer the squares on the waxed paper-lined baking sheets; let chill thoroughly. Submerge each candy into the melted candy coating. Place in the refrigerator until firm.

Nutrition Information

- Calories: 93 calories
- Cholesterol: 12mg cholesterol
- Protein: 1g protein.
- Total Fat: 7g fat (3g saturated fat)

224. Dark Chocolate Raspberry Fudge

Serving: 3 pounds (81 pieces). | Prep: 15mins | Cook: 5mins | Ready in:

Ingredients

- 1 package (10 to 12 ounces) white baking chips
- 1 teaspoon butter, softened
- 3 cups dark chocolate chips
- 1 can (14 ounces) sweetened condensed milk
- 1/4 cup raspberry liqueur
- 1/8 teaspoon salt

Direction

- Scatter a single layer of baking chips over a small baking sheet. Put in the freezer for half an hour. Use foil to line a pan of 9 inches square; butter the foil.
- Mix milk and dark chocolate chips in a microwaveable bowl. Heat in the microwave on high without covering for 2 minutes and stir. Microwave in intervals of 30 seconds while whisking until smooth. Mix in salt and liqueur. Put in white baking chips; whisk until partly melted. Pour mixture into prepped pan. Put in the refrigerator till firm, about an hour.
- Take the fudge out of the pan by lifting with foil. Peel off the foil and slice into square pieces of an inch. Keep refrigerated in a tightly sealed container to store.

Nutrition Information

- Calories: 85 calories
- Total Fat: 5g fat (3g saturated fat)
- Sodium: 13mg sodium

- Fiber: 0 fiber)
- Total Carbohydrate: 10g carbohydrate (9g sugars
- Cholesterol: 2mg cholesterol
- Protein: 1g protein.

- Fiber: 1g fiber)
- Total Carbohydrate: 19g carbohydrate (16g sugars
- Cholesterol: 10mg cholesterol
- Protein: 1g protein.
- Total Fat: 12g fat (6g saturated fat)

225. Dipped Peanut Butter Logs

Serving: about 4 dozen. | Prep: 20mins | Cook: 0mins | Ready in:

Ingredients

- 1 cup butter, melted
- 1/2 cup chunky peanut butter
- 3-3/4 cups confectioners' sugar
- 10 ounces sweetened shredded coconut (about 3-1/2 cups)
- 1 cup chopped pecans
- 1/2 cup graham cracker crumbs (about 8 squares)
- 2 teaspoons vanilla extract
- 2 cups (12 ounces) semisweet chocolate chips
- 2 tablespoons shortening

Direction

- Mix together the first seven ingredients in a large bowl. Chill until firm enough to shape, for about 1 hour.
- Make 2-inch logs out of the mixture; put on a baking sheet lined with waxed paper. Melt together chocolate chips and shortening in a microwave; stir till smooth.
- Into chocolate, dip one end of each log; let the excess drip off or drizzle chocolate onto the logs. Take them back to sheet lined with waxed paper; chill until chocolate sets.

Nutrition Information

- Calories: 181 calories
- Sodium: 77mg sodium

226. Double Decker Fudge

Serving: 3-1/2 pounds. | Prep: 20mins | Cook: 0mins | Ready in:

Ingredients

- 1 tablespoon plus 1/2 cup butter, divided
- 4-1/2 cups sugar
- 1 can (12 ounces) evaporated milk
- 1 jar (7 ounces) marshmallow creme
- 2 cups peanut butter chips, divided
- 1/2 cup baking cocoa
- 1 teaspoon vanilla extract

Direction

- Line a 9-inch square pan using foil and butter the foil with a tablespoon butter; put aside. Mix 1/4 cup butter, marshmallow creme, milk and sugar in a heavy saucepan. Cook and mix over medium heat until the sugar dissolves. Heat up to a rapid boil for 5 minutes, mixing continuously. Take off from the heat.
- Into a bowl, put 3 cups of hot mixture; put in one cup peanut butter chips. Mix until chips melts and mixture turns smooth. Put into lined pan.
- Put leftover butter and chips, the vanilla and cocoa into the leftover hot mixture; mix until chips and butter melt and turn smooth. Put evenly on top of peanut butter layer in pan. Let cool. Take fudge out of pan with foil. Slice into 1-inch squares. Chill in airtight containers.

Nutrition Information

- Calories: 121 calories

- Total Fat: 4g fat (2g saturated fat)
- Sodium: 40mg sodium
- Fiber: 1g fiber)
- Total Carbohydrate: 21g carbohydrate (19g sugars
- Cholesterol: 6mg cholesterol
- Protein: 2g protein.

227. Double Nut English Toffee

Serving: 3-1/2 pounds. | Prep: 15mins | Cook: 20mins | Ready in:

Ingredients

- 1-1/2 teaspoons plus 2 cups butter, softened, divided
- 2 cups sugar
- 1 cup chopped almonds, toasted
- 1 package (12 ounces) semisweet chocolate chips, divided
- 2 cups ground walnuts or pecans, divided

Direction

- Use 1 1/2 teaspoons butter to butter a 15x10x1-inch pan; put aside. Put leftover butter and sugar together in heavy saucepan, mix and cook on medium heat till it reaches a soft-crack stage or candy thermometer reads 290°. Take off from heat; mix in almonds. Put in prepped pan immediately.
- Sprinkle 1 cup chocolate chips over; stand till chips are glossy. Evenly spread on top; sprinkle 1 cup walnuts over. Cover; refrigerate for 1 hour till set.
- Melt leftover chips in a microwave; mix till smooth. Spread on toffee; sprinkle leftover walnuts over. Cover; refrigerate for 30 minutes till set. Break to 2-inch pieces; keep in airtight container.

Nutrition Information

- Calories:
- Sodium:
- Fiber:
- Total Carbohydrate:
- Cholesterol:
- Protein:
- Total Fat:

228. Easy Chocolate Drops

Serving: 18 | Prep: | Cook: |Ready in:

Ingredients

- 3 tablespoons margarine
- 3 tablespoons peanut butter
- 1 cup semisweet chocolate chips
- 3 cups whole wheat flake cereal

Direction

- Mix chocolate chips, peanut butter and margarine in a medium-sized saucepan. Cook on low heat, while mixing often till becomes melted. Take out of the heat and mix in cereal. Drop by spoonfuls onto wax paper or the greased cookie sheets, and keep chilled in the refrigerator till becomes set.

Nutrition Information

- Calories: 95 calories;
- Protein: 1.6
- Total Fat: 6.1
- Sodium: 69
- Total Carbohydrate: 10.5
- Cholesterol: 0

229. Easy Chocolate Truffles

Serving: 48 | Prep: | Cook: |Ready in:

Ingredients

- 8 ounces good-quality semi- or bittersweet chocolate, coarsely chopped
- 4 ounces unsweetened chocolate
- 8 tablespoons unsalted butter
- 1 (14 ounce) can sweetened condensed milk
- Your choice of flavoring (see below)
- Your choice of coating (see below)

Direction

- Heat milk, butter and chocolates in pan till butter and chocolates melt partially. Take off heat; mix till melted completely. Whisk desired flavoring in till smooth and creamy.
- Put in bowl; let stand for about 2 hours till firm enough to hold its own shape.
- 1 level tbsp. at a time, use tbsp. (spring action 1 tbsp. scoop is preferred) to mold chocolate to balls. Put onto greased parchment paper-lined cookie sheet.
- Put preferred coating into small bowl. One by one, drop truffles in bowl using greased fingertips. Shake the bowl back and forth to completely coat truffles. By hand, roll truffles to make round if needed. Put back on parchment. Can be refrigerated for up to 5 days in airtight container/frozen for up to 1 month. Let stand to slightly soften at room temperature before serving.

Nutrition Information

- Calories: 78 calories;
- Protein: 1.3
- Total Fat: 5.4
- Sodium: 11
- Total Carbohydrate: 7.8
- Cholesterol: 8

230. Easy Double Decker Fudge

Serving: about 1-1/2 pounds. | Prep: 15mins | Cook: 0mins | Ready in:

Ingredients

- 1 teaspoon butter
- 1 cup peanut butter chips
- 1 can (14 ounces) sweetened condensed milk, divided
- 1 teaspoon vanilla extract, divided
- 1 cup (6 ounces) semisweet chocolate chips

Direction

- Use foil to line an 8 in. square pan; butter the foil and set aside.
- Mix 2/3 cup milk and peanut butter chips in a microwave safe bowl. Microwave for a minute on high; stir. Microwave at additional intervals of 15 second; stir till the mixture becomes smooth. Add half a teaspoon of vanilla and stir. Transfer the mixture to the prepared square pan. Chill in the fridge for 10 minutes.
- At the same time, mix the remaining milk and chocolate chips in a microwave-safe bowl. Microwave for a minute on high; stir. Microwave at additional intervals of 15 second; stir till the mixture becomes smooth. Add the remaining vanilla and stir. Spread the mixture over the peanut butter layer.
- Chill in the fridge for an hour or until firm. Get fudge out of pan by using foil. Divide into 1 in. squares.

Nutrition Information

- Calories: 47 calories
- Total Carbohydrate: 6g carbohydrate (6g sugars
- Cholesterol: 2mg cholesterol
- Protein: 1g protein. Diabetic Exchanges: 1/2 starch.
- Total Fat: 2g fat (1g saturated fat)

- Sodium: 15mg sodium
- Fiber: 0 fiber)

231. Easy Holiday Fudge

Serving: about 2-1/2 pounds. | Prep: 5mins | Cook: 5mins | Ready in:

Ingredients

- 1 teaspoon butter
- 1 can (14 ounces) sweetened condensed milk
- 2 cups (12 ounces) semisweet chocolate chips
- 1 cup butterscotch chips
- 1 cup chopped pecans
- 1/2 cup raisins
- 1 teaspoon vanilla extract

Direction

- Use foil to line a 9-in. square baking pan. Grease foil using butter; put aside.
- Mix together the chips and milk in a large microwave-safe bowl. Microwave, uncovered, for 1 minute on high; stir the mix. Cook for another 30-60 seconds or until chips are melted, stirring every 30 seconds. Stir the pecans, raisins and vanilla into the mixture. Transfer the mixture into the prepared pan. Refrigerate, covered, for 2 hours or until firm.
- Lift fudge out of the pan using foil. Take off the foil gently; slice the fudge into 1-in. squares. For storage, keep in an airtight container.

Nutrition Information

- Calories: 82 calories
- Fiber: 1g fiber)
- Total Carbohydrate: 10g carbohydrate (9g sugars
- Cholesterol: 3mg cholesterol
- Protein: 1g protein. Diabetic Exchanges: 1 fat
- Total Fat: 5g fat (2g saturated fat)

- Sodium: 12mg sodium

232. Easy Marshmallow Fudge

Serving: 5 dozen. | Prep: 15mins | Cook: 0mins | Ready in:

Ingredients

- 1 tablespoon plus 2 cups butter, divided
- 1 package (10-1/2 ounces) pastel miniature marshmallows
- 1 package (12 ounces) semisweet chocolate chips
- 1 package (11 ounces) butterscotch chips
- 1 cup peanut butter

Direction

- Use the foil to line the 13x9-inch pan; use 1 tablespoon of the butter grease foil. Put the marshmallows into the prepped pan.
- In the saucepan on low heat, melt leftover butter, peanut butter and chips, whisk continuously. Add on top of the marshmallows. Tap the pan gently on the working surface. Chill.
- With the foil, lift the fudge from the pan. Chop into the square pieces. Keep in airtight container in the fridge.

Nutrition Information

- Calories: 152 calories
- Fiber: 1g fiber)
- Total Carbohydrate: 12g carbohydrate (10g sugars
- Cholesterol: 17mg cholesterol
- Protein: 2g protein.
- Total Fat: 12g fat (7g saturated fat)
- Sodium: 91mg sodium

233. Easy Microwave Caramels

Serving: about 2-3/4 lbs. | Prep: 30mins | Cook: 0mins | Ready in:

Ingredients

- 1 cup unsalted butter
- 2-1/3 cups (1 pound) brown sugar, firmly packed
- 1 cup light corn syrup
- 1 can (14 ounces) sweetened condensed milk
- 1/8 teaspoon salt
- 1 teaspoon vanilla extract
- 1/2 cup chopped walnuts, optional

Direction

- Mix salt, milk, syrup, sugar and butter in a microwavable, 2-quart pitcher. Microwave for 2 to 3 minutes on high, mixing once after each minute. Once butter has melted, mix thoroughly. Add in a microwave candy thermometer. Microwave for about 8 minutes on high or till mixture attains 245° for firm-ball stage. Do not mix. Take out of microwave; mix in walnuts and vanilla. Rest for ten minutes, mixing thoroughly a few times. Put to buttered pan, 13x9-inch in size; 11x7-inch pan makes thicker candy. Chill till cool. Flip pan over. Cautiously tap entire block of candy out; slice into squares. Use waxed paper to wrap and keep refrigerated. Alternately, preserve in freezer.

Nutrition Information

- Calories:
- Protein:
- Total Fat:
- Sodium:
- Fiber:
- Total Carbohydrate:
- Cholesterol:

234. Easy Microwave Mint Fudge

Serving: about 3 pounds (117 pieces). | Prep: 10mins | Cook: 5mins | Ready in:

Ingredients

- 2 teaspoons butter
- 7-1/2 cups confectioners' sugar
- 1 cup baking cocoa
- 15 tablespoons butter, softened
- 7 tablespoons 2% milk
- 2 teaspoons vanilla extract
- 1 cup Andes creme de menthe baking chips

Direction

- Use foil to line a 13x9 in. pan; use 2 teaspoons butter to grease foil.
- Sift cocoa and confectioners' sugar together in a large microwave safe bowl. Pour in milk and butter (remember not to stir). Microwave on high for 2 - 2 and a half minute. Get the bowl out of the microwave; stir till the mixture is blended. Add vanilla and stir. Spread the mixture into the prepared pan. Use baking chips to sprinkle, press chips lightly into fudge. Chill in the fridge for an hour till firm.
- Lift fudge out of pan by foil. Get rid of foil; chop fudge into 1 in. squares. Keep in an airtight container and store in the fridge.
- To prepare in advance: Place layers of fudge between waxed paper and store an airtight container in the fridge. Serve at room temperature.
- To store in the freezer: Use waxed paper then foil to wrap fudge. Put wrapped fudge in freezer containers and put the containers in the freezer. To thaw, bring the wrapped fudge to sit at room temperature.

Nutrition Information

- Calories:
- Protein:
- Total Fat:
- Sodium:
- Fiber:
- Total Carbohydrate:
- Cholesterol:

235. Eggnog Fudge

Serving: 24 | Prep: 15mins | Cook: 10mins | Ready in:

Ingredients

- 1 cooking spray
- 1 cup eggnog
- 3 cups white sugar
- 1 1/2 cups miniature marshmallows
- 1/2 teaspoon ground cinnamon
- 1/2 teaspoon ground nutmeg
- 1/8 cup butter, chilled
- 1/2 (11 ounce) package white chocolate chips
- 1 cup chopped almonds

Direction

- Use aluminum foil to line a 9 x 13 inch baking pan and put aside.
- Use cooking spray to coat a large saucepan's bottom and sides. Heat together eggnog and sugar on medium heat. Heat till it reaches a rolling boil, stir continuously using a wooden spoon. Boil for about 2 minutes.
- Fold marshmallows, cinnamon and nutmeg into the mixture. Bring back to a boil for 6 minutes, stir continuously. The mixture will turn brown as it boils. Take off from heat and stir the butter, white chocolate chips and almonds quickly into the mixture. Stir till well combined and glossy.
- Transfer into the prepared pan quickly.
- Let it cool down at room temperature. Take out of pan, take off the foil and slice into squares.

Nutrition Information

- Calories: 190 calories;
- Total Fat: 6
- Sodium: 23
- Total Carbohydrate: 33.5
- Cholesterol: 10
- Protein: 1.7

236. Family Favorite Cinnamon Candy

Serving: 3-1/2 pounds. | Prep: 10mins | Cook: 40mins | Ready in:

Ingredients

- 1 tablespoon butter
- 3-3/4 cups sugar
- 1-1/4 cups light corn syrup
- 1 cup water
- 3 packages (6 ounces each) Red Hots
- 1/4 cup confectioners' sugar

Direction

- Use butter to grease 2 15x10x1-inch pans.
- Put water, corn syrup and sugar together in a big heavy saucepan and boil on medium heat, constantly mixing to melt sugar. Add red hots; boil for 10 minutes, carefully mixing till Red Hots melt. It'll be very hot; to avoid burns, wear oven mitt while mixing. Cook without mixing till it reaches a hard-crack stage or candy thermometer reads 300°.
- Take off from heat; divide it to prepped pans immediately. Fully cool for 1 hour.
- Break candy to pieces. In big resealable bag, put confectioners' sugar; add candy in batches. Toss to lightly coat.

Nutrition Information

- Calories:
- Sodium:

- Fiber:
- Total Carbohydrate:
- Cholesterol:
- Protein:
- Total Fat:

237. Festive Holiday Fruitcake Bark

Serving: 2 pounds. | Prep: 10mins | Cook: 0mins | Ready in:

Ingredients

- 2/3 cup chopped mixed candied fruit
- 2 tablespoons brandy
- 1/2 cup walnut pieces, toasted, divided
- 20 ounces white candy coating, coarsely chopped
- 2/3 cup miniature marshmallows
- 10 shortbread cookies, coarsely chopped

Direction

- Mix brandy and candied fruit in a small bowl. Cover and chill for 2 hours, stirring sometimes.
- Use waxed paper to line a 15x10x1-inch baking pan. For topping, set aside 2 tablespoons walnuts and 2 tablespoons of candied fruit. Microwave candy coating to melt; mix until smooth. Mix in walnuts, the rest of fruit, cookie pieces and marshmallows.
- Pour into prepped baking pan but do not full fill. Scatter with the saved walnuts and fruit; push into melted candy coating. Put aside to set. Slice or break into pieces. Keep in a tightly closed container to store.

Nutrition Information

- Calories:
- Sodium:
- Fiber:
- Total Carbohydrate:
- Cholesterol:
- Protein:
- Total Fat:

238. Fruit 'n' Nut Clusters

Serving: 1 dozen. | Prep: 10mins | Cook: 0mins | Ready in:

Ingredients

- 1 cup vanilla or white chips
- 1/3 cup dried cranberries
- 1/3 cup salted whole cashews

Direction

- Melt chips in a microwave-safe bowl; mix until smooth. Stir in cranberries and cashews. Drop onto a baking sheet that is lined with a waxed paper by tablespoonfuls. Chill in the refrigerator until firm. Keep in an airtight container.

Nutrition Information

- Calories: 113 calories
- Sodium: 41mg sodium
- Fiber: 0 fiber
- Total Carbohydrate: 12g carbohydrate (11g sugars
- Cholesterol: 2mg cholesterol
- Protein: 2g protein. Diabetic Exchanges: 1-1/2 fat
- Total Fat: 7g fat (3g saturated fat)

239. Fudge Drops

Serving: about 2-1/4 pounds. | Prep: 30mins | Cook: 0mins | Ready in:

Ingredients

- 1-2/3 cups sugar
- 1 can (5 ounces) evaporated milk
- 2 tablespoons butter
- 1/2 teaspoon salt
- 2-3/4 cups miniature marshmallows
- 2 cups (12 ounces) semisweet chocolate chips
- 1/2 cup coarsely chopped walnuts
- 1/2 cup raisins

Direction

- In a heavy saucepan, combine the salt, butter, milk, and sugar. Heat the mixture until it boils over medium heat while stirring frequently. Boil and stir the mixture for 5 minutes.
- Remove it from the heat and mix in the rest of the ingredients. Stir thoroughly until the marshmallows are partly melted, for about 1 minute. Drop onto baking sheets that are lined with waxed papers by tablespoonfuls. Let it sit at room temperature until cool. Keep in a cool, dry place in airtight containers.

Nutrition Information

- Calories: 120 calories
- Fiber: 1g fiber)
- Total Carbohydrate: 20g carbohydrate (18g sugars
- Cholesterol: 3mg cholesterol
- Protein: 1g protein.
- Total Fat: 5g fat (2g saturated fat)
- Sodium: 46mg sodium

240. Fudge With Candy Bar Bits

Serving: about 1-1/2 pounds. | Prep: 20mins | Cook: 0mins | Ready in:

Ingredients

- 1 teaspoon butter
- 1 cup semisweet chocolate chips
- 1 cup butterscotch chips
- 1 can (16 ounces) chocolate fudge frosting
- 2 Snickers candy bars (2.07 ounces each), cut into 1/4-inch chunks, divided

Direction

- Use foil to line a 9x9-inch pan and use butter to grease the foil then put aside.
- Microwave butterscotch chips and chocolate in a big microwavable-safe bowl until melted; mix until smooth. Mix in 1/2 candy bar pieces and frosting. Pour into pan. Drizzle the rest of candy bar pieces on top. Put in the refrigerator until set, about 60 minutes.
- Use a cookie cutter with a heart shape to cut the fudge. Put into a tightly closed container and chill to store.

Nutrition Information

- Calories: 93 calories
- Sodium: 30mg sodium
- Fiber: 0 fiber)
- Total Carbohydrate: 13g carbohydrate (11g sugars
- Cholesterol: 1mg cholesterol
- Protein: 0 protein.
- Total Fat: 5g fat (3g saturated fat)

241. Fudgy Christmas Wreath

Serving: about 24 servings. | Prep: 30mins | Cook: 0mins | Ready in:

Ingredients

- 1 can (14 ounces) sweetened condensed milk
- 2 cups (12 ounces) semisweet chocolate chips
- 1 cup chopped walnuts
- 1/2 teaspoon vanilla extract
- Red and green maraschino cherries

Direction

- Cook chocolate chips and milk over low heat in a saucepan for about 6 minutes, stirring, until chocolate is melted and mixture thickens lightly. Put off the heat; whisk in vanilla and nuts. Allow mixture to cool for about 15 minutes, until it begins to firm. Line waxed paper on a baking sheet. Place chocolate mixture into small mounds by 2 tablespoonfuls to shape a wreath. Garnish with cherries. Refrigerate until solid; serve cold.

Nutrition Information

- Calories: 152 calories
- Total Fat: 9g fat (4g saturated fat)
- Sodium: 23mg sodium
- Fiber: 1g fiber)
- Total Carbohydrate: 18g carbohydrate (17g sugars
- Cholesterol: 6mg cholesterol
- Protein: 3g protein.

242. Golden Walnut Caramel Squares

Serving: 6-1/2 dozen. | Prep: 40mins | Cook: 40mins | Ready in:

Ingredients

- 1 cup all-purpose flour
- 3 tablespoons sugar
- 1/2 cup cold butter
- 1/3 cup semisweet chocolate chips
- CARAMEL LAYER:
- 1-1/3 cups sugar
- 1 cup butter, cubed
- 1 cup heavy whipping cream
- 1/3 cup corn syrup
- 2-1/2 cups chopped walnuts
- 1 ounce unsweetened chocolate, chopped

Direction

- Line foil on a baking pan, 9-inch in size and oil the foil; put aside.
- Mix sugar and flour in a big bowl. Cut in butter till mixture looks much like coarse crumbs. Pat into prepped pan; use a fork to puncture crust. Bake for 18 to 22 minutes at 350° till set and edges start to turn brown.
- Quickly scatter chocolate chips over top. Soften chips for several minutes, then smear on crust; put aside.
- Cook sugar over moderately-low heat in a heavy, big skillet till liquified. Do not mix. Turn the heat to low; cook till golden brown, about five minutes.
- Mix cream, corn syrup and butter in a big saucepan. Gently add cooked sugar. Cook and ix over moderate heat till a candy thermometer registers 240° for soft-ball stage. Take away from heat; mix in walnuts. Put on top of prepped crust.
- Liquify chocolate in microwave; mix till smooth. Sprinkle on top of caramel layer. Refrigerate with a cover till firm, about 2 hours.
- Remove candy from pan with foil. Slowly remove foil; slice candy into squares.

Nutrition Information

- Calories: 96 calories
- Protein: 1g protein. Diabetic Exchanges: 1 fat
- Total Fat: 7g fat (3g saturated fat)
- Sodium: 27mg sodium
- Fiber: 0 fiber)
- Total Carbohydrate: 7g carbohydrate (5g sugars
- Cholesterol: 13mg cholesterol

243. Goody Goody Gumdrops

Serving: about 1 pound (64 pieces). | Prep: 10mins | Cook: 10mins | Ready in:

Ingredients

- 3 envelopes unflavored gelatin
- 1-1/4 cups water, divided
- 1-1/2 cups sugar
- 1/4 to 1/2 teaspoon peppermint extract
- 4 drops each red and green food coloring
- Additional sugar

Direction

- Scatter gelatin on top of 1/2 cup water in a small bowl; let sit 5 minutes. Heat up sugar and leftover 3/4 cup water to a boil in a small saucepan over medium heat, mixing continuously. Put in gelatin mixture; simmer and mix over low heat about 5 minutes until gelatin is fully dissolved. Take off from heat; mix in extract.
- Split mixture among 2 bowls; dye one red and the one green using food coloring. Put each into a greased 8x4-inch loaf pan; let cool completely. Cover and chill for 3 hours or until set.
- Loosen sides from pan using a knife; flip onto a cutting board dusted with sugar. Slice into 1/2-inch cubes; toss in more sugar.
- Let sit at room temperature 3-4 hours, with no cover, or until all sides are dry, flipping every 60 minutes.

Nutrition Information

- Calories: 23 calories
- Total Fat: 0 fat (0 saturated fat)
- Sodium: 3mg sodium
- Fiber: 0 fiber)
- Total Carbohydrate: 5g carbohydrate (5g sugars
- Cholesterol: 0 cholesterol
- Protein: 1g protein.

244. Grandma's Hazelnut Candies

Serving: about 4-1/2 dozen. | Prep: 15mins | Cook: 10mins | Ready in:

Ingredients

- 1 package (10 to 12 ounces) white baking chips
- 3/4 cup Nutella
- 1-1/2 cups chopped hazelnuts, toasted, divided

Direction

- In a small saucepan, mix Nutella and baking chips over low heat and cook and stir until smooth. Take off from the heat. Mix in 1 cup of hazelnuts.
- Drop onto the baking sheets that are lined with a waxed paper by tablespoonfuls; sprinkle the remaining hazelnuts on top. Put in the refrigerator until firm. Keep in an airtight container.

Nutrition Information

- Calories: 69 calories
- Total Carbohydrate: 6g carbohydrate (5g sugars
- Cholesterol: 1mg cholesterol
- Protein: 1g protein. Diabetic Exchanges: 1/2 starch
- Total Fat: 5g fat (1g saturated fat)
- Sodium: 6mg sodium
- Fiber: 0 fiber)

245. Green Mint Bark

Serving: 1-1/2 pounds. | Prep: 15mins | Cook: 5mins | Ready in:

Ingredients

- 1 package (10 to 12 ounces) white baking chips

- 12 ounces green candy coating disks
- 1 teaspoon peppermint extract
- 2 to 3 candy canes, crushed

Direction

- Line foil on a baking sheet; put aside. Melt chips in a microwave; mix till smooth. Spread into 13x9-inch rectangle on prepped baking sheet.
- Melt candy coating in microwave; mix till smooth. Mix in extract. Spread on white layer; sprinkle candy over.
- Chill till firm for 10 minutes; break to pieces. Keep in airtight container.

Nutrition Information

- Calories: 171 calories
- Total Fat: 9g fat (7g saturated fat)
- Sodium: 32mg sodium
- Fiber: 0 fiber)
- Total Carbohydrate: 21g carbohydrate (20g sugars
- Cholesterol: 3mg cholesterol
- Protein: 1g protein. Diabetic Exchanges: 2 fat

246. Hard Candy Peppermint Twists

Serving: about 1/2 pound. | Prep: 60mins | Cook: 40mins | Ready in:

Ingredients

- 1 cup water
- 1 tablespoon white vinegar
- 2 cups sugar
- 1-1/2 teaspoons peppermint extract
- 1/8 teaspoon red food coloring

Direction

- Grease 2 9-inch square pans with cooking spray; put aside. (Don't use butter or foil to prepare pans.). Combine vinegar and water in a heavy saucepan over medium heat. Put in sugar. Cook and mix for about 8 minutes until mixture comes to a boil and sugar is dissolved. (Cover saucepan for 1-1/2 to 2 minutes to let steam wash crystals down if sugar crystals are present.) Cook for about 26 minutes, until a candy thermometer registers 300° (hard-crack stage), without stirring.
- Mix food coloring and peppermint extract together. Take syrup away from the heat; mix in peppermint mixture until thoroughly combined (mixture will be a little bubbly). Put into greased pans quickly and carefully (don't scrape saucepan or tilt pans to spread mixture evenly). Let cool for 1-1/2 to 2 minutes.
- Score candy into 1/2-in.to 3/4-in.-wide pieces, about 3-in. long using a sharp knife. Put the two pans in a warm oven for about 5 minutes (150 degrees or your oven's lowest temperature), until candy is warm enough to slice but cool enough to handle.
- Snip along scored lines with a heavy-duty kitchen scissors, a piece at a time. Wrap each piece around the handle of a wooden spoon immediately; take out candy and put on waxed paper to set. Repeat until mixture in pan starts to firm up. Put pan bank into oven for no less than 5 minutes.
- In the meantime, take out second pan from oven. Cut and wrap like the first pan until mixture starts to firm up. Put back to oven and keep cutting and wrapping with the first pan. Repeat until all is cut and formed into twists.

Nutrition Information

- Calories: 198 calories
- Sodium: 1mg sodium
- Fiber: 0 fiber)
- Total Carbohydrate: 50g carbohydrate (48g sugars
- Cholesterol: 0 cholesterol
- Protein: 0 protein.
- Total Fat: 0 fat (0 saturated fat)

247. Hazelnut Toffee

Serving: 2 pounds. | Prep: 15mins | Cook: 15mins | Ready in:

Ingredients

- 1-3/4 cups finely chopped hazelnuts
- 1-1/2 cups sugar
- 1/2 cup water
- 1/3 cup light corn syrup
- 1 cup butter
- 1/4 teaspoon salt
- 1/4 teaspoon baking soda
- 1/4 teaspoon orange extract
- 1 cup (6 ounces) semisweet chocolate chips

Direction

- In a 15x10x1-inch baking pan that is greased, put the hazelnuts. Bake in the oven for about 15 minutes at 300°F until toasted; reserve.
- Mix corn syrup, water and sugar in a large heavy saucepan; make it boil over medium heat. Then cover and boil for 2 minutes. Mix in butter; and cook over medium heat, whisking occasionally, until thermometer registers 300°F-310°F (hard crack stage). Take away from heat; instantly mix in 1-1/4 cups toasted hazelnuts, orange extract, baking soda and salt.
- Transfer onto a baking sheet that is greased and spread to a thickness of 1/4-inch. Dust with chocolate chips. Allow to stand for about 5 minutes, until chocolates liquefied; place chocolate over toffee and spread. Dust with remaining hazelnuts. Allow to stand for 1 hour. Then crumble into pieces.

Nutrition Information

- Calories: 163 calories
- Total Fat: 11g fat (5g saturated fat)
- Sodium: 77mg sodium
- Fiber: 1g fiber)
- Total Carbohydrate: 17g carbohydrate (15g sugars
- Cholesterol: 15mg cholesterol
- Protein: 1g protein.

248. Holiday Divinity

Serving: 1-1/4 pounds. | Prep: 25mins | Cook: 15mins | Ready in:

Ingredients

- 2 cups sugar
- 1/2 cup water
- 1/3 cup light corn syrup
- 2 egg whites
- 1 teaspoon vanilla extract
- 1/8 teaspoon salt
- 1 cup chopped walnuts, toasted
- 1/4 cup diced candied cherries
- 1/4 cup diced candied pineapple

Direction

- Mix the corn syrup, water and sugar in a heavy saucepan; cook and mix until sugar dissolves and mixture boils. Cook over medium heat, without mixing, until a candy thermometer registers 250° (hard-ball stage). Take off from the heat.
- In the meantime, whip the egg whites in a stand mixer until stiff peak create. Add hot syrup cautiously in a slow, steady stream into the mixing bowl with mixer running on high speed. Put in salt and vanilla. Whip on high speed about 10 minutes just until candy loses its shine and keeps its shape. Mix in fruit and nuts.
- Put by teaspoonfuls onto waxed paper. Put in airtight containers to store.

Nutrition Information

- Calories: 289 calories

- Total Carbohydrate: 56g carbohydrate (49g sugars
- Cholesterol: 0 cholesterol
- Protein: 4g protein.
- Total Fat: 7g fat (0 saturated fat)
- Sodium: 59mg sodium
- Fiber: 1g fiber)

249. Holiday Pecan Logs

Serving: about 3-1/4 pounds. | Prep: 25mins | Cook: 10mins | Ready in:

Ingredients

- 2 teaspoons plus 1/2 cup butter, softened, divided
- 3-3/4 cups confectioners' sugar
- 1/2 cup nonfat dry milk powder
- 1/2 cup sugar
- 1/2 cup light corn syrup
- 1 teaspoon vanilla extract
- 1 package (14 ounces) caramels
- 1 tablespoon milk or half-and-half cream
- 2 cups chopped pecans

Direction

- Use 2 teaspoons butter to grease an 8-inch square pan; put aside. Mix together confectioners' sugar and milk powder; put aside. Mix together 1/2 cup butter, sugar and corn syrup in a heavy saucepan; cook and stir till sugar dissolves and the mixture reaches a boil. Stir the confectioners' sugar mixture into the mix, about 1/3 at a time, till incorporated.
- Take off from heat; stir vanilla into the mixture. Keep on stirring until the mixture slightly mounds when dropped down from a spoon. Spread into the prepared pan. Let it cool down.
- Chop the candy into four strips; then halve each strip. Roll each one into a log; use waxed paper to wrap and twist the ends. Freeze or chill in refrigerator until firm.
- In the meantime, melt caramels and milk in a microwave, stir often. Roll the logs into the caramel mixture, then into the pecans. Wrap them in waxed paper. For storage, keep at room temperature in airtight containers. Use a serrated knife to cut into slices.

Nutrition Information

- Calories: 264 calories
- Protein: 2g protein.
- Total Fat: 12g fat (4g saturated fat)
- Sodium: 96mg sodium
- Fiber: 1g fiber)
- Total Carbohydrate: 40g carbohydrate (35g sugars
- Cholesterol: 12mg cholesterol

250. Holiday Truffles

Serving: about 7 dozen. | Prep: 45mins | Cook: 0mins | Ready in:

Ingredients

- 3 packages (12 ounces each) semisweet chocolate chips, divided
- 2-1/4 cups sweetened condensed milk, divided
- 1/2 teaspoon orange extract
- 1/2 teaspoon peppermint extract
- 1/2 teaspoon almond extract
- 1-1/2 pounds white candy coating, melted
- 3/4 pound dark chocolate candy coating, melted
- 1/3 cup crushed peppermint candies
- 1/2 cup ground almonds
- 1/3 cup sweetened shredded coconut
- Paste food coloring, optional

Direction

- Melt 1 package of chips in a microwaveable bowl; mix until smooth. Pour 3/4 cup milk

and stir well. Mix in orange extract. Keep adding and mixing two more times, putting peppermint extract to 1 portion and almond extract to the other.
- Chill for 45 minutes, covered, until firm enough to form into 1-in. balls.
- Put on 3 separate waxed paper-lined baking sheets. Refrigerate for 1-2 hours or until set.
- Plunge orange-flavored truffles in white candy coating twice; let excess fall off. Put on waxed paper; let sit until firm.
- Plunge peppermint-flavored truffles in dark chocolate coating; let excess fall off. Top with peppermint candies.
- Plunge almond-flavored truffles in dark chocolate; let excess fall off. Top with coconut or almonds. Dye white coating with food coloring; sprinkle on top of white truffles (optional).

Nutrition Information

- Calories: 117 calories
- Cholesterol: 3mg cholesterol
- Protein: 1g protein.
- Total Fat: 6g fat (4g saturated fat)
- Sodium: 12mg sodium
- Fiber: 0 fiber
- Total Carbohydrate: 16g carbohydrate (15g sugars

251. Homemade Gumdrops

Serving: About 1-3/4 pounds. | Prep: 35mins | Cook: 0mins | Ready in:

Ingredients

- 2-1/2 cups sugar, divided
- 1-1/3 cups applesauce
- 2 packages (3 ounces each) red or green gelatin
- 2 envelopes unflavored gelatin
- 1 teaspoon lemon juice

Direction

- Mix together lemon juice, unflavored gelatin, red or green gelatin, applesauce and two cups of sugar in a big saucepan; let sit for a minute. Boil while stirring frequently on medium heat. Keep boiling for a minute. Quickly transfer to a cold 11x7-inch baking dish sprayed with cooking spray. Put in the refrigerator to firm up for 3 hours.
- Separate gelatin from the pan's sides with a spatula. Turn upside down onto waxed paper to take out of the pan. Cut into shapes or 1-in squares with small sharp cookie cutters or kitchen scissors dipped on hot water.
- Put on waxed paper. Let sit at room temperature to dry until slightly sticky, about 8 hours. Cover with remaining sugar. Keep in a tightly sealed container to store.

Nutrition Information

- Calories: 35 calories
- Cholesterol: 0 cholesterol
- Protein: 0 protein.
- Total Fat: 0 fat (0 saturated fat)
- Sodium: 3mg sodium
- Fiber: 0 fiber
- Total Carbohydrate: 9g carbohydrate (8g sugars

252. Honey Almond Nougats

Serving: about 1 pound. | Prep: 20mins | Cook: 10mins | Ready in:

Ingredients

- 1-1/2 teaspoons butter
- 2/3 cup superfine sugar
- 2 teaspoons cornstarch
- 1/2 cup honey
- 2 egg whites
- 2 cups ground almonds

- 1 teaspoon ground cinnamon
- 1 cup finely chopped almonds

Direction

- Use the butter to coat a large bowl; then put aside. Mix honey, cornstarch, and sugar in a large heavy saucepan on medium heat. Stir and cook until the mixture boils and sugar dissolves. Put a cover on and boil for a minute. Remove the cover; cook but don't stir until reaching the soft-crack stage or a candy thermometer registers 286 degrees.
- Whisk egg whites in a stand mixer to form stiff peaks. Add the hot sugar mixture steadily and slowly using a mixer at high speed into the mixing bowl. Whisk on high and scrape the sides of the bowl from time to time until the mixture becomes lukewarm and maintains its shape, or for 10 minutes.
- Mix in the cinnamon and ground almonds; fold. Place onto the buttered bowl; allow to cool to room temperature. Form into 1-inch balls; then roll them in the chopped almonds. Place into an airtight container to store.

Nutrition Information

- Calories: 66 calories
- Protein: 2g protein. Diabetic Exchanges: 1/2 starch
- Total Fat: 4g fat (0 saturated fat)
- Sodium: 4mg sodium
- Fiber: 1g fiber
- Total Carbohydrate: 8g carbohydrate (6g sugars
- Cholesterol: 0 cholesterol

253. Honey Cream Taffy

Serving: about 5 dozen. | Prep: 01hours45mins | Cook: 0mins | Ready in:

Ingredients

- 1 tablespoon butter, softened
- 1 cup heavy whipping cream
- 2 cups honey
- 1 cup sugar

Direction

- Use butter to grease a 15x10x1-inch pan; put it into the refrigerator. Mix together cream and honey in a large deep heavy saucepan. Add sugar into the mix; cook on medium heat and stir using a wooden spoon till sugar melts and the mixture boils.
- Use a tight-fitting lid to cover the pan and boil for 1 minute. Take off the lid; cook, without mixing, until it reaches a soft-crack stage (a candy thermometer reads 290°). Take off from heat and transfer into the prepared pan (do not scrape the saucepan's sides). Let it cool down for 5 minutes. Use a wooden spoon to bring the honey mixture's edges into the center of pan. Let it cool down for another 5-10 minutes or until cool enough to work with.
- Butter your hands then pull and stretch the taffy until it forms ridges. (Taffy will no longer be glossy and turn into light tan-color.) Pull it into 1/2 inch thick ropes. Butter a kitchen scissors and cut into 1-in.ch pieces. Wrap each in waxed paper or plastic wrap.

Nutrition Information

- Calories: 63 calories
- Sodium: 4mg sodium
- Fiber: 0 fiber
- Total Carbohydrate: 13g carbohydrate (12g sugars
- Cholesterol: 6mg cholesterol
- Protein: 0 protein.
- Total Fat: 2g fat (1g saturated fat)

254. Honey Peanut Squares

Serving: about 4 dozen. | Prep: 15mins | Cook: 0mins | Ready in:

Ingredients

- 4 cups honey-roasted peanuts, divided
- 1 can (14 ounces) sweetened condensed milk
- 1 package (10-1/2 ounces) miniature marshmallows
- 1 package (10 ounces) peanut butter chips
- 1/2 cup butter, cubed
- 1/2 cup peanut butter

Direction

- Use foil to line a 13-inch x 9-inch pan and spray with cooking spray. Scatter 2 cups peanuts in the pan.
- Mix the peanut butter, butter, peanut butter chips, marshmallows and milk in a saucepan. Cook and mix until smooth. Put on top of peanuts, scatter evenly. Scatter with remaining peanuts; push down. Chill for no less than 45 minutes, with cover.
- Take foil out of pan; slice into squares. Put in an airtight container to store.

Nutrition Information

- Calories: 185 calories
- Total Fat: 11g fat (3g saturated fat)
- Sodium: 104mg sodium
- Fiber: 2g fiber
- Total Carbohydrate: 18g carbohydrate (13g sugars
- Cholesterol: 9mg cholesterol
- Protein: 5g protein.

255. Layered Peanut Butter Chocolate Fudge

Serving: About 2-1/2 pounds. | Prep: 25mins | Cook: 0mins | Ready in:

Ingredients

- 1-1/2 teaspoons butter, softened
- 2-2/3 cups milk chocolate chips
- 1 cup creamy peanut butter, divided
- 2 tablespoons shortening, divided
- 2-2/3 cups vanilla or white chips

Direction

- Using foil, line a 13-in. x 9-in. tray; butter the foil and put aside. Melt a tablespoon shortening, half cup peanut butter and the milk chocolate chips in a big heavy saucepan over low heat; cook and mix continuously until smooth. Put into lined pan. Chill for 10 minutes or until set.
- In the meantime, melt the shortening, the leftover peanut butter and vanilla chips in the microwave at 70% power for a minute; mix. Microwave at extra 10- to 20-second intervals, mixing until smooth.
- Put over the chocolate layer evenly. Chill for half an hour or until set. Take fudge out of the pan using foil. Discard the foil gently; slice into 1-in. squares.

Nutrition Information

- Calories: 56 calories
- Fiber: 0 fiber)
- Total Carbohydrate: 5g carbohydrate (2g sugars
- Cholesterol: 2mg cholesterol
- Protein: 1g protein.
- Total Fat: 4g fat (2g saturated fat)
- Sodium: 17mg sodium

256. Lime In The Coconut Almond Bark

Serving: about 1 pound. | Prep: 10mins | Cook: 5mins | Ready in:

Ingredients

- 1 package (10 to 12 ounces) white baking chips
- 4 teaspoons shortening
- 2 to 4 drops green food coloring, optional
- 1/2 cup sweetened shredded coconut, toasted
- 1/2 cup chopped almonds, toasted
- 4 teaspoons grated lime zest

Direction

- Prepare a 9x9-inch baking pan by lining with foil; put aside. Microwave shortening and chips until melted; mix until smooth. Mix in food coloring (optional). Mix in lime zest, almonds and coconut. Transfer to the lined baking pan and spread out. Put in the refrigerator till firm or for 10 to 15 minutes.
- Break the bar into small pieces. Keep in a tightly close container and store at room temperature.

Nutrition Information

- Calories: 143 calories
- Sodium: 24mg sodium
- Fiber: 1g fiber)
- Total Carbohydrate: 13g carbohydrate (12g sugars
- Cholesterol: 2mg cholesterol
- Protein: 2g protein.
- Total Fat: 10g fat (5g saturated fat)

257. Macadamia & Coconut Caramels

Serving: 1-1/2 pounds. | Prep: 25mins | Cook: 25mins | Ready in:

Ingredients

- 1 teaspoon plus 1/2 cup butter, divided
- 1 cup packed light brown sugar
- 1/2 cup light corn syrup
- 1/4 teaspoon cream of tartar
- 3/4 cup sweetened condensed milk
- 1/2 cup sweetened shredded coconut
- 1/2 cup chopped macadamia nuts
- 1/2 teaspoon vanilla extract

Direction

- Use foil to line an 8-inch square baking dish, and grease the foil with 1 tsp. butter; put to one side.
- Combine remaining butter, cream of tartar, corn syrup, and brown sugar in a large, heavy saucepan; bring mixture to a boil over medium heat, stirring continuously. Turn off the heat; slowly mix in milk. Cook, stirring over medium-low heat until a candy thermometer reaches 244° (this is called firm-ball stage).
- Turn the heat off; mix in remaining ingredients. Transfer the mixture to the prepared dish. Chill in the fridge for at least 2 hours until set.
- Gently lift candy out of the dish using foil. Take off the foil; slice caramel into 1-inch squares. Use waxed paper to wrap cut candies separately. Twist 2 ends. Keep them in an air-tight container.

Nutrition Information

- Calories: 56 calories
- Protein: 0 protein.
- Total Fat: 3g fat (1g saturated fat)
- Sodium: 23mg sodium
- Fiber: 0 fiber)
- Total Carbohydrate: 8g carbohydrate (6g sugars
- Cholesterol: 5mg cholesterol

258. Macadamia Almond Brittle

Serving: about 1 pound. | Prep: 10mins | Cook: 10mins | Ready in:

Ingredients

- 1 cup sugar
- 1/2 cup light corn syrup
- 3/4 cup coarsely chopped macadamia nuts
- 3/4 cup coarsely chopped almonds
- 1 tablespoon butter
- 2 teaspoons vanilla extract
- 1 teaspoon baking soda

Direction

- Mix corn syrup and sugar in a 1-1/2 quart microwave-safe bowl. Microwave for 3 minutes at high level. Mix in nuts then microwave again until a candy thermometer reads 300° (hard-crack stage), or for 2 to 3 minutes. Quickly mix in baking soda, vanilla and butter until the mixture gets foamy and light.
- Grease a baking sheet. When the bubbles subside, pour the mixture into a prepared baking sheet, use metal spatula to spread as thinly as possible. Let cool completely then smash into pieces. Put waxed paper between layers and keep them in an airtight container.

Nutrition Information

- Calories: 220 calories
- Total Fat: 11g fat (2g saturated fat)
- Sodium: 154mg sodium
- Fiber: 2g fiber)
- Total Carbohydrate: 30g carbohydrate (24g sugars
- Cholesterol: 3mg cholesterol
- Protein: 2g protein.

259. Macadamia Fudge

Serving: about 2 pounds. | Prep: 20mins | Cook: 0mins | Ready in:

Ingredients

- 1-1/2 teaspoons butter, softened
- 3 cups (18 ounces) semisweet chocolate chips
- 1 can (14 ounces) sweetened condensed milk
- Pinch salt
- 1 cup chopped macadamia nuts
- 1-1/2 teaspoons vanilla extract

Direction

- Use a foil to line an 8-inch square pan and coat the foil with butter; put aside.
- Add salt, milk and chocolate chips in a heavy saucepan. Stir and cook over low heat until melted chips. Take out from the heat, mix in vanilla and nuts. Add the mixture into the prepared pan. Let chill until set, or for 2 hours.
- Take the fudge out from the pan with foil. Carefully remove foil, divide fudge into 1-inch squares.

Nutrition Information

- Calories: 74 calories
- Cholesterol: 2mg cholesterol
- Protein: 1g protein.
- Total Fat: 5g fat (2g saturated fat)
- Sodium: 17mg sodium
- Fiber: 1g fiber)
- Total Carbohydrate: 9g carbohydrate (8g sugars

260. Macadamia Coconut Candy Clusters

Serving: 3-1/2 dozen. | Prep: 25mins | Cook: 0mins | Ready in:

Ingredients

- 1 package (10 to 12 ounces) white baking chips
- 2 teaspoons shortening
- 1 cup sweetened shredded coconut, toasted
- 1/2 cup crisp rice cereal
- 1/2 cup chopped macadamia nuts, toasted

Direction

- Melt shortening and baking chips in a microwave; mix till smooth. Add nuts, cereal and coconut.
- Drop onto waxed paper by teaspoonfuls; stand till set. Keep at room temperature in airtight container.

Nutrition Information

- Calories: 62 calories
- Protein: 1g protein.
- Total Fat: 4g fat (2g saturated fat)
- Sodium: 19mg sodium
- Fiber: 0 fiber)
- Total Carbohydrate: 6g carbohydrate (5g sugars
- Cholesterol: 1mg cholesterol

261. Maple Pralines

Serving: about 1 pound. | Prep: 10mins | Cook: 10mins | Ready in:

Ingredients

- 1 cup sugar
- 2/3 cup milk
- 1/2 cup maple syrup
- 2 tablespoons butter
- 3/4 cup coarsely chopped pecans, toasted

Direction

- Mix syrup, milk and sugar in a heavy 1-quart saucepan. Cook and mix over medium heat until the mixture boils. Turn down heat to medium-low. Cook, with no cover, until a candy thermometer registers 234° (soft-ball stage), mixing from time to time.
- Take off from the heat. Put butter; don't stir. Let cool to 160°, without mixing. Mix in pecans. Whip using a wooden spoon robustly until mixture just starts to thicken but is still glossy. Put onto waxed paper by spoonfuls immediately. Let cool. Put in an airtight container to store.

Nutrition Information

- Calories: 132 calories
- Sodium: 20mg sodium
- Fiber: 1g fiber)
- Total Carbohydrate: 20g carbohydrate (19g sugars
- Cholesterol: 5mg cholesterol
- Protein: 1g protein.
- Total Fat: 6g fat (1g saturated fat)

262. Maple Walnut Crisps

Serving: 44 crisps. | Prep: 15mins | Cook: 10mins | Ready in:

Ingredients

- 44 Club crackers (2-1/2x1 inch)
- 1 cup unsalted butter, cubed
- 1 cup packed brown sugar
- 2 tablespoons maple syrup
- 1/2 cup chopped pecans
- 1/2 cup chopped walnuts
- 1/3 cup finely chopped almonds
- 1/4 teaspoon maple flavoring

Direction

- Put the crackers in a single layer into a 15x10x1-in. baking pan lined with parchment paper. Put aside.

- Melt butter over medium heat in a small heavy saucepan. Mix in syrup and brown sugar. Heat until boiling; cook and stir until sugar dissolves for 3-4 minutes. Stir the rest of the ingredients into the mixture. Evenly spread atop the crackers.
- Bake until top appears dry at 350° for about 10-12 minutes or. Let it cool down thoroughly on a wire rack. Crack into pieces. For storage, keep in an airtight container.

Nutrition Information

- Calories: 104 calories
- Total Fat: 8g fat (3g saturated fat)
- Sodium: 47mg sodium
- Fiber: 0 fiber)
- Total Carbohydrate: 9g carbohydrate (6g sugars
- Cholesterol: 11mg cholesterol
- Protein: 1g protein. Diabetic Exchanges: 1 fat

263. Marshmallow Chocolate Covered Cherries

Serving: about 4-1/2 dozen. | Prep: 25mins | Cook: 0mins | Ready in:

Ingredients

- 1/2 cup butter, softened
- 2 cups marshmallow creme
- Pinch salt
- 1 teaspoon almond extract
- 4 cups confectioners' sugar
- 1 jar (16 ounces) maraschino cherries, well drained
- 2 cups (12 ounces) semisweet chocolate chips
- 2 tablespoons shortening

Direction

- Cream butter in a bowl. Add sugar, extract, salt and marshmallow crème; combine well. Knead into a large ball; chill for an hour. Shape into 1-in. balls; make them into 2-in. flat circles. Wrap around cherries with circles and form into balls carefully. Arrange in a baking sheet lined with waxed paper. Loosely cover; keep in the fridge for 4 hours or overnight. In a microwave-safe bowl or a double boiler, melt shortening and chocolate chips. Coat cherries with chocolate; arrange on waxed paper to harden. Keep in a container with cover in the fridge for 1-2 weeks before serving.

Nutrition Information

- Calories: 106 calories
- Cholesterol: 5mg cholesterol
- Protein: 0 protein.
- Total Fat: 4g fat (2g saturated fat)
- Sodium: 24mg sodium
- Fiber: 0 fiber)
- Total Carbohydrate: 19g carbohydrate (17g sugars

264. Marshmallow Puffs

Serving: 3 dozen. | Prep: 10mins | Cook: 0mins | Ready in:

Ingredients

- 36 large marshmallows
- 1-1/2 cups semisweet chocolate chips
- 1/2 cup chunky peanut butter
- 2 tablespoons butter

Direction

- Using foil, line a 9-in. square pan; butter the foil. Place marshmallow in pan. Melt butter, peanut butter and chocolate chips in a microwave; stir until smooth. Pour over the marshmallows and spread. Chill completely. Cut into 1-1/2-in. squares.

Nutrition Information

- Calories: 83 calories
- Sodium: 28mg sodium
- Fiber: 1g fiber)
- Total Carbohydrate: 11g carbohydrate (8g sugars
- Cholesterol: 2mg cholesterol
- Protein: 1g protein.
- Total Fat: 5g fat (2g saturated fat)

265. Marzipan Yule Logs

Serving: 2 yule logs (10 servings each). | Prep: 60mins | Cook: 0mins | Ready in:

Ingredients

- 3 tablespoons golden raisins
- 3 tablespoons golden or light rum
- 1 teaspoon meringue powder
- 1 tablespoon water
- 1 cup blanched almonds
- 1 cup confectioners' sugar
- 1 teaspoon almond extract
- 1 teaspoon corn syrup
- 3 tablespoons chopped candied orange peel
- 4 ounces semisweet chocolate, melted
- Pecan halves and halved candied cherries

Direction

- Mix rum and raisins in a small bowl; cover. Stand overnight. Drain; keep liquid.
- Melt meringue powder in water in another small bowl. Pulse 1/2 cup confectioners' sugar and almonds till almonds are ground finely in a food processor. Add leftover confectioners' sugar; pulse till blended. Add meringue mixture, corn syrup and extract; process till it makes a ball. Remove; in plastic, wrap. Refrigerate till firm for 1 hour.
- Crumble almond paste into big bowl; knead in candied peel and drained raisins. As needed, add enough reserved rum to soften if it is too

stiff. Halve mixture; form each to 6-in. log. In plastic, wrap; refrigerate till firm for 4 hours – overnight.
- Unwrap logs; brush melted chocolate on all sides. Put onto waxed paper; use cherries and pecans to decorate. Crosswise cut to slices; serve.

Nutrition Information

- Calories:
- Total Carbohydrate:
- Cholesterol:
- Protein:
- Total Fat:
- Sodium:
- Fiber:

266. Melting Snowmen

Serving: 2 dozen. | Prep: 01hours30mins | Cook: 0mins | Ready in:

Ingredients

- 3/4 cup sweetened condensed milk
- 1-1/2 teaspoons peppermint extract
- 2-1/4 to 2-1/2 cups confectioners' sugar
- 1/2 cup baking cocoa
- 1 pound white candy coating, chopped, divided
- 7 to 8 gumdrops or Starburst candies (orange for noses and colors of your choice for earmuffs)
- 1/3 cup dark chocolate chips

Direction

- Mix together extract and milk in a small bowl. Mix in cocoa and two cups confectioners' sugar until a dough is formed. Lightly dust a surface with confectioners' sugar and place the dough. Add in enough remaining confectioners' sugar and knead until a soft

dough is achieved (make sure to have a non-sticky dough).
- Split into three portions. Form one piece into 24 balls (half inch in size). Form remaining dough pieces into 24 balls (1 inch in size). Flatten each 1-in ball into 1 1/2-inch uneven circles on baking sheets lined with waxed paper.
- Microwave 2 oz. white candy coating in a microwaveable bowl until melted. Stick a 1/2-inch ball near the edge of each circle with melted coating. Let sit for an hour to dry.
- Make earmuffs and noses as you like out of gumdrops. Heat the remaining white candy coating until melted and allow to slightly cool. Pour candy coating onto snowmen, working in batches of 6; let the coating drape over each until covered completely. Quickly press in earmuffs and noses. Place at room temperature for an hour until dry when touched.
- Microwave chocolate chips until melted; whisk until smooth. To create tops of earmuffs, arms, buttons, mouths and eyes, draw using melted chocolate and a toothpick.

Nutrition Information

- Calories: 205 calories
- Sodium: 12mg sodium
- Fiber: 0 fiber)
- Total Carbohydrate: 34g carbohydrate (31g sugars
- Cholesterol: 3mg cholesterol
- Protein: 1g protein.
- Total Fat: 8g fat (6g saturated fat)

267. Microwave Mint Fudge

Serving: 2-1/4 pounds. | Prep: 15mins | Cook: 0mins | Ready in:

Ingredients

- 1-1/2 cups sugar
- 1 can (5 ounces) evaporated milk
- 1/4 cup butter, cubed
- 5 cups miniature marshmallows
- 1 package (10 ounces) mint chocolate chips
- 1 packet (1 ounce) pre-melted baking chocolate
- 1/2 cup chopped walnuts
- 1 teaspoon vanilla extract
- 1/2 teaspoon peppermint extract

Direction

- Mix butter, milk and sugar together in a 2-qt. microwave-safe bowl. Microwave on high, stirring after 2 1/2 minutes, till the mixture comes to a full rolling boil. Cook for 3 more minutes, stirring after 1 minutes. Put in marshmallows; mix till melted. Mix in chocolate and chips till smooth. Mix in extracts and nuts. Transfer to a greased 11x7-in. pan immediately. Chill till firm. Cut into squares. Refrigerate for storing.

Nutrition Information

- Calories: 75 calories
- Protein: 0 protein.
- Total Fat: 3g fat (2g saturated fat)
- Sodium: 12mg sodium
- Fiber: 0 fiber)
- Total Carbohydrate: 12g carbohydrate (10g sugars
- Cholesterol: 3mg cholesterol

268. Milk Chocolate Truffles

Serving: 3 dozen. | Prep: 30mins | Cook: 0mins | Ready in:

Ingredients

- 3 cups (18 ounces) milk chocolate chips
- 1 carton (8 ounces) frozen whipped topping, thawed

- 1/2 cup vanilla wafer crumbs (about 15 wafers)

Direction

- In double boiler/microwave, melt chocolate chips; cool. Beat whipped topping and melted chocolate in a bowl. Form to 1/2-in. balls. Roll into vanilla wafer crumbs then freeze/refrigerate.

Nutrition Information

- Calories: 96 calories
- Total Fat: 6g fat (4g saturated fat)
- Sodium: 17mg sodium
- Fiber: 1g fiber)
- Total Carbohydrate: 11g carbohydrate (9g sugars
- Cholesterol: 3mg cholesterol
- Protein: 1g protein.

269. Minty Chocolate Crackles

Serving: about 4 dozen. | Prep: 25mins | Cook: 15mins | Ready in:

Ingredients

- 1 cup (6 ounces) semisweet chocolate chips
- 1/2 cup plus 4-1/2 teaspoons shortening
- 3/4 cup sugar
- 1 egg
- 1/4 cup light corn syrup
- 1 teaspoon peppermint extract
- 1 teaspoon vanilla extract
- 2 cups all-purpose flour
- 1/2 teaspoon baking soda
- 1/4 teaspoon salt
- 1/4 cup crushed peppermint candy
- Additional sugar

Direction

- Melt chocolate chips in a double boiler or a microwave; slightly cool the melted chocolate. Cream sugar and shortening in a bowl, beat in extract and melted chocolate, corn syrup and egg. Mix salt, baking soda and flour; add the flour mixture to the cream mixture slowly. Fold in candy. Make 1-in. balls by rolling the mixture then roll I sugar. Place balls 2 in. apart from each other on ungreased baking sheets. Put baking sheets into the oven and bake for 12 to 14 minutes at 350 degrees till surface cracks and edges becomes firm (the center will still be soft). Cool it for 5 minutes then transfer to wire racks.

Nutrition Information

- Calories: 157 calories
- Total Carbohydrate: 22g carbohydrate (13g sugars
- Cholesterol: 9mg cholesterol
- Protein: 2g protein.
- Total Fat: 7g fat (3g saturated fat)
- Sodium: 59mg sodium
- Fiber: 1g fiber)

270. Minty Snowmen

Serving: 8-9 snowmen. | Prep: 30mins | Cook: 0mins | Ready in:

Ingredients

- 1 tablespoon butter, softened
- 1 tablespoon light corn syrup
- 1/2 teaspoon mint extract
- 1/8 teaspoon salt
- 1 cup confectioners' sugar
- Red, green, blue and/or purple liquid or gel food coloring
- Colored sprinkles, nonpareils and cake decorator candies

Direction

- Mix the salt, extract, corn syrup and butter in a small bowl. Mix in confectioners' sugar slowly. Knead for 1-2 minutes by hand or until mixture becomes elastic.
- Mix a tablespoon of dough with food coloring for each color of dough; knead until combined. Keep leftover dough plain. Shape white dough into a log; take out 1/4 of the log and put aside.
- Split the leftover log into 8-9 pieces and shape into balls for the snowmen's bodies. Split the saved dough into 8-9 pieces and shape into balls for the snowmen's heads. Put 1 smaller ball over each bigger ball.
- To make hats, scarves and earmuffs, use the tinted dough as desired. Make buttons, noses and eyes using candies.

Nutrition Information

- Calories: 80 calories
- Protein: 0 protein.
- Total Fat: 1g fat (1g saturated fat)
- Sodium: 55mg sodium
- Fiber: 0 fiber)
- Total Carbohydrate: 17g carbohydrate (15g sugars
- Cholesterol: 4mg cholesterol

271. Mocha Cream Truffles

Serving: about 4 dozen. | Prep: 60mins | Cook: 0mins | Ready in:

Ingredients

- 1 package (15-1/2 ounces) Oreo cookies
- 1 package (8 ounces) cream cheese, softened
- 3 tablespoons instant espresso powder
- 1 teaspoon boiling water
- 1/2 cup chocolate-covered coffee beans, coarsely chopped, optional
- 3-1/2 cups semisweet chocolate chips
- 2 tablespoons plus 1-1/2 teaspoons shortening

Direction

- In food processor, process sandwich cookies till chopped finely, covered. In boiling water, dissolve espresso powder. Add cream cheese and espresso mixture in cookie crumbs; process till smooth, covered. If desired, mix coffee beans in.
- Form to 1-inch balls. Put onto baking sheets; refrigerate for 1 hour minimum, covered.
- Melt shortening and chocolate chips in microwave; mix till smooth. In chocolate, dip balls; let excess drip off. Put onto waxed paper; let stand till set. Keep in an airtight container in the fridge.

Nutrition Information

- Calories: 122 calories
- Sodium: 65mg sodium
- Fiber: 1g fiber)
- Total Carbohydrate: 14g carbohydrate (10g sugars
- Cholesterol: 5mg cholesterol
- Protein: 1g protein.
- Total Fat: 8g fat (4g saturated fat)

272. Molasses Fudge

Serving: about 4 dozen. | Prep: 25mins | Cook: 20mins | Ready in:

Ingredients

- 1 teaspoon plus 2 tablespoons butter, divided
- 1 cup sugar
- 1 cup packed brown sugar
- 1/2 cup half-and-half cream
- 2 tablespoons molasses
- 1/2 teaspoon ground cinnamon
- 1/4 teaspoon ground nutmeg
- 1/8 teaspoon ground cloves
- 1-1/2 teaspoons vanilla extract
- 1/2 cup coarsely chopped walnuts

Direction

- Use foil to line a 9x5-inch loaf pan. Use half tsp. of butter to grease the foil; put aside.
- Use half tsp. of butter to grease sides of a big heavy saucepan. Put in spices, molasses, cream and sugars. Cook and whisk on medium heat till the mixture boils and the sugar dissolves. Cook on medium low heat till the candy thermometer reaches 240 degrees (at the soft-ball stage), whisk frequently.
- Take it off the heat. Put in the leftover butter and vanilla (don't whisk). Let cool down (do not whisk) to 110 degrees for roughly 55 minutes.
- Take the thermometer out; whip vigorously using the wooden spoon till the mixture starts to become thick; put in the walnuts. Whip for roughly 10 minutes or till the mixture starts to lose the gloss and the fudge becomes very thick.
- Rapidly add to the prepped pan. While still warm, score into 1-inch square pieces. Once the fudge firm up, use foil to lift the candy from the pan; chop into square pieces. Keep stored in an airtight container.

Nutrition Information

- Calories: 52 calories
- Sodium: 7mg sodium
- Fiber: 0 fiber)
- Total Carbohydrate: 10g carbohydrate (9g sugars
- Cholesterol: 3mg cholesterol
- Protein: 0 protein.
- Total Fat: 2g fat (1g saturated fat)

273. Mounds Balls

Serving: about 7 dozen candies. | Prep: 40mins | Cook: 0mins | Ready in:

Ingredients

- 1/2 pound unsalted butter
- 3-3/4 cups confectioners' sugar
- 1 pound sweetened shredded coconut
- 1/2 cup sweetened condensed milk
- 1 cup chopped walnuts
- 1 teaspoon vanilla extract
- CHOCOLATE COATING:
- 2 cups (12 ounces) semisweet chocolate chips
- 4 ounces unsweetened chocolate
- 2 -inch x 1-inch x 1/2-inch piece paraffin wax
- Round wooden toothpicks
- Styrofoam sheets

Direction

- Cream sugar and butter together in bowl. Put in vanilla, walnuts, milk and coconut. Then stir until blended. Let chill until firm slightly. Form into the walnut-sized balls. Put a toothpick into each ball. Arrange balls on the baking sheets. Place in the freezer. In double boiler, melt paraffin wax, chocolate squares and chocolate chips over the simmering water. Over the hot water, keep warm. Submerge the frozen balls into the chocolate mixture with picks as handles. Stick the picks upright into the wax paper-wrapped Styrofoam sheet. Let chill until firm. Discard package candy and picks in the individual paper liners. (It may also be frozen.)

Nutrition Information

- Calories: 111 calories
- Sodium: 18mg sodium
- Fiber: 1g fiber)
- Total Carbohydrate: 12g carbohydrate (10g sugars
- Cholesterol: 7mg cholesterol
- Protein: 1g protein.
- Total Fat: 7g fat (4g saturated fat)

274. No Fuss Truffles

Serving: about 4-1/2 dozen. | Prep: 50mins | Cook: 0mins | Ready in:

Ingredients

- 2 packages (10 to 12 ounces each) milk chocolate or butterscotch chips
- 1 carton (8 ounces) frozen whipped topping, thawed
- 1-1/4 cups ground toasted almonds, graham cracker crumbs or finely chopped salted peanuts

Direction

- Melt chips in microwave-safe bowl; mix till smooth. Cool for 30 minutes, mixing several times, to room temperature.
- Fold whipped topping in; drop on waxed paper-lined baking sheets by rounded teaspoonfuls. Freeze till firm or for 1 1/2 hours.
- Form to balls; roll in peanuts/crumbs/almonds. Refrigerate/freeze in airtight container. Remove from freezer about 30 minutes prior to serving if frozen.

Nutrition Information

- Calories: 103 calories
- Protein: 2g protein.
- Total Fat: 7g fat (4g saturated fat)
- Sodium: 9mg sodium
- Fiber: 1g fiber)
- Total Carbohydrate: 9g carbohydrate (7g sugars
- Cholesterol: 2mg cholesterol

275. Nut Goody Bars

Serving: 12 | Prep: | Cook: | Ready in:

Ingredients

- 4 cups semisweet chocolate chips
- 2 cups butterscotch chips
- 2 cups crunchy peanut butter
- 1 cup walnuts
- 6 cups miniature marshmallows

Direction

- Over low heat, melt the chips and then mix in walnuts and peanut butter. Remove the pan from the heat source and quickly pour in mini marshmallows. Toss until the marshmallows are covered completely. Transfer into a 9x13 inch pan that is greased and then place in a fridge.

Nutrition Information

- Calories: 817 calories;
- Total Fat: 51.8
- Sodium: 266
- Total Carbohydrate: 84.3
- Cholesterol: 0
- Protein: 14.4

276. Nutty Chocolate Peanut Clusters

Serving: 2-3/4 pounds. | Prep: 10mins | Cook: 10mins | Ready in:

Ingredients

- 1 pound white candy coating, chopped
- 2 cups (12 ounces) semisweet chocolate chips
- 1 jar (16 ounces) dry roasted peanuts

Direction

- Melt chocolate chips and candy coating in a metal bowl or double boiler over hot water; mix until smooth. Take off from the heat; mix in peanuts.
- Dollop by rounded teaspoonfuls onto waxed paper-lined baking sheets. Chill for 10-15

minutes or until firm. Put in airtight containers to store.

Nutrition Information

- Calories:
- Sodium:
- Fiber:
- Total Carbohydrate:
- Cholesterol:
- Protein:
- Total Fat:

| 277. | Nutty Citrus Candy |

Serving: 8 dozen. | Prep: 15mins | Cook: 0mins | Ready in:

Ingredients

- 3-3/4 cups confectioners' sugar
- 1 package (12 ounces) vanilla wafers, crushed
- 1 can (6 ounces) frozen orange juice concentrate, thawed
- 1/2 cup butter, melted
- 1-1/2 to 2 cups ground walnuts

Direction

- Mix the butter, juice concentrate, wafer crumbs and confectioners' sugar in a bowl. Roll into 3/4-inch balls, then toss in walnuts. Chill with cover for no less than one day before enjoying. Put in an airtight container to store in the fridge.

Nutrition Information

- Calories: 53 calories
- Protein: 0 protein.
- Total Fat: 2g fat (1g saturated fat)
- Sodium: 21mg sodium
- Fiber: 0 fiber.
- Total Carbohydrate: 8g carbohydrate (6g sugars
- Cholesterol: 3mg cholesterol

| 278. | Nutty Sticky Bun Candies |

Serving: 2-1/4 pounds. | Prep: 20mins | Cook: 15mins | Ready in:

Ingredients

- 2 teaspoons plus 1/2 cup softened butter, divided
- 3-3/4 cups confectioners' sugar
- 1/2 cup nonfat dry milk powder
- 1/2 cup granulated sugar
- 1/2 cup light corn syrup
- 1 teaspoon vanilla extract
- FILLING:
- 1/4 cup granulated sugar
- 1 teaspoon ground cinnamon
- 2-1/4 cups deluxe mixed nuts, divided
- 1 tablespoon light corn syrup

Direction

- Grease an 8x8-inch square pan with 2 teaspoons butter; put aside.
- Combine milk powder and confectioners' sugar. Combine remaining butter, 1/2 cup corn syrup, and 1/2 cup granulated sugar in a large heavy saucepan; cook, stirring, until mixture gets to a boil and sugar is dissolved. Mix in confectioners' sugar mixture, approximately 1/3 each time, until incorporated.
- Put off the heat. Mix in vanilla. Keep stirring until mixture mounds slightly when dropped from a spoon and a thermometer registers 150°. Spread mixture over the bottom of the prepared pan. Allow to cool for 15 minutes.
- To make filling, combine cinnamon and 1/4 cup granulated sugar. Pour 3/4 cup nuts in a food processor; put on the lid and process until ground.

- Divide cooled candy into 4 equal portions. Roll each portion into a 9x5-inch rectangle. Scatter each rectangle with ground nuts and 1/4 sugar mixture to within 1/2 inch of edges. Starting with a long side, roll up tightly jelly-roll style.
- Chop the remainder of nuts. Brush corn syrup over each roll; roll in chopped nuts. Cut roll into 1/2-inch slices with a serrated knife. Store in an airtight container at room temperature.

Nutrition Information

- Calories: 71 calories
- Total Carbohydrate: 11g carbohydrate (10g sugars
- Cholesterol: 4mg cholesterol
- Protein: 1g protein.
- Total Fat: 3g fat (1g saturated fat)
- Sodium: 28mg sodium
- Fiber: 0 fiber)

279. Old Fashioned Peppermint Taffy

Serving: 1-3/4 pounds. | Prep: 01hours30mins | Cook: 20mins | Ready in:

Ingredients

- 1 tablespoon plus 1/4 cup butter, cubed
- 2 cups light corn syrup
- 1-1/2 cups sugar
- 2 teaspoons peppermint extract
- 1/2 teaspoon salt
- 6 drops red food coloring

Direction

- Use 1 tablespoon butter to grease a 15x10x1-inch pan; put aside.
- Put sugar and corn syrup together in a small, heavy saucepan and boil on medium heat. Add leftover butter; mix till melted. Mix and cook till it reaches hard ball stage or candy thermometer reads 250°.
- Take off from heat; mix in food coloring, salt and extract. Put into prepped pan; stand till cool enough to handle for 5-10 minutes. Divide to 4 portions.
- Pull 1 candy portion quickly with well-buttered fingers till firm yet pliable; color will be light pink. Pull to 1/2-inch wide rope and repeat with leftover candy; cut to 1-inch pieces. Use waxed paper to wrap each.

Nutrition Information

- Calories: 23 calories
- Fiber: 0 fiber)
- Total Carbohydrate: 5g carbohydrate (3g sugars
- Cholesterol: 1mg cholesterol
- Protein: 0 protein.
- Total Fat: 0 fat (0 saturated fat)
- Sodium: 13mg sodium

280. Old Time Butter Crunch Candy

Serving: about 2 pounds. | Prep: 15mins | Cook: 25mins | Ready in:

Ingredients

- 1 cup butter
- 1-1/4 cup sugar
- 2 tablespoons light corn syrup
- 2 tablespoons water
- 2 cups finely chopped toasted almonds
- 8 milk chocolate candy bars (1.55 ounces each)

Direction

- Using foil, line a 13x9-in. pan; put aside. Grease the sides of a large heavy saucepan with part of the butter. Add the rest of the butter to the saucepan; over low heat, melt.

- Add water, corn syrup and sugar. Over medium heat, cook while stirring until a candy thermometer registers 300° (hard-crack stage).
- Take out of the heat; stir in almonds. Transfer to the lined pan quickly; spread to cover the bottom of the pan. Completely cool. Turn the pan upside down carefully to remove the candy in one piece; get rid of foil.
- In a microwave-safe bowl or double boiler, melt 1/2 of the chocolate; top over candy. Allow to cool. Turn candy over and do the same with the rest of the chocolate; cool. Break into 2-in. pieces. Keep in an airtight container.

Nutrition Information

- Calories: 375 calories
- Cholesterol: 35mg cholesterol
- Protein: 5g protein.
- Total Fat: 26g fat (12g saturated fat)
- Sodium: 137mg sodium
- Fiber: 3g fiber)
- Total Carbohydrate: 34g carbohydrate (29g sugars

281. Orange Cappuccino Creams

Serving: about 4 dozen. | Prep: 10mins | Cook: 20mins | Ready in:

Ingredients

- 12 ounces white baking chocolate, chopped
- 6 tablespoons heavy whipping cream, divided
- 1-1/2 teaspoons orange juice
- 1/2 teaspoon orange extract
- 1-1/2 teaspoons finely grated orange zest
- 1/4 cup finely chopped walnuts
- 2 teaspoons instant coffee granules
- 4 ounces semisweet chocolate, chopped

Direction

- Melt white chocolate in a small heavy saucepan together with 1/4 cup cream, orange juice, extract and zest on low heat. Stir till the chocolate melts. Take off from heat; stir walnuts into the mixture. Let it cool down for about 10-12 minutes.
- Fill the foil or paper candy cups with cooled chocolate mixture two-thirds full using a small spoon. Refrigerate for about 30 minutes.
- In the meantime, mix together coffee granules and remaining cream in a small saucepan. Cook and stir on low heat until the coffee dissolves. Add semisweet chocolate into the mix; cook and stir till chocolate melts. Spoon 1/2 teaspoon of the mix on top of each cup. For storage, keep at room temperature in an airtight container.

Nutrition Information

- Calories: 17 calories
- Fiber: 0 fiber)
- Total Carbohydrate: 1g carbohydrate (1g sugars
- Cholesterol: 3mg cholesterol
- Protein: 0 protein.
- Total Fat: 1g fat (1g saturated fat)
- Sodium: 1mg sodium

282. Orange Coconut Creams

Serving: 9 dozen. | Prep: 60mins | Cook: 0mins | Ready in:

Ingredients

- 1 can (14 ounces) sweetened condensed milk
- 1/2 cup butter, cubed
- 1 package (2 pounds) confectioners' sugar
- 1 cup sweetened shredded coconut
- 1-1/2 teaspoons orange extract
- 2 cups (12 ounces) semisweet chocolate
- 8 ounces German sweet chocolate, chopped
- 2 tablespoons shortening

Direction

- Mix and cook butter and milk in a small saucepan on low heat till butter melts. Put confectioners' sugar in a big bowl. Add milk mixture; beat till smooth. Add orange extract and coconut; stir well. Roll to 1-inch balls; put onto waxed paper-lined baking sheets and refrigerate for 1 hour till firm.
- Melt shortening, chocolate and chips in microwave; mix till smooth. In chocolate, dip balls; let excess drip off. Put on waxed paper and let stand till set.

Nutrition Information

- Calories: 79 calories
- Total Carbohydrate: 13g carbohydrate (13g sugars
- Cholesterol: 4mg cholesterol
- Protein: 1g protein.
- Total Fat: 3g fat (2g saturated fat)
- Sodium: 16mg sodium
- Fiber: 0 fiber)

283. Orange Fantasy Fudge

Serving: 2-1/4 pounds. | Prep: 10mins | Cook: 15mins | Ready in:

Ingredients

- 1-1/2 teaspoons plus 1/2 cup butter, softened, divided
- 1-1/2 cups sugar
- 1 can (5 ounces) evaporated milk
- 2 cups (12 ounces) semisweet chocolate chips
- 1 jar (7 ounces) marshmallow creme
- 3 teaspoons orange extract
- 1 teaspoon vanilla extract

Direction

- Use the foil to line the 9-inch square pan; use 1.5 teaspoons of the butter to grease the foil and put aside. In the heavy saucepan, mix leftover butter, milk and sugar. Cook and whisk on medium heat till the sugar dissolves. Let come to a rapid boil; boil for 5 minutes; whisk continuously.
- Lower the heat to low; whisk in the marshmallow crème and chocolate chips till blended and melted. Take out of heat; whisk in the extracts. Add to the prepped pan. Chill till firm or overnight.
- With the foil, lift the fudge out of the pan; gently peel off the foil. Chop the fudge into 1-inch square pieces. Keep in fridge.

Nutrition Information

- Calories: 56 calories
- Fiber: 0 fiber)
- Total Carbohydrate: 9g carbohydrate (8g sugars
- Cholesterol: 4mg cholesterol
- Protein: 0 protein.
- Total Fat: 3g fat (2g saturated fat)
- Sodium: 16mg sodium

284. Orange Walnut Candy

Serving: 8 dozen. | Prep: 30mins | Cook: 0mins | Ready in:

Ingredients

- 3-3/4 cups confectioners' sugar
- 1 package (12 ounces) vanilla wafers, crushed
- 1 can (6 ounces) frozen orange juice concentrate, thawed
- 1/2 cup butter, melted
- 1-1/2 to 2 cups ground walnuts

Direction

- Mix the butter, orange juice concentrate, wafer crumbs and sugar in a bowl. Roll into 3/4-inch balls; toss in walnuts. Chill with cover in an airtight container for no less than a day before enjoying.

Nutrition Information

- Calories: 53 calories
- Protein: 0 protein.
- Total Fat: 2g fat (1g saturated fat)
- Sodium: 21mg sodium
- Fiber: 0 fiber)
- Total Carbohydrate: 8g carbohydrate (6g sugars
- Cholesterol: 3mg cholesterol

285. Orange Almond Chocolate Logs

Serving: 2 dozen. | Prep: 30mins | Cook: 0mins | Ready in:

Ingredients

- 1/3 cup butter, softened
- 1/4 cup almond paste
- 2 teaspoons grated orange zest, divided
- 9 ounces white baking chocolate, chopped
- 2 tablespoons orange juice
- 3 tablespoons coarse sugar
- 1-1/2 cups dark chocolate chips
- 1-1/2 teaspoons shortening

Direction

- Cream 1/2 tsp. orange zest, almond paste and butter till fluffy and light in small bowl. Melt white baking chocolate in microwave; mix till smooth. Add to creamed mixture slowly. Mix orange juice in slowly; beat till smooth. Cover; refrigerate till easy to handle, occasionally mixing, for 20 minutes.
- Form to 2-in. logs; put onto waxed paper-lined baking sheets. Cover loosely; refrigerate till firm for 30 minutes. Mix leftover orange zest and coarse sugar; put aside.
- Melt shortening and chocolate chips in microwave; mix till smooth. Dip logs into chocolate; let excess drip off. Put onto waxed paper-lined sheets. Sprinkle sugar mixture on. Let stand till firm.

Nutrition Information

- Calories: 182 calories
- Total Fat: 12g fat (7g saturated fat)
- Sodium: 29mg sodium
- Fiber: 0 fiber)
- Total Carbohydrate: 18g carbohydrate (16g sugars
- Cholesterol: 9mg cholesterol
- Protein: 2g protein.

286. Orange Pistachio Divinity

Serving: about 4 dozen (1-1/3 pounds). | Prep: 15mins | Cook: 20mins | Ready in:

Ingredients

- 2 large egg whites
- 2-2/3 cups sugar
- 2/3 cup light corn syrup
- 1/2 cup water
- 1 teaspoon grated orange zest
- 1 teaspoon vanilla extract
- 2/3 cup pistachios, coarsely chopped

Direction

- Stand egg whites for 30 minutes in stand mixer's bowl at room temperature. Meanwhile, line waxed paper on 2 15x10x1-in. pans.
- Mix and cook water, corn syrup and sugar in a big heavy saucepan till it boils and sugar dissolves; cook without mixing on medium heat till it hits hard-ball stage and thermometer reads 252°. Beat egg whites till stiff peaks form on medium speed before the temperature is reached.

- In a thin stream, add hot sugar mixture slowly on egg whites with mixer on high speed, constantly beating, occasionally scraping sides of bowl. Add vanilla and orange zest; beat for 5-6 minutes till it starts to lose its gloss and candy holds it shapes. Don't overbeat; it'll crumble and stiffen. Fold in pistachios immediately.
- By tablespoonfuls, drop mixture onto prepped pans quickly; stand till dry to touch at room temperature. Keep between waxed paper layers in airtight container in room temperature.

Nutrition Information

- Calories: 68 calories
- Sodium: 13mg sodium
- Fiber: 0 fiber)
- Total Carbohydrate: 15g carbohydrate (15g sugars
- Cholesterol: 0 cholesterol
- Protein: 1g protein.
- Total Fat: 1g fat (0 saturated fat)

287. Oreos And Candy Cane Chocolate Bark

Serving: about 1-1/2 pounds. | Prep: 15mins | Cook: 0mins | Ready in:

Ingredients

- 2 packages (10 ounces each) dark chocolate chips
- 10 candy cane or chocolate mint creme Oreo cookies, split and chopped
- 1/3 cup white baking chips
- 1/8 teaspoon peppermint extract
- 2 candy canes, crushed

Direction

- Line parchment paper on 15x10x1-in. baking pan. Melt dark chocolate in top of double boiler/metal bowl above hot water; mix till smooth. Take off heat; mix cookies in. Spread on prepped pan.
- Microwave white baking chips, mixing every 30 seconds, on high till melted. Mix extract in; drizzle dark chocolate mixture on. Sprinkle crushed candy canes on; cool. Refrigerate till set for an hour.
- Break to pieces; keep in airtight container.

Nutrition Information

- Calories: 141 calories
- Total Carbohydrate: 19g carbohydrate (16g sugars
- Cholesterol: 0 cholesterol
- Protein: 2g protein.
- Total Fat: 8g fat (5g saturated fat)
- Sodium: 32mg sodium
- Fiber: 2g fiber)

288. Peanut Butter Chocolate Cups

Serving: 1 dozen. | Prep: 20mins | Cook: 0mins | Ready in:

Ingredients

- 1 milk chocolate candy bar (7 ounces)
- 1/4 cup butter
- 1 tablespoon shortening
- 1/4 cup creamy peanut butter

Direction

- Melt shortening, butter and chocolate in a microwave. Stir until they become smooth. Put paper miniature baking cups or foil into miniature muffin tin. Add one tablespoon chocolate mixture to each cup.

- Melt peanut butter in a microwave. Stir until they become smooth. Pour into cups. Add the remaining chocolate mixture on top. If necessary, remelt the chocolate mixture. Place in the refrigerator until firm, about half an hour.

Nutrition Information

- Calories: 93 calories
- Total Carbohydrate: 3g carbohydrate (2g sugars
- Cholesterol: 11mg cholesterol
- Protein: 2g protein.
- Total Fat: 9g fat (4g saturated fat)
- Sodium: 66mg sodium
- Fiber: 0 fiber)

289. Peanut Butter Clusters

Serving: 36 | Prep: | Cook: | Ready in:

Ingredients

- 1 (10 ounce) package Reese's Peanut Butter Chips
- 1/2 cup dry-roasted unsalted peanuts
- 1/2 cup regular oats, uncooked
- 1/2 cup raisins
- 1 teaspoon cinnamon

Direction

- Place chips in a bowl and microwave on high power for 1 1/2 minutes until melted. Mix. Put in the rest of ingredients; stir well. Firmly roll into 1-inch balls with your hands. Let cool.

Nutrition Information

- Calories: 65 calories;
- Total Fat: 3.2
- Sodium: 19
- Total Carbohydrate: 6.7

- Cholesterol: 0
- Protein: 2.3

290. Peanut Butter Pinecones

Serving: about 2 dozen. | Prep: 60mins | Cook: 0mins | Ready in:

Ingredients

- 1/2 cup butter, softened
- 1/2 cup creamy peanut butter
- 1 cup plus 2 tablespoons confectioners' sugar
- 1-1/2 cups graham cracker crumbs
- 1/2 cup ground almonds
- 1-3/4 cups sliced almonds, toasted
- 1 package (11-1/2 ounces) milk chocolate chips
- 2 tablespoons shortening

Direction

- Cream together the butter, peanut butter and confectioners' sugar in a small bowl till smooth. Stir cracker crumbs and ground almonds into the mixture. Make a cone shape out of rounded tablespoonfuls of the dough; refrigerate until easy to work with.
- Push the sliced almonds' pointed end into the dough to make a pinecone; put onto pans lined with waxed paper. Melt together chocolate chips and shortening in a microwave-safe bowl; stir till smooth.
- Push a toothpick into each pinecone's bottom. Holding over a bowl, spoon the melted chocolate onto the almonds (if necessary, to fully cover the almonds, spread the chocolate out using another toothpick). Return to pan lined with waxed paper; refrigerate until firm. For storage, keep in an airtight container in the refrigerator.

Nutrition Information

- Calories: 221 calories

- Fiber: 2g fiber)
- Total Carbohydrate: 19g carbohydrate (13g sugars
- Cholesterol: 12mg cholesterol
- Protein: 4g protein.
- Total Fat: 15g fat (6g saturated fat)
- Sodium: 98mg sodium

291. Peanut Butter Snowballs

Serving: 2 dozen. | Prep: 15mins | Cook: 0mins | Ready in:

Ingredients

- 1 cup confectioners' sugar
- 1/2 cup creamy peanut butter
- 3 tablespoons butter, softened
- 1 pound white candy coating, coarsely chopped

Direction

- Mix butter, peanut butter and sugar in a bowl. Form to 1-in. balls; put onto waxed paper-lined baking sheet. Chill till firm or for 30 minutes.
- Meanwhile, melt candy coating in microwave-safe bowl then dip balls; put on waxed paper. Let harden.

Nutrition Information

- Calories: 164 calories
- Protein: 1g protein.
- Total Fat: 10g fat (6g saturated fat)
- Sodium: 39mg sodium
- Fiber: 0 fiber)
- Total Carbohydrate: 19g carbohydrate (18g sugars
- Cholesterol: 4mg cholesterol

292. Peanut Butter Swirled Fudge

Serving: 4-3/4 pounds. | Prep: 20mins | Cook: 35mins | Ready in:

Ingredients

- 1 teaspoon plus 1 cup butter, divided
- 4 cups sugar
- 1 cup half-and-half cream
- 3/4 cup baking cocoa
- 1/2 cup dark corn syrup
- 1/8 teaspoon salt
- 1 jar (7 ounces) marshmallow creme
- 1 cup creamy peanut butter
- 2 packages (10 ounces each) peanut butter chips, divided

Direction

- Line a 13-inch x 9-inch pan using foil and butter the foil with a teaspoon butter; put aside.
- Mix the leftover butter, corn syrup, cocoa, salt, cream and sugar in a big heavy saucepan. Heat up to a boil over medium heat, mixing until sugar dissolves. Cook over medium-low heat, without mixing until a candy thermometer registers 234° (soft-ball stage). Take off from the heat; mix in a package chips, peanut butter and marshmallow creme.
- Whip with a hand mixer about 6-8 minutes, until mixture starts to lose its gloss. Fold in leftover chips. Put into lined pan. Chill for 2 hours or until set.
- Take fudge out of pan with foil. Throw the foil; slice fudge into 1-inch squares. Put in an airtight container to store.

Nutrition Information

- Calories: 93 calories
- Sodium: 41mg sodium
- Fiber: 0 fiber)
- Total Carbohydrate: 12g carbohydrate (11g sugars

- Cholesterol: 5mg cholesterol
- Protein: 2g protein.
- Total Fat: 4g fat (2g saturated fat)

293. Peanut Buttercream Candy

Serving: about 7 dozen. | Prep: 40mins | Cook: 0mins | Ready in:

Ingredients

- 1 cup butter, softened
- 7-1/2 cups confectioners' sugar
- 2 tablespoons half-and-half cream
- 1 teaspoon vanilla extract
- 3 cups milk chocolate chips
- 2 teaspoons shortening
- 2-1/2 cups finely chopped peanuts

Direction

- Cream butter till fluffy and light in a big bowl. Add vanilla, cream and confectioners' sugar slowly; beat for 3-4 minutes on medium speed. Form to 3/4-inch balls.
- Melt shortening and chocolate chips in a microwave/heavy saucepan; mix till smooth. In melted chocolate, dip balls; roll in peanuts. Put on wax paper-lined baking sheets and refrigerate till set. Keep in refrigerator in airtight container.

Nutrition Information

- Calories: 348 calories
- Cholesterol: 22mg cholesterol
- Protein: 4g protein.
- Total Fat: 18g fat (8g saturated fat)
- Sodium: 82mg sodium
- Fiber: 1g fiber)
- Total Carbohydrate: 45g carbohydrate (40g sugars

294. Pecan Brittle

Serving: about 1 pound. | Prep: 5mins | Cook: 10mins | Ready in:

Ingredients

- 2 teaspoons plus 1 tablespoon butter, divided
- 1 cup sugar
- 1/2 cup light corn syrup
- 1 cup pecan halves
- 1 teaspoon baking soda
- 1 teaspoon vanilla extract

Direction

- Using 2 teaspoons butter, grease a 15x10x1-inch pan; put aside.
- Mix corn syrup and sugar in a 2-quart microwaveable glass dish. Microwave for 4 mins, uncovered, on high or until a candy thermometer registers 238° or it reaches soft-ball stage.
- Put in pecans. Heat in the microwave for 4 minutes or until a candy thermometer registers 300° or it reaches hard-crack stage. It will be very hot. Mix in the leftover butter, vanilla and baking soda robustly until combined.
- Put into greased pan immediately; spread using a metal spatula as thin as possible. Let cool completely; crack into pieces. Put in an airtight container to store with waxed paper placed between layers.

Nutrition Information

- Calories: 136 calories
- Fiber: 1g fiber)
- Total Carbohydrate: 21g carbohydrate (16g sugars
- Cholesterol: 2mg cholesterol
- Protein: 1g protein.
- Total Fat: 6g fat (1g saturated fat)
- Sodium: 90mg sodium

295. Pecan Candy Clusters

Serving: 16 candies. | Prep: 30mins | Cook: 0mins | Ready in:

Ingredients

- 2 cups milk chocolate chips, divided
- 64 pecan halves (about 1-1/2 cups)
- 28 caramels
- 2 tablespoons heavy whipping cream

Direction

- Use waxed paper to line a baking tray; put aside. Microwave a cup chocolate chips to melt; mix until smooth. Put chocolate by tablespoonfuls onto lined baking tray. Put 4 pecans over each chocolate drop quickly.
- In a 1-quart microwaveable pan, put the caramels; pour in cream. Microwave on high, with no cover, for 2 minutes, mixing once. Scoop onto the center of each cluster.
- Melt the leftover chocolate chips; mix until smooth. Smear on top of caramel. Let sit until firm.

Nutrition Information

- Calories:
- Sodium:
- Fiber:
- Total Carbohydrate:
- Cholesterol:
- Protein:
- Total Fat:

296. Pecan Caramel Clusters

Serving: about 2 pounds. | Prep: 25mins | Cook: 0mins | Ready in:

Ingredients

- 1 package (14 ounces) caramels
- 2 tablespoons water
- 2 tablespoons butter
- 2 cups coarsely chopped pecans
- 4 ounces white candy coating, coarsely chopped
- 4 ounces dark chocolate candy coating, coarsely chopped

Direction

- Mix the butter, water and caramels in a microwaveable bowl. Microwave on high, uncovered, for 3 to 3-1/2 minutes, mixing every half a minute. Mix in pecans.
- Dollop by tablespoonfuls onto greased baking sheets. Freeze until set, 15-20 minutes.
- Mix candy coatings in a microwaveable bowl. Microwave on high, uncovered, for 1-2 minutes, mixing every 15 seconds; mix until smooth. Plunge caramel clusters in coating; let excess drip off. Put on baking sheets lined with waxed paper. Refrigerate until set.

Nutrition Information

- Calories: 152 calories
- Total Fat: 10g fat (4g saturated fat)
- Sodium: 40mg sodium
- Fiber: 1g fiber)
- Total Carbohydrate: 17g carbohydrate (14g sugars
- Cholesterol: 3mg cholesterol
- Protein: 1g protein.

297. Pecan Caramels

Serving: about 2-1/2 pounds. | Prep: 20mins | Cook: 35mins | Ready in:

Ingredients

- 1 tablespoon butter, softened

- 1 cup sugar
- 1 cup light corn syrup
- 2 cups heavy whipping cream, divided
- 1 can (14 ounces) sweetened condensed milk
- 2 cups chopped pecans
- 1 teaspoon vanilla extract

Direction

- Use foil to line a 13x9 in. pan; use butter to grease the foil. Set aside.
- Mix a cup of cream, corn syrup, sugar in a large heavy saucepan. Bring to a boil on medium heat. Cook and stir for 10 minutes till everything is blended and the mixture becomes smooth. Add the remaining cream, milk and stir. Bring to a boil on medium low heat, remember to stir constantly. Cook and stir for 25 minutes till a candy thermometer reaches 238 degrees (this is the soft ball stage).
- Get the pan off heat; put in vanilla, pecans and stir. Transfer the mixture into the prepared pan (remember not to scrape the saucepan). Cool, lift candy out of pan; chop into 1 in. squares. Use waxed paper to wrap each candy.

Nutrition Information

- Calories: 66 calories
- Protein: 1g protein.
- Total Fat: 4g fat (2g saturated fat)
- Sodium: 12mg sodium
- Fiber: 0 fiber
- Total Carbohydrate: 7g carbohydrate (6g sugars
- Cholesterol: 9mg cholesterol

298. Pecan Chocolate Candies

Serving: 3 dozen. | Prep: 25mins | Cook: 5mins |Ready in:

Ingredients

- 1 can (5 ounces) evaporated milk
- 1/2 cup sugar
- 1 cup (6 ounces) semisweet chocolate chips
- 2 teaspoons vanilla extract
- 2-1/2 cups crushed vanilla wafers (about 75 wafers)
- 1-1/2 cups chopped pecans, divided

Direction

- Boil sugar and milk in big saucepan on medium heat; take off heat. Mix vanilla and chocolate chips in till smooth. Add 1/3 cup pecans and vanilla wafers; mix till combined well. Put in bowl; refrigerate till set for 30 minutes.
- Form to 3/4-in. balls. Coat by rolling in leftover pecans. Put onto waxed paper-lined baking sheets then refrigerate till set.

Nutrition Information

- Calories: 108 calories
- Protein: 1g protein. Diabetic Exchanges: 1 starch
- Total Fat: 6g fat (2g saturated fat)
- Sodium: 29mg sodium
- Fiber: 1g fiber)
- Total Carbohydrate: 13g carbohydrate (9g sugars
- Cholesterol: 2mg cholesterol

299. Pecan Cinnamon Fudge

Serving: about 1-1/4 pounds. | Prep: 15mins | Cook: 0mins |Ready in:

Ingredients

- 1 teaspoon plus 1/2 cup butter, divided
- 1/4 cup milk
- 1-1/2 teaspoons vanilla extract
- 3 cups confectioners' sugar
- 1/2 cup baking cocoa
- 1 teaspoon ground cinnamon

- 1 cup chopped pecans

Direction

- Use 1 teaspoon butter to grease an 8-inch square dish; put aside. Mix together milk and remaining butter in a microwave-safe bowl. Microwave on high, with no cover, until butter melts, for 1 to 1-1/2 minutes. Stir vanilla into the mixture.
- Mix together the confectioners' sugar, cocoa and cinnamon in a bowl; mix in the milk mixture till incorporated. Stir pecans into the mixture. Transfer into the prepared pan. Chill in refrigerator for about 8 hours or overnight. Slice into squares.

Nutrition Information

- Calories: 324 calories
- Sodium: 100mg sodium
- Fiber: 2g fiber)
- Total Carbohydrate: 40g carbohydrate (34g sugars
- Cholesterol: 26mg cholesterol
- Protein: 2g protein.
- Total Fat: 19g fat (7g saturated fat)

300. Pecan Clusters

Serving: about 4 dozen. | Prep: 15mins | Cook: 20mins | Ready in:

Ingredients

- 3 cups chopped pecans
- 3 tablespoons butter, melted
- 12 ounces milk or dark chocolate candy coating, melted

Direction

- In a 15x10x1-inch baking pan, stir pecans with butter. Bake for 20-30 minutes at 250°, mixing every 10 minutes.
- Take out of oven; add to a bowl. Put in candy coating and mix until coated evenly. Put by rounded teaspoonfuls onto waxed paper. Let cool completely. Put in an airtight container to store.

Nutrition Information

- Calories: 94 calories
- Cholesterol: 2mg cholesterol
- Protein: 1g protein.
- Total Fat: 8g fat (3g saturated fat)
- Sodium: 7mg sodium
- Fiber: 1g fiber)
- Total Carbohydrate: 6g carbohydrate (5g sugars

301. Pecan Delights

Serving: about 4 dozen. | Prep: 15mins | Cook: 60mins | Ready in:

Ingredients

- 2-1/4 cups packed brown sugar
- 1 cup butter, cubed
- 1 cup light corn syrup
- 1/8 teaspoon salt
- 1 can (14 ounces) sweetened condensed milk
- 1 teaspoon vanilla extract
- 1-1/2 pounds whole pecans
- 1 cup (6 ounces) semisweet chocolate chips
- 1 cup milk chocolate chips
- 2 tablespoons shortening

Direction

- Combine first 4 ingredients in a large saucepan. Over medium heat, cook until all the sugar dissolves. Put in milk gradually and mix well. Keep cooking till a candy thermometer registers 248° (firm-ball stage).
- Discard from heat; mix in the vanilla until it is blended. Then fold in pecans. Drop onto a

parchment-lined or oiled baking sheets by tablespoonfuls. Let chill until firm. Then loosen from the paper.
- In a microwave-safe bowl, melt shortening and chocolate chips. Drizzle over every cluster. Allow to cool.

Nutrition Information

- Calories: 255 calories
- Sodium: 71mg sodium
- Fiber: 2g fiber)
- Total Carbohydrate: 26g carbohydrate (22g sugars
- Cholesterol: 14mg cholesterol
- Protein: 2g protein.
- Total Fat: 17g fat (5g saturated fat)

302. Pecan Divinity

Serving: 4 dozen. | Prep: 10mins | Cook: 15mins | Ready in:

Ingredients

- 2 cups sugar
- 1 cup water
- 1 jar (7 ounces) marshmallow creme
- 1 teaspoon vanilla extract
- 1-1/2 cups chopped pecans

Direction

- In a large heavy saucepan, combine the water and sugar. Cook on medium heat, do not stir until it reaches into a hard-ball stage (a candy thermometer reads 250°).
- Take off from the heat; mix in the pecans, vanilla, and marshmallow creme. Keep on stirring until the candy cools down and when it's dropped from the spoon, it starts to hold its shape.
- Drop onto a baking sheet that is lined with a waxed paper quickly by heaping teaspoonfuls. Keep at room temperature in an airtight container.

Nutrition Information

- Calories: 72 calories
- Sodium: 4mg sodium
- Fiber: 0 fiber)
- Total Carbohydrate: 12g carbohydrate (11g sugars
- Cholesterol: 0 cholesterol
- Protein: 0 protein.
- Total Fat: 3g fat (0 saturated fat)

303. Penuche Fudge

Serving: 24 | Prep: 20mins | Cook: 20mins | Ready in:

Ingredients

- 1 1/2 cups white sugar
- 1 cup brown sugar
- 1/3 cup half-and-half cream
- 1/3 cup milk
- 2 tablespoons margarine
- 1 teaspoon vanilla extract
- 1/2 cup pecan halves

Direction

- Use butter to grease a baking sheet. Butter a heavy, 2-quart saucepan's sides.
- Stir together the margarine, brown sugar, cream, milk and white sugar in the saucepan and heat till boiling over medium heat. Cook, do not stir, till it reaches temperature between 112 to 116°C (234 to 240°F), the mixture tests done when you drop a small portion of syrup into cold water and it forms a soft ball that flattens when you take it out onto a flat surface. Take off from heat and cool to lukewarm (110 degrees).
- Stir vanilla into the mix and beat vigorously till mixture is no longer glossy. Quickly stir

pecans into the mix and spread it onto the prepared sheet. Score it into squares while still warm; then cut when firm.

Nutrition Information

- Calories: 113 calories;
- Total Fat: 3
- Sodium: 16
- Total Carbohydrate: 22.1
- Cholesterol: 2
- Protein: 0.4

304. Peppermint Candy

Serving: about 1-1/2 pounds (64 pieces). | Prep: 25mins | Cook: 0mins | Ready in:

Ingredients

- 1 cup semisweet chocolate chips
- 1 can (14 ounces) sweetened condensed milk, divided
- 1 cup white baking chips
- 3 teaspoons peppermint extract
- 2 to 3 drops green food coloring

Direction

- Melt the chocolate chips with 3/4 cup of the condensed milk in a small saucepan over low heat, stirring occasionally. Line waxed paper on an 8-inch square dish; coat the paper with butter.
- Spread pan with 1/2 melted chocolate mixture; let chill for 5 to 10 mins (allow the remaining melted chocolate mixture to stand at the room temperature).
- Melt the white baking chips in another saucepan. Mix in the remaining condensed milk until they become smooth. Discard from heat. Put in food coloring and extract. Place in the refrigerator until set. Spread over chocolate layer; spread with reserved

chocolate mixture. Place in the refrigerator until set. Cut into 1-inch pieces.

Nutrition Information

- Calories: 51 calories
- Total Carbohydrate: 7g carbohydrate (5g sugars
- Cholesterol: 3mg cholesterol
- Protein: 1g protein.
- Total Fat: 2g fat (1g saturated fat)
- Sodium: 11mg sodium
- Fiber: 0 fiber)

305. Peppermint Fudge

Serving: 24 | Prep: 10mins | Cook: 5mins | Ready in:

Ingredients

- 1 2/3 cups granulated sugar
- 2/3 cup NESTLE® CARNATION® Evaporated Milk
- 2 tablespoons butter or margarine
- 1/4 teaspoon salt
- 2 cups miniature marshmallows
- 1 1/2 cups NESTLE® TOLL HOUSE® Semi-Sweet Chocolate Morsels
- 1/2 teaspoon vanilla extract
- 1/4 teaspoon peppermint extract
- 1/4 cup crushed, hard peppermint candy

Direction

- Use foil to line an 8-in square baking pan.
- In a medium heavy-duty saucepan, mix together salt, butter, evaporated milk and sugar. Put over medium heat and bring to a full rolling boil while stirring continuously. Boil for 4-5 minutes while stirring continuously. Put off the heat.
- Whisk in peppermint extract, vanilla extract, morsels and marshmallows. Vigorously whisk to melt marshmallows, about a minute.

Transfer to the lined baking pan and allow to cool for a minute. Place candy on top, lightly press into the mixture. Put in the refrigerator to firm up for 2 hours. Take out of the pan and discard foil. Slice into 48 pieces.

Nutrition Information

- Calories: 150 calories;
- Cholesterol: 5
- Protein: 1.3
- Total Fat: 4.6
- Sodium: 45
- Total Carbohydrate: 27.3

306. Peppermint Fudge Truffles

Serving: 4 dozen. | Prep: 25mins | Cook: 0mins | Ready in:

Ingredients

- 1 cup milk chocolate chips
- 1 can (16 ounces) chocolate frosting
- 1-1/2 cups peppermint crunch baking chips, divided
- 1/2 cup chopped walnuts or pecans
- 1/8 teaspoon peppermint extract

Direction

- Melt milk chocolate chips in microwave-safe bowl; mix till smooth. Mix extract, walnuts, 1/2 cup peppermint chips and frosting in; cover. Chill till firm enough to shape to balls for 30 minutes.
- Chop leftover peppermint chips coarsely; form chocolate mixture to 1-in. balls then roll into chopped chips. Keep in airtight container in the fridge.

Nutrition Information

- Calories:
- Protein:
- Total Fat:
- Sodium:
- Fiber:
- Total Carbohydrate:
- Cholesterol:

307. Peppermint Swirl Fudge

Serving: about 1-1/2 pounds. | Prep: 10mins | Cook: 5mins | Ready in:

Ingredients

- 1 teaspoon butter
- 1 package (10 to 12 ounces) white baking chips
- 1 can (16 ounces) vanilla frosting
- 1/2 teaspoon peppermint extract
- 8 drops red food coloring
- 2 tablespoons crushed peppermint candies

Direction

- Use foil to line a 9-in. square pan and use butter to grease the foil; put aside.
- Melt chips in a small saucepan; stir till smooth. Take off from heat. Stir frosting and extract into the mixture. Spread it into the prepared pan. Sparsely dot drops of food coloring atop the fudge; using a knife, cut through the fudge to swirl. Sprinkle the top with candies. Refrigerate till set for about 1 hour.
- Lift the fudge out of pan with foil. Take off foil carefully; slice fudge into 1-in. squares. For storage, keep in an airtight container.

Nutrition Information

- Calories: 45 calories
- Sodium: 17mg sodium
- Fiber: 0 fiber)
- Total Carbohydrate: 6g carbohydrate (5g sugars

- Cholesterol: 1mg cholesterol
- Protein: 0 protein.
- Total Fat: 3g fat (1g saturated fat)

- Cholesterol: 0 cholesterol
- Protein: 2g protein.
- Total Fat: 4g fat (1g saturated fat)
- Sodium: 34mg sodium

308. Pine Nut Divinity

Serving: about 3 dozen. | Prep: 30mins | Cook: 0mins | Ready in:

Ingredients

- 3 cups sugar
- 2/3 cup water
- 1/2 cup light corn syrup
- 2 egg whites
- 1/8 teaspoon salt
- 1 teaspoon vanilla extract
- 1 cup pine nuts, toasted

Direction

- Mix corn syrup, water and sugar in a big saucepan; heat up to a boil over medium-high heat, mixing continuously. Cook over medium heat about 10-15 minutes (don't mix) until a candy thermometer registers 260° (hard-ball stage). Take off from the heat.
- Whip salt and egg whites in a big bowl, until stiff peak create. Whip on high and add hot sugar mixture in a thin stream on top of egg whites slowly; keep whipping for about 3 minutes. Put in vanilla; whip about 5 minutes just until candy begins to lose its shine. Mix in the pine nuts.
- Quickly put by tablespoonfuls onto waxed paper; or pour into a 9-inch square pan greased with butter and slice into serving size pieces. Cover tightly and store.

Nutrition Information

- Calories: 200 calories
- Fiber: 0 fiber)
- Total Carbohydrate: 41g carbohydrate (37g sugars

309. Pineapple Fudge

Serving: 28 | Prep: | Cook: |Ready in:

Ingredients

- 1 cup evaporated milk
- 3 cups white sugar
- 2 tablespoons butter
- 1 cup crushed pineapple, drained
- 2 teaspoons lemon juice

Direction

- Grease a 9-inch square pan with butter. Put aside.
- Mix butter, sugar, and milk together. Heat to boiling point slowly.
- Mix in drained crushed pineapple and cook to soft ball stage over medium heat, 236 degrees (113 degrees C), mixing frequently for about 25 minutes to avoid burning. Cool. Mix in lemon juice. Whip until mixture is lost its shine and becomes smooth.
- Transfer into greased pan. Cool, then slice into squares.

Nutrition Information

- Calories: 108 calories;
- Total Fat: 1.5
- Sodium: 15
- Total Carbohydrate: 23.8
- Cholesterol: 5
- Protein: 0.7

310. Pistachio Coconut Chews

Serving: 2-1/4 pounds. | Prep: 20mins | Cook: 0mins | Ready in:

Ingredients

- 8 cups unsweetened finely shredded coconut
- 3 cups confectioners' sugar
- 1/2 cup coconut milk
- 1/3 cup light corn syrup
- 1/2 cup chopped pistachios
- 2 teaspoons matcha (green tea powder)
- 1/2 teaspoon almond extract
- 1/4 teaspoon ground cardamom
- Confectioners' sugar

Direction

- Mix corn syrup, coconut milk, confectioners' sugar and coconut in a big bowl; press 1/2 of it into 9-in. greased square pan.
- Add cardamom, extract, matcha and pistachios to leftover coconut mixture; press over top in an even layer. Cover; refrigerate till firm for 2 hours. Cut to 1-in. squares. In confectioners' sugar, dip bottoms.

Nutrition Information

- Calories:
- Protein:
- Total Fat:
- Sodium:
- Fiber:
- Total Carbohydrate:
- Cholesterol:

311. Pistachio Cranberry Bark

Serving: about 1 pound. | Prep: 20mins | Cook: 0mins | Ready in:

Ingredients

- 2 cups (12 ounces) semisweet chocolate chips
- 1 cup chopped pistachios, toasted, divided
- 3/4 cup dried cranberries, divided
- 5 ounces white candy coating, melted

Direction

- Microwave chocolate chips in a microwaveable bowl until melted; mix until smooth. Mix in 1/2 of the cranberries and 3/4 cup of pistachios; smear onto a waxed paper-lined baking tray. Sprinkle with melted candy coating. Slice through layers, using a knife to swirl.
- Scatter with the leftover pistachios and cranberries. Chill until set.
- Break or slice into pieces. Put in an airtight container in the fridge to store.

Nutrition Information

- Calories: 215 calories
- Fiber: 2g fiber)
- Total Carbohydrate: 28g carbohydrate (24g sugars
- Cholesterol: 0 cholesterol
- Protein: 3g protein.
- Total Fat: 12g fat (6g saturated fat)
- Sodium: 36mg sodium

312. Pulled Molasses Taffy

Serving: 14-1/2 dozen. | Prep: 02hours00mins | Cook: 0mins | Ready in:

Ingredients

- 5 teaspoons butter, softened, divided
- 1/4 cup water
- 1-1/4 cups packed brown sugar
- 2 tablespoons cider vinegar
- 1/4 teaspoon salt
- 1/3 cup molasses

Direction

- Use 3 teaspoons butter to grease a 15x10x1-in. pan; put aside. Mix together the water, brown sugar, vinegar and salt in a heavy saucepan. Heat until boiling on medium heat. Cook and stir until firm-ball stage (a candy thermometer reads 245°), stir from time to time. Add molasses and the remaining butter into the mixture. Cook, uncovered, until hard-ball stage (a candy thermometer reads 260°), stir from time to time. Take off from heat; transfer into the prepared pan. Let it cool down until cool enough to handle for about 5 minutes.
- Butter your fingers and quickly pull half of the candy till it becomes firm but pliable. Pull the candy and shape it into a 1/2-in. rope. Slice into 1-1/4-in. pieces. Continue with the rest of the taffy. Use foil or waxed paper to wrap each piece; twist the ends. For storage, keep in airtight containers in the refrigerator. Take out of the refrigerator 30 minutes before serving.

Nutrition Information

- Calories: 17 calories
- Protein: 0 protein.
- Total Fat: 0 fat (0 saturated fat)
- Sodium: 11mg sodium
- Fiber: 0 fiber
- Total Carbohydrate: 4g carbohydrate (4g sugars
- Cholesterol: 1mg cholesterol

313. Pumpkin Seed Toffee

Serving: 2 pounds. | Prep: 10mins | Cook: 20mins | Ready in:

Ingredients

- 2 teaspoons plus 2 cups butter, softened, divided
- 2 cups sugar
- 1 tablespoon corn syrup
- 1 teaspoon pumpkin pie spice
- 1/4 teaspoon salt
- 1 cup roasted pumpkin seeds or pepitas

Direction

- Use 2 teaspoons butter to grease 15x10x1-inch pan; put aside. Melt leftover butter in a heavy saucepan; mix in salt, pie spice, corn syrup and sugar. Mix and cook on medium heat till it reach a hard-crack stage or candy thermometer reads 300°.
- Take off from heat; mix in pumpkin seeds. Put in prepped pan immediately; stand for 1 hour at room temperature till cool. Break to bite-sized pieces; keep at room temperature in airtight container.

Nutrition Information

- Calories: 380 calories
- Total Fat: 29g fat (16g saturated fat)
- Sodium: 284mg sodium
- Fiber: 1g fiber)
- Total Carbohydrate: 28g carbohydrate (26g sugars
- Cholesterol: 61mg cholesterol
- Protein: 5g protein.

314. Puttin' On The Ritz Candy

Serving: 3 dozen. | Prep: 45mins | Cook: 0mins | Ready in:

Ingredients

- 1 jar (12-1/4 ounces) caramel ice cream topping
- 1 cup chopped pecans
- 36 butter-flavored crackers
- 1 cup (6 ounces) semisweet chocolate chips
- 1 tablespoon shortening

Direction

- Heat pecans and caramel topping in microwave-safe bowl for 5-7 minutes on high, frequently mixing till mixture thickens; cool for 5 minutes. Put crackers on wax paper-lined baking sheets. On each cracker, put 1 teaspoon caramel mixture; refrigerate it for 1 hour.
- Melt shortening and chocolate chips in a microwave; mix till smooth. Dip bottom of every cracker in chocolate and shake excess off. Put on wax paper-lined pans, caramel side down; refrigerate till set for 1 hour. Keep in airtight container.

Nutrition Information

- Calories: 90 calories
- Sodium: 65mg sodium
- Fiber: 1g fiber)
- Total Carbohydrate: 12g carbohydrate (9g sugars
- Cholesterol: 0 cholesterol
- Protein: 1g protein.
- Total Fat: 5g fat (1g saturated fat)

315. Quick Butterscotch Fudge

Serving: 2-1/2 pounds. | Prep: 20mins | Cook: 0mins | Ready in:

Ingredients

- 1 teaspoon plus 1/2 cup butter, divided
- 2 cups sugar
- 1 cup evaporated milk
- 1 package (10 to 11 ounces) butterscotch chips
- 1-1/2 cups graham cracker crumbs

Direction

- Use foil to line an 8-in. square pan and grease the foil using 1 teaspoon of butter; put aside. In a small heavy saucepan, combine the remaining butter, milk and sugar. Heat until boiling; cook for 5 minutes. Take off the heat. Add graham cracker crumbs and butterscotch chips; mix until chips melt.
- Transfer to prepared pan. Chill in refrigerator until firm. Lift the fudge out of the pan using foil. Remove foil; slice fudge into 1-in. squares. Store, refrigerated in an airtight container.

Nutrition Information

- Calories: 75 calories
- Fiber: 0 fiber)
- Total Carbohydrate: 11g carbohydrate (10g sugars
- Cholesterol: 6mg cholesterol
- Protein: 1g protein.
- Total Fat: 3g fat (2g saturated fat)
- Sodium: 34mg sodium

316. Quick Coconut Bonbons

Serving: about 21 dozen. | Prep: 25mins | Cook: 0mins | Ready in:

Ingredients

- 1/2 cup butter, softened
- 2 pounds confectioners' sugar
- 1 can (14 ounces) sweetened condensed milk
- 4 cups chopped pecans
- 3-1/2 cups sweetened shredded coconut (about 10 ounces)
- 1 teaspoon vanilla extract
- 2 cups (12 ounces) semisweet chocolate chips
- 1 tablespoon shortening

Direction

- Cream sugar and butter till fluffy and light in a big bowl. Add vanilla, coconut, pecans and milk; stir well. Form to 1-inch balls; refrigerate till firm for 30-45 minutes.
- Melt shortening and chips in a microwave/heavy saucepan; mix till smooth.

Dip balls; put to set on waxed paper; keep in an airtight container.

Nutrition Information

- Calories: 48 calories
- Protein: 0 protein.
- Total Fat: 3g fat (1g saturated fat)
- Sodium: 9mg sodium
- Fiber: 0 fiber)
- Total Carbohydrate: 6g carbohydrate (5g sugars
- Cholesterol: 2mg cholesterol

317. Raisin Cashew Drops

Serving: 2-1/2 pounds. | Prep: 10mins | Cook: 10mins | Ready in:

Ingredients

- 2 cups (12 ounces) semisweet chocolate chips
- 1 can (14 ounces) sweetened condensed milk
- 1 tablespoon light corn syrup
- 1 teaspoon vanilla extract
- 2 cups coarsely chopped cashews
- 2 cups raisins

Direction

- Melt chocolate chips with corn syrup and milk in a heavy saucepan over low heat for 10-12 minutes, mixing from time to time. Take off from the heat; mix in vanilla until combined. Mix in raisins and cashews.
- Put by teaspoonfuls onto waxed paper-lined baking trays. Chill for 3 hours or until set. Put in the fridge to store.

Nutrition Information

- Calories:
- Sodium:
- Fiber:
- Total Carbohydrate:
- Cholesterol:
- Protein:
- Total Fat:

318. Raspberry Rocky Road Fudge

Serving: about 3-1/2 pounds. | Prep: 20mins | Cook: 0mins | Ready in:

Ingredients

- 1-1/2 teaspoons plus 1/2 cup butter, softened, divided
- 2 cups sugar
- 12 large marshmallows
- 1 can (5 ounces) evaporated milk
- 1/4 teaspoon salt
- 1 package (12 ounces) semisweet chocolate chips, divided
- 1 cup raspberry chocolate chips
- 3/4 cup creamy peanut butter
- 1 teaspoon vanilla extract
- 1-2/3 cups salted peanuts, crushed

Direction

- Line a 13-in. x 9-in. pan using foil and use 1-1/2 teaspoons butter to grease the foil; put aside. Mix together the rest of the butter, marshmallows, milk, salt and sugar in a large saucepan. Heat until boiling on medium heat, stir continuously. Cook and stir till smooth.
- Take off from heat. Stir the chips, peanut butter and vanilla into the mixture till smooth. Fold peanuts into the mix. Spread it into the prepared pan. Refrigerate till set for about 2 hours. Lift the fudge out of pan with the foil; slice it into 1-in. squares. For storage, keep refrigerated in an airtight container.

Nutrition Information

- Calories:
- Protein:
- Total Fat:
- Sodium:
- Fiber:
- Total Carbohydrate:
- Cholesterol:

319. Reindeer Treats

Serving: 3-1/2 dozen. | Prep: 10mins | Cook: 5mins | Ready in:

Ingredients

- 6 cups chocolate-flavored crisp rice cereal
- 1 cup packed brown sugar
- 1 cup light corn syrup
- 1 cup peanut butter
- 40 miniature pretzels, halved
- 80 miniature peanut butter candies
- 40 red-hot candies

Direction

- Put cereal in a large bowl; put aside. In a large saucepan, mix corn syrup and brown sugar. Heat to a boil; cook and stir in 2 minutes. Take away from the heat; blend in peanut butter until smooth. Transfer over cereal and stir until covered.
- Form into 1 1/2 -inch balls; arrange on baking sheets lined with waxed paper. Allow to stand until firm. Arrange 2 pretzel halves in each ball for antlers. Put 2 peanut butter candies on each for eyes and 1 red-hot for the nose.

Nutrition Information

- Calories: 351 calories
- Sodium: 280mg sodium
- Fiber: 2g fiber
- Total Carbohydrate: 53g carbohydrate (38g sugars
- Cholesterol: 2mg cholesterol
- Protein: 7g protein.
- Total Fat: 15g fat (4g saturated fat)

320. Ribbon Fantasy Fudge

Serving: 49 pieces. | Prep: 10mins | Cook: 10mins | Ready in:

Ingredients

- 2 teaspoons plus 3/4 cup butter, cubed, divided
- 3 cups sugar
- 1 can (5 ounces) evaporated milk
- 1 jar (7 ounces) marshmallow creme
- 1 cup (6 ounces) semisweet chocolate chips
- 1 teaspoon vanilla extract, divided
- 1/2 cup peanut butter

Direction

- Use foil to line a 9-in. square pan; with 2 teaspoons of butter, grease the foil; put aside. Mix the rest of the butter, milk and sugar in a large heavy saucepan. Bring to a full rolling boil; stir constantly. Boil over medium heat for 4 minutes; stir to prevent scorching. Take out of the heat; put aside.
- Split marshmallow crème into 2 heat-resistant bowls; add half teaspoon vanilla and chocolate chips to one bowl, the rest of vanilla and peanut butter to the second one. Place 1/2 of sugar mixture into each bowl.
- Stir chocolate mixture until smooth; transfer to lined pan; mix peanut butter mixture; pour over chocolate layer carefully. Keep in the fridge until firm.
- Lift fudge out of pan with foil. Get rid of foil; slice fudge into 1-1/4-in. squares.

Nutrition Information

- Calories: 99 calories
- Fiber: 0 fiber

- Total Carbohydrate: 15g carbohydrate (14g sugars
- Cholesterol: 7mg cholesterol
- Protein: 1g protein.
- Total Fat: 4g fat (2g saturated fat)
- Sodium: 39mg sodium

321. Rich Peanut Clusters

Serving: about 15 dozen. | Prep: 15mins | Cook: 5mins | Ready in:

Ingredients

- 2 packages (12 ounces each) semisweet chocolate chips
- 2 packages (10 to 12 ounces each) vanilla or white chips
- 1 tablespoon shortening
- 1 teaspoon vanilla extract
- 1/2 teaspoon butter, softened
- 2 cans (12 ounces each) salted peanuts

Direction

- Melt chips and shortening in a microwave; stir till smooth. Stir vanilla and butter into the mixture. Add peanuts into the mix; combine thoroughly.
- Drop teaspoonfuls onto pans lined with waxed paper. Refrigerate till set. For storage, keep in an airtight container.

Nutrition Information

- Calories: 58 calories
- Sodium: 20mg sodium
- Fiber: 1g fiber)
- Total Carbohydrate: 5g carbohydrate (4g sugars
- Cholesterol: 0 cholesterol
- Protein: 1g protein.
- Total Fat: 4g fat (2g saturated fat)

322. Rich Pistachio Brittle

Serving: about 1-1/2 pounds. | Prep: 10mins | Cook: 30mins | Ready in:

Ingredients

- 1-1/4 cups sugar
- 1/3 cup water
- 1/3 cup light corn syrup
- 1 teaspoon salt
- 1/2 cup butter, cubed
- 2 cups pistachios, toasted
- 1/2 teaspoon baking soda
- 1/2 teaspoon vanilla extract

Direction

- Butter a 15x10x1 in. pan. Mix salt, corn syrup, water and sugar in a large saucepan. Cook on medium heat till a candy thermometer reaches 240 degrees (this is the soft ball stage). Put in pistachio and butter carefully; cook and stir till the temperature of the mixture reaches 284 degrees (this is the soft crack stage).
- Get the saucepan off heat; mix in vanilla, baking soda. Transfer the mixture into the prepared pan immediately. Spread to of 1/4 in. thickness. Cool then crack the cool mixture into pieces. Keep in an airtight container to store.

Nutrition Information

- Calories: 161 calories
- Protein: 3g protein.
- Total Fat: 9g fat (3g saturated fat)
- Sodium: 215mg sodium
- Fiber: 1g fiber)
- Total Carbohydrate: 18g carbohydrate (14g sugars
- Cholesterol: 11mg cholesterol

323. Rocky Road Fudge

Serving: | Prep: | Cook: | Ready in:

Ingredients

- 2 cups one 12 ounce bag nestle semisweet morsels
- 1 can sweetened condensed milk, 14 ounces
- 1 teaspoon vanilla extract
- 2 cups mini marshamallows, rounded
- 1 1/2 cups salted coctail peanuts, coarsely chopped, flat, instead do fw salted toasted almonds

Direction

- Preparation:
- LINE 13 x 9-inch baking pan using foil; lightly grease. MICROWAVE the sweetened condensed milk and morsels on HIGH (100%) power in a big, uncovered, microwave-safe bowl for a minute; MIX. Some of morsels may retain their original form. Microwave for another 10 to 15-second intervals if needed, mixing until morsels are melted. Mix in the vanilla extract. Fold in nuts and marshmallows. PUSH the blend into the prepared baking pan. Refrigerate until ready to eat. Take out of the pan; discard the foil. Slice into pieces.
- We prefer in 7 x 11 Pyrex plate (so I reduce the marshmallows from 3 cups in the original recipe to 2).
- I process in the microwave at 50% power.
- Distribute in a pan with green spatula, after an hour in the refrigerator, cut quickly 8 by 4, lifted using med offset then place in the containers, return to the refrigerator.
- The longer it sets the better. In other words, the time should be more than 2 hours, or else the consistency will too soft.

324. Rocky Toffee Fudge

Serving: 2-1/2 pounds. | Prep: 5mins | Cook: 5mins | Ready in:

Ingredients

- 1 teaspoon butter
- 1 can (14 ounces) sweetened condensed milk
- 2 cups (12 ounces) dark chocolate chips
- 1 cup (6 ounces) semisweet chocolate chips
- 1 cup miniature marshmallows
- 1/2 cup milk chocolate English toffee bits
- 1/3 cup Kahlua (coffee liqueur)

Direction

- Use foil to line a 9-inch square baking pan. Use butter to grease the foil; put aside.
- Mix the chips and milk in a big microwave-safe bowl. Microwave, uncovered, on high setting for 60 seconds; whisk. Cook till the chips melt or for 30 to 60 seconds more, whisking every 30 seconds. Whisk in Kahlua, toffee bits and marshmallows.
- Move into the prepped pan. Keep covered and refrigerated till firm or for 2 hours. Lift the fudge from pan using the foil. Lightly peel off the foil; chop the fudge into 1-inch square pieces. Keep stored in an airtight container.

Nutrition Information

- Calories:
- Sodium:
- Fiber:
- Total Carbohydrate:
- Cholesterol:
- Protein:
- Total Fat:

325. S'more Drops

Serving: 2-1/2 dozen. | Prep: 20mins | Cook: 0mins | Ready in:

Ingredients

- 4 cups Golden Grahams
- 1-1/2 cups miniature marshmallows
- 1 cup (6 ounces) semisweet chocolate chips
- 1/3 cup light corn syrup
- 1 tablespoon butter
- 1/2 teaspoon vanilla extract

Direction

- Mix marshmallows and cereal in a big bowl; put aside. In 1-quart microwave-safe dish, put butter, corn syrup and chocolate chips.
- Microwave on high, with no cover, mixing every 30 seconds, till smooth for 1-2 minutes; mix in vanilla. Put on cereal mixture; mix well. Drop on wax paper-lined baking sheets by tablespoonfuls and cool.

Nutrition Information

- Calories: 68 calories
- Protein: 1g protein.
- Total Fat: 2g fat (1g saturated fat)
- Sodium: 58mg sodium
- Fiber: 0 fiber)
- Total Carbohydrate: 13g carbohydrate (8g sugars
- Cholesterol: 1mg cholesterol

326. Salted Peanut Chews

Serving: 2 dozen. | Prep: 25mins | Cook: 15mins | Ready in:

Ingredients

- 1-1/2 cups all-purpose flour
- 1/2 cup packed brown sugar
- 3/4 cup butter, softened, divided
- 3 cups miniature marshmallows
- 2 cups peanut butter chips
- 2/3 cup corn syrup
- 2 teaspoons vanilla extract
- 2 cups crisp rice cereal
- 2 cups salted peanuts

Direction

- Mix 1/2 cup butter, brown sugar and flour in a big bowl; press into 13x9-inch ungreased baking pan. Bake it at 350° till light brown for 12-15 minutes.
- Sprinkle marshmallows over; put back in oven till marshmallows start to melt for 3-5 minutes. Put aside.
- Mix and cook leftover butter, vanilla, corn syrup and peanut butter chips till smooth in a big saucepan; take off from heat. Mix in peanuts and cereal. Put on prepped crust; scatter to cover. Cool before cutting to bars on wire rack.

Nutrition Information

- Calories: 290 calories
- Total Fat: 16g fat (6g saturated fat)
- Sodium: 182mg sodium
- Fiber: 3g fiber)
- Total Carbohydrate: 33g carbohydrate (17g sugars
- Cholesterol: 15mg cholesterol
- Protein: 7g protein.

327. Salted Peanut Rolls

Serving: 15 | Prep: 15mins | Cook: | Ready in:

Ingredients

- 24 ounces salted peanuts
- 2 cups peanut butter chips
- 1 (7 ounce) jar marshmallow creme

- 1 (14 ounce) can sweetened condensed milk

Direction

- Spread 3 cups chopped peanuts on bottom of 9x13-in. glass pan. Melt peanut butter chips in saucepan on low heat/microwave. Take off heat; mix condensed milk and marshmallow cream in. Put on peanut layers; sprinkle leftover 1 cup peanuts over. Chill till set; cut to bars.

Nutrition Information

- Calories: 573 calories;
- Total Fat: 33.9
- Sodium: 492
- Total Carbohydrate: 50.2
- Cholesterol: 9
- Protein: 19.7

328. Saltine Toffee Bark

Serving: 2 pounds. | Prep: 15mins | Cook: 10mins | Ready in:

Ingredients

- 40 saltines
- 1 cup butter, cubed
- 3/4 cup sugar
- 2 cups (12 ounces) semisweet chocolate chips
- 1 package (8 ounces) milk chocolate English toffee bits

Direction

- Use a heavy-duty foil to line a 15x10x1-inch baking pan. Place saltines on top of foil in one layer and put aside.
- Heat butter over medium heat in a large heavy saucepan until melted. Mix in sugar. Boil the mixture; cook while stirring to dissolve sugar, about 1 to 2 minutes. Spread evenly onto crackers.
- Bake at 350 degrees until it bubbles, about 8 to 10 minutes. Quickly put chocolate chips on top. Wait several minutes until chips turn soft, then spread chocolate all over the surface. Garnish with toffee bits. Allow to cool.
- Chill, covered, in the refrigerator until firm for about an hour. Cut into pieces. Keep in a tightly sealed container to store.

Nutrition Information

- Calories: 171 calories
- Total Carbohydrate: 18g carbohydrate (11g sugars
- Cholesterol: 21mg cholesterol
- Protein: 1g protein.
- Total Fat: 12g fat (7g saturated fat)
- Sodium: 119mg sodium
- Fiber: 1g fiber)

329. Simple Macadamia Nut Fudge

Serving: about 5 pounds. | Prep: 15mins | Cook: 0mins | Ready in:

Ingredients

- 2 teaspoons plus 1/2 cup butter, divided
- 4-1/2 cups granulated sugar
- 1 can (12 ounces) evaporated milk
- 3 cups chopped macadamia nuts, divided
- 12 ounces German sweet chocolate, chopped
- 1 package (12 ounces) semisweet chocolate chips
- 1 jar (7 ounces) marshmallow creme
- 2 teaspoons vanilla extract
- 1/2 teaspoon salt, optional

Direction

- Line two 9-inch square pans with aluminum foil. Brush the foil with 2 tsp. butter. Put to one side.

- Combine remaining butter, milk, and sugar in a large heavy saucepan. Bring the mixture to a gentle boil. Cook and stir continuously for 5 minutes. Turn off the heat; mix in vanilla, marshmallow creme, chocolate chips, chopped chocolate, 2 cups of nuts and salt if desired.
- Transfer fudge to the two pans; scatter remaining nuts on top and press them lightly into the mixture. Chill until firm. Once firm, lift the fudge out of the pans using foil. Remove the foil; slice fudge into 1-inch square bars. Preserve them in an air-tight container.

Nutrition Information

- Calories: 72 calories
- Total Carbohydrate: 10g carbohydrate (9g sugars
- Cholesterol: 2mg cholesterol
- Protein: 1g protein. Diabetic Exchanges: 1 fat
- Total Fat: 4g fat (1g saturated fat)
- Sodium: 14mg sodium
- Fiber: 0 fiber)

330. Snowball

Serving: about 3 dozen. | Prep: 20mins | Cook: 0mins | Ready in:

Ingredients

- 1/2 cup butter, cubed
- 1 can (14 ounces) sweetened condensed milk
- 3 tablespoons baking cocoa
- 1 teaspoon vanilla extract
- 2 cups graham cracker crumbs (about 32 squares)
- 3-1/2 cups sweetened shredded coconut, divided
- 32 to 35 large marshmallows

Direction

- Line waxed paper on a baking sheet; put aside.
- Put vanilla, cocoa, milk and butter together in a big saucepan; mix and cook on medium heat till it is smooth and butter melts. Take off from heat; mix in 1 1/2 cups coconut and cracker crumbs. Stand till cool enough to handle.
- Wrap 1 tablespoon mixture around every marshmallow with moistened hands; to avoid sticking, dip hands into water often. Roll in leftover coconut; put on prepped baking sheet. Cover; freeze till firm. Keep in an airtight container in freezer/fridge. Can be frozen for maximum of 2 months.

Nutrition Information

- Calories: 145 calories
- Total Fat: 7g fat (5g saturated fat)
- Sodium: 95mg sodium
- Fiber: 1g fiber)
- Total Carbohydrate: 19g carbohydrate (14g sugars
- Cholesterol: 11mg cholesterol
- Protein: 2g protein.

331. Sour Cream Walnut Fudge

Serving: about 1-1/2 pounds. | Prep: 30mins | Cook: 0mins | Ready in:

Ingredients

- 1 teaspoon plus 2 tablespoons butter, divided
- 2 cups sugar
- 1/2 cup sour cream
- 1/3 cup light corn syrup
- 1/4 teaspoon salt
- 2 teaspoons vanilla extract
- 1 cup chopped walnuts

Direction

- Line the 8-inch square pan with the foil and grease foil using 1 teaspoon of the butter; put

aside. In the big and heavy saucepan, mix leftover butter, salt, corn syrup, sour cream and sugar. Boil on medium heat; cook till the candy thermometer reaches 238 degrees (a soft-ball stage).
- Take out of heat; whisk in the vanilla. Allow it to rest, no whisking, for 15 minutes. Put in the walnuts. Use wooden spoon to whip roughly for 8 minutes or till creamy and thicken. Add to the prepped pan. Keep in the refrigerator till firm.
- With the foil, lift the fudge out of the pan. Get rid of the foil; chop the fudge into 1-inch square pieces. Keep in the airtight container in fridge.

Nutrition Information

- Calories: 49 calories
- Total Carbohydrate: 8g carbohydrate (7g sugars
- Cholesterol: 2mg cholesterol
- Protein: 1g protein.
- Total Fat: 2g fat (1g saturated fat)
- Sodium: 17mg sodium
- Fiber: 0 fiber)

332. Speedy Oven Fudge

Serving: 3 pounds. | Prep: 10mins | Cook: 15mins | Ready in:

Ingredients

- 1/2 cup milk
- 1 cup butter
- 2/3 cup baking cocoa
- 2 pounds confectioners' sugar
- 2 teaspoons vanilla extract
- 1 cup chopped nuts

Direction

- In a 3-quart baking dish, put first 4 ingredients in order listed (without stirring). Bake for 15 mins in a 350° oven, until the butter melts.
- Place into a bowl carefully. Put in vanilla, then beat for 2 mins on high. Mix in nuts. Transfer to a buttered 11x7-inch dish. Let cool. Cut and serve.

Nutrition Information

- Calories: 128 calories
- Sodium: 40mg sodium
- Fiber: 0 fiber)
- Total Carbohydrate: 20g carbohydrate (18g sugars
- Cholesterol: 11mg cholesterol
- Protein: 1g protein.
- Total Fat: 5g fat (3g saturated fat)

333. Spiced Almond Brittle

Serving: 1-1/4 pounds. | Prep: 15mins | Cook: 15mins | Ready in:

Ingredients

- 1 cup sugar
- 1/2 cup light corn syrup
- 1/4 cup water
- 1/4 teaspoon salt
- 1-1/2 cups unblanched almonds
- 2 tablespoons butter
- 1/2 teaspoon pumpkin pie spice
- 1/4 teaspoon cayenne pepper
- 1/4 teaspoon dried rosemary, crushed
- 1/8 teaspoon ground nutmeg
- 1 teaspoon baking soda

Direction

- Line a 15x10x1-in. pan using parchment paper (Don't grease or spray.). Mix salt, corn syrup, water and sugar in a big heavy saucepan. Heat up to a boil, mixing frequently until sugar is

dissolved. Brush down the sides of the pan with a pastry brush dipped in water to get rid of sugar crystals. Cook over medium heat without mixing until a candy thermometer registers 260° (hard-ball stage).
- Mix in seasonings, butter and almonds; cook until thermometer registers 300° (hard-crack stage), about 8 minutes more, mixing constantly.
- Take off from heat; mix in baking soda. (Mixture will be frothy.) Pour onto lined pan immediately, spreading as thin as can be. Let cool entirely.
- Crack brittle into pieces. Place between layers of waxed paper in airtight containers to store.

Nutrition Information

- Calories: 139 calories
- Cholesterol: 3mg cholesterol
- Protein: 2g protein.
- Total Fat: 7g fat (1g saturated fat)
- Sodium: 109mg sodium
- Fiber: 1g fiber)
- Total Carbohydrate: 19g carbohydrate (17g sugars

334. Spiced Almond Butter Candy

Serving: 3-1/2 pounds. | Prep: 10mins | Cook: 30mins | Ready in:

Ingredients

- 1-1/2 teaspoons butter
- 2-1/2 cups almond butter
- 2 cups salted roasted almonds, coarsely chopped
- 2 teaspoons ground cinnamon
- 1/2 teaspoon ground nutmeg
- 1/2 teaspoon vanilla extract
- 1/4 teaspoon ground allspice
- 2 cups sugar
- 1-1/2 cups light corn syrup
- 1/4 cup water
- 1-1/2 teaspoons baking soda
- 1 cup (6 ounces) semisweet chocolate chips or 60% cacao bittersweet chocolate baking chips, melted

Direction

- Use foil to line a 15x10x1-inch pan then butter the foil. Mix the allspice, vanilla, nutmeg, cinnamon, almonds and almond butter in a big bowl; put aside.
- Mix the water, corn syrup and sugar in a big heavy saucepan; cook and mix over medium heat until sugar dissolves. Heat up to a boil. Brush down the sides of the pan with a pastry brush dipped in water to remove sugar crystals. Cook, without mixing, until a candy thermometer registers 300° (hard-crack stage).
- Take off from the heat. Mix in baking soda and almond butter mixture quickly. Scatter into lined pan. Let cool completely. Crack candy into pieces. Sprinkle with chocolate. Let sit at room temperature until firm. Put in airtight containers to store.

Nutrition Information

- Calories:
- Sodium:
- Fiber:
- Total Carbohydrate:
- Cholesterol:
- Protein:
- Total Fat:

335. Strawberry Parfait Holiday Bark

Serving: about 3/4 pound. | Prep: 10mins | Cook: 0mins | Ready in:

Ingredients

- 10 ounces white candy coating
- 2/3 cup chopped walnuts, toasted
- 2/3 cup freeze-dried strawberries, chopped
- 1/2 cup miniature marshmallows
- 1/2 cup coarsely chopped pretzels

Direction

- Use parchment paper to line a 15x10x1-inch pan.
- Microwave candy coating until melted; mix till smooth. Mix in pretzels, marshmallows, strawberries and walnuts then transfer to lined pan. Allow to cool. Let sit in the refrigerator until set, about an hour. Divide into pieces by breaking apart. Keep in a tightly closed container to store.

Nutrition Information

- Calories:
- Protein:
- Total Fat:
- Sodium:
- Fiber:
- Total Carbohydrate:
- Cholesterol:

336. Sugar Cone Spruce Trees

Serving: 8 trees. | Prep: 60mins | Cook: 0mins | Ready in:

Ingredients

- 8 sugar ice cream cones
- 1 can (16 ounces) vanilla frosting, divided
- 1/2 cup confectioners' sugar
- Green gel food coloring
- Assorted candy decorations

Direction

- Score carefully and cut ice cream cones to preferred heights with a serrated knife. Mix together confectioners' sugar and 3/4 cup of frosting in a small bowl, then tint green. Set leftover frosting aside.
- In the corner of a plastic bag or pastry, cut a hole, then insert star tip #77. Fill with green frosting, then pipe the cones with frosting in overlapping rows. Use candies to garnish.
- Once the frosting on trees is dry, spread a big serving platter with white frosting to look like snow. Place trees on frosted platter.

Nutrition Information

- Calories: 320 calories
- Protein: 1g protein.
- Total Fat: 10g fat (3g saturated fat)
- Sodium: 149mg sodium
- Fiber: 0 fiber)
- Total Carbohydrate: 54g carbohydrate (42g sugars
- Cholesterol: 0 cholesterol

337. Sugarless Licorice Stars

Serving: 7-9 dozen. | Prep: 15mins | Cook: 0mins | Ready in:

Ingredients

- 2 envelopes unflavored gelatin
- 4 cups diet cherry soda, divided
- 3 packages (.3 ounce each) sugar-free cherry gelatin
- 2 teaspoons anise flavoring

Direction

- Place 1/2 cup of soda in a large bowl, soften in gelatin. Boil the remaining soda in a small saucepan. Take away from the heat; put into the gelatin mixture; stir properly. Mix in the flavored gelatin till dissolved. Put in anise.
- Skim foam if necessary. Transfer into a 13x9-in. pan. Keep chilled till firm. Cut into 1-in. squares with any holiday cutters or a small

star-shaped one. Place in the refrigerator for storage.

Nutrition Information

- Calories: 3 calories
- Total Fat: 0 fat (0 saturated fat)
- Sodium: 7mg sodium
- Fiber: 0 fiber)
- Total Carbohydrate: 0 carbohydrate (0 sugars
- Cholesterol: 0 cholesterol
- Protein: 0 protein.

338. Sugarplums

Serving: 24 | Prep: | Cook: 20mins | Ready in:

Ingredients

- 4 ounces dried figs, (⅔ cup)
- ⅓ cup whole or slivered almonds (2 ounces), toasted (see Tip)
- 2 tablespoons cocoa powder
- ½ teaspoon ground cinnamon
- ¼ cup honey
- 1 tablespoon freshly grated orange zest
- 2 teaspoons amaretto, or ¼ teaspoon almond extract
- ¼ cup sugar

Direction

- In a food processor, mix cinnamon, cocoa, figs, and almonds and pulse until the figs and almonds are the size of peppercorns. Add amaretto (or almond extract), honey, and orange zest and then pulse 3 or 4 times more, just until mixed in.
- Spread sugar in a shallow dish or pie plate. Shape the fig mixture into 1-inch balls and then fold in sugar.

Nutrition Information

- Calories: 42 calories;
- Saturated Fat: 0
- Cholesterol: 0
- Protein: 1
- Sugar: 7
- Total Fat: 1
- Sodium: 1
- Fiber: 1
- Total Carbohydrate: 9

339. Sweetheart Fudge

Serving: about 5 dozen. | Prep: 30mins | Cook: 0mins | Ready in:

Ingredients

- 1-1/2 teaspoons plus 1/4 cup butter, divided
- 3 cups sugar
- 2/3 cup baking cocoa
- 1/8 teaspoon salt
- 1-1/2 cups milk
- 1 teaspoon vanilla extract

Direction

- Line an 8-inch square pan using foil then coat the foil using 1-1/2 teaspoons butter; put aside. Mix salt, cocoa and sugar in a heavy saucepan. Mix in milk until smooth; bring to a rapid boil over medium heat, mixing constantly. Cook without mixing until reaching 234 ° (soft-ball stage) on a candy thermometer. Take away from the heat; put in the leftover butter and vanilla (don't blend).
- Cool down to 110 ° (for 5 minutes). Beat using a spoon until the fudge becomes thick and starts losing its gloss. Spread instantly into prepared pan. Cool. Lift the fudge out of the pan with foil. Remove the foil; slice fudge into 1-inch squares.

Nutrition Information

- Calories: 106 calories
- Total Carbohydrate: 22g carbohydrate (20g sugars
- Cholesterol: 6mg cholesterol
- Protein: 1g protein.
- Total Fat: 2g fat (1g saturated fat)
- Sodium: 33mg sodium
- Fiber: 0 fiber)

340. Swirled Peppermint Marshmallows

Serving: 1-1/2 pounds. | Prep: 30mins | Cook: 25mins | Ready in:

Ingredients

- 2 teaspoons butter
- 3 envelopes unflavored gelatin
- 1 cup cold water, divided
- 2 cups sugar
- 1 cup light corn syrup
- 1/4 teaspoon salt
- 3/4 teaspoon peppermint extract
- 10 to 12 drops food coloring
- 1/4 cup confectioners' sugar
- 1/4 cup finely ground peppermint candies

Direction

- Use foil to line a 13x9-inch pan and butter the foil to grease; put aside.
- Scatter gelatin over half a cup of water in a big metal bowl and let sit. Mix together remaining water, salt, corn syrup and sugar in a big heavy saucepan. Boil the mixture and stir from time to time. Cook but do not stir until the mixture reaches soft ball stage at 240 degrees.
- Take it away from the heat and slowly pour into gelatin. On high speed, beat the mixture for 15 minutes until thickened and doubled in volume. Add extract and beat. Pour into prepped pan. Immediately add food coloring onto candy; to swirl, cut a knife through. Let sit while covered for 6 hours or overnight at room temperature.
- Mix together peppermint candies and confectioners' sugar. Take the marshmallows out of the pan using the foil. Cut into 1-in square pieces using a pizza cutter of knife sprayed with cooking spray; stir in confectioners' sugar mixture. Keep in a tightly sealed container and store in a cool and dry place.

Nutrition Information

- Calories: 24 calories
- Protein: 0 protein.
- Total Fat: 0 fat (0 saturated fat)
- Sodium: 8mg sodium
- Fiber: 0 fiber)
- Total Carbohydrate: 6g carbohydrate (6g sugars
- Cholesterol: 0 cholesterol

341. Tempting Truffles

Serving: 1 dozen. | Prep: 10mins | Cook: 0mins | Ready in:

Ingredients

- 1/4 cup heavy whipping cream
- 1-1/2 teaspoons butter
- 1/4 teaspoon almond extract
- 2 milk chocolate candy bars (1.55 ounces each), chopped
- 2 ounces semisweet chocolate, chopped
- 1/3 cup finely chopped hazelnuts or almonds

Direction

- Place butter and cream in a small saucepan over medium heat for 2-3 minutes or until bubbles appear around the edge of pan, whisking constantly. Separate from heat. Mix in candy bars, extract and semisweet chocolate. Mix until smooth. Push plastic wrap

onto surface of mixture. Keep in the refrigerator for 2 hours or until simple to handle.
- Form into 12 balls; roll in nuts. Keep in the refrigerator for 2 hours or until solid. Then refrigerate.

Nutrition Information

- Calories: 96 calories
- Sodium: 13mg sodium
- Fiber: 0 fiber)
- Total Carbohydrate: 8g carbohydrate (0 sugars
- Cholesterol: 10mg cholesterol
- Protein: 1g protein.
- Total Fat: 7g fat (4g saturated fat)

342. Terrific Truffles

Serving: about 5 dozen. | Prep: 45mins | Cook: 0mins | Ready in:

Ingredients

- 1 package (8 ounces) cream cheese, softened
- 3 cups confectioners' sugar
- 12 ounces semisweet chocolate, chopped
- 1-1/2 teaspoons vanilla extract
- 3/4 cup crushed peppermint candy, unsweetened shredded coconut or ground nuts

Direction

- Beat cream cheese in a large bowl until fluffy. Gradually beat confectioners' sugar into the mixture till smooth.
- Melt chocolate in a microwave; stir till smooth. Add the chocolate and vanilla into the cream cheese mixture; beat until incorporated. Refrigerate for about 1 hour.
- Make 1-in. balls out of the dough. Roll them into the crushed peppermint, coconut or nuts. For storage, keep in an airtight container in the refrigerator.

Nutrition Information

- Calories: 64 calories
- Sodium: 11mg sodium
- Fiber: 0 fiber)
- Total Carbohydrate: 10g carbohydrate (9g sugars
- Cholesterol: 4mg cholesterol
- Protein: 1g protein. Diabetic Exchanges: 1/2 starch
- Total Fat: 3g fat (2g saturated fat)

343. Three Layer Fudge

Serving: 1 pound. | Prep: 0mins | Cook: 0mins | Ready in:

Ingredients

- CHOCOLATE LAYER:
- 2 teaspoons plus 2 tablespoons butter, divided
- 2 cups sugar
- 3/4 cup half-and-half cream
- 2 ounces unsweetened chocolate
- 2 tablespoons light corn syrup
- 1/2 teaspoon salt
- 1/2 teaspoon vanilla extract
- CHERRY ALMOND LAYER:
- 1 teaspoon plus 2 tablespoons butter, divided
- 2 cups sugar
- 3/4 cup half-and-half cream
- 2 tablespoons light corn syrup
- 1/2 teaspoon salt
- 1/4 cup chopped maraschino cherries, drained and patted dry
- 1/2 teaspoon almond extract
- 2 to 3 drops food coloring, optional
- COCONUT VANILLA LAYER:
- 1 teaspoon plus 2 tablespoons butter, divided
- 2 cups sugar
- 3/4 cup half-and-half cream
- 2 tablespoons light corn syrup
- 1/2 teaspoon salt

- 1/2 cup flaked coconut
- 1 teaspoon vanilla extract

Direction

- Use foil to line a 9-inch square pan; use 1 tsp. of butter to grease foil. Put aside.
- For the chocolate layer, butter sides of a big heavy saucepan using 1 tsp. of butter; put in salt, corn syrup, chocolate, cream and sugar. Cook and whisk on medium heat till the sugar dissolves. Boil. Boil till the mixture reaches 236 degrees (at the soft-ball stage), whisk once in a while. Take it off the heat.
- Put in the leftover butter and vanilla (don't whisk). Let cool down to 110 degrees, do not whisk. Whisk using a clean dry wooden spoon till the fudge starts to become thick; put in the nuts. Keep whisking for roughly 10 minutes or till the fudge thickens and starts to lose the gloss. Instantly spread to the prepped pan; put aside.
- For the cherry almond layer, use 1 tsp. of butter to grease sides of a clean big heavy saucepan; put in salt, corn syrup, cream and sugar. Cook and whisk on medium heat till the sugar dissolves. Boil. Boil till the mixture reaches 236 degrees (at the soft-ball stage), whisk once in a while. Take it off the heat.
- Put in the leftover butter and almond extract (don't whisk). Let cool to 110 degrees, do not whisk. Whisk using a clean dry wooden spoon till the fudge starts to become thick; put in the food coloring (optional) and cherries. Keep whisking for roughly 8 minutes or till the fudge thickens and starts to lose the gloss. Instantly spread on top of the first layer.
- For the coconut vanilla layer, use 1 tsp. of butter to grease sides of a clean big heavy saucepan; put in salt, corn syrup, cream and sugar. Cook and whisk on medium heat till the sugar dissolves. Boil. Boil till the mixture reaches 236 degrees (at the soft-ball stage), whisk once in a while. Take it off the heat.
- Put in the leftover butter and vanilla (don't whisk). Let cool to 110 degrees, do not whisk. Whisk using a clean dry wooden spoon till the fudge starts to become thick; put in the coconut. Keep whisking for roughly 8 minutes or till the fudge thickens and starts to lose the gloss. Instantly spread on top of the second layer.
- Score into square pieces while still warmed. With the foil, lift the fudge from the pan. Get rid of the foil; chop the fudge into 1-inch square pieces. Keep stored in an airtight container.

Nutrition Information

- Calories:
- Protein:
- Total Fat:
- Sodium:
- Fiber:
- Total Carbohydrate:
- Cholesterol:

344. Three Chocolate Fudge

Serving: about 5-1/2 pounds. | Prep: 15mins | Cook: 20mins | Ready in:

Ingredients

- 1 tablespoon butter
- 3-1/3 cups sugar
- 1 cup packed dark brown sugar
- 1 can (12 ounces) evaporated milk
- 1 cup butter, cubed
- 32 large marshmallows, halved
- 1 teaspoon vanilla extract
- 2 cups (12 ounces) semisweet chocolate chips
- 14 ounces milk chocolate, chopped
- 2 ounces semisweet chocolate, chopped
- 2 cups chopped pecans, toasted

Direction

- Line foil over a 15x10x1-inch pan; use 1 tablespoon butter to grease the foil.

- Combine cubed butter, milk, and sugar in a heavy large saucepan. Heat over medium heat, stirring constantly, until mixture comes to a rolling bowl; cook while stirring, for 5 minutes. Turn off the heat. Mix in vanilla and marshmallows until combined.
- Slowly whisk in chopped chocolate and chocolate chips until melted. Mix in pecans. Instantly pour mixture into the buttered pan, spreading evenly. Chill in the fridge until set, about 1 hour. Take fudge out of the pan using foil. Take off the foil; divide the fudge into squares about 1 inch. Place fudges between layers of waxed paper in an airtight container to store.

Nutrition Information

- Calories: 79 calories
- Total Fat: 4g fat (2g saturated fat)
- Sodium: 16mg sodium
- Fiber: 0 fiber)
- Total Carbohydrate: 11g carbohydrate (10g sugars
- Cholesterol: 5mg cholesterol
- Protein: 1g protein.

345. Toasted Coconut Truffles

Serving: about 5-1/2 dozen. | Prep: 30mins | Cook: 0mins | Ready in:

Ingredients

- 4 cups (24 ounces) semisweet chocolate chips
- 1 package (8 ounces) cream cheese, softened and cubed
- 3/4 cup sweetened condensed milk
- 3 teaspoons vanilla extract
- 2 teaspoons water
- 1 pound white candy coating, coarsely chopped
- 2 tablespoons sweetened shredded coconut, finely chopped and toasted

Direction

- Melt chocolate chips in a microwave-safe bowl; mix till smooth. Add water, vanilla, milk and cream cheese; use hand mixer to beat till blended. Cover; refrigerate for 1 1/2 hours till easy to handle.
- Form to 1-inch balls; put on waxed paper-lined baking sheets. Cover loosely; refrigerate till firm for 1-2 hours.
- Melt candy coating in the microwave; mix till smooth. In coating, dip balls; let excess drip off. Put onto waxed paper-lined baking sheets then sprinkle coconut. Refrigerate for 15 minutes till firm. Keep in the fridge in an airtight container.

Nutrition Information

- Calories: 220 calories
- Sodium: 32mg sodium
- Fiber: 1g fiber)
- Total Carbohydrate: 27g carbohydrate (25g sugars
- Cholesterol: 10mg cholesterol
- Protein: 2g protein.
- Total Fat: 13g fat (9g saturated fat)

346. Toffee Peanut Clusters

Serving: 5 dozen. | Prep: 30mins | Cook: 0mins | Ready in:

Ingredients

- 1-1/2 pounds milk chocolate candy coating, coarsely chopped
- 1 jar (16 ounces) dry roasted peanuts
- 1 package (8 ounces) milk chocolate English toffee bits

Direction

- Put candy coating in a microwave, melt the candy coating and stir it till becomes smooth.

Mix in toffee bits and peanuts. Line baking sheets by waxed paper and use the toffee mixture to make rounded tablespoonful drops on the baking sheets. Allow the drops to sit till they are set. Keep in an airtight container.

Nutrition Information

- Calories: 123 calories
- Protein: 2g protein. Diabetic Exchanges: 1-1/2 fat
- Total Fat: 8g fat (4g saturated fat)
- Sodium: 78mg sodium
- Fiber: 1g fiber)
- Total Carbohydrate: 11g carbohydrate (9g sugars
- Cholesterol: 3mg cholesterol

347. Tootsie Roll Fudge

Serving: about 2 pounds. | Prep: 15mins | Cook: 15mins | Ready in:

Ingredients

- 1 teaspoon plus 2 tablespoons butter, divided
- 2 cups Tootsie Roll Midgees
- 2 tablespoons peanut butter
- 3-3/4 cups confectioners' sugar
- 2 tablespoons milk
- 1 teaspoon vanilla extract
- 1 cup chopped pecans
- 1/3 cup green and red M&M's

Direction

- Use foil to line a 9-in. square pan. Use 1 teaspoon butter to grease the foil; put aside. Melt the Tootsie Rolls, peanut butter and the rest of the butter together in a heavy saucepan on low heat, stir continuously. Stir the confectioners' sugar, milk and vanilla slowly into the mix (the mixture will thicken a lot). Fold the pecans into the mixture.

- Spread this mixture into the prepared pan. Score the surface into 1-in. squares with a sharp knife. Push an M&M's candy into each square's center. Let it cool down. Take the fudge out of pan using the foil; slice into squares. For storage, keep in an airtight container.

Nutrition Information

- Calories:
- Cholesterol:
- Protein:
- Total Fat:
- Sodium:
- Fiber:
- Total Carbohydrate:

348. Trail Mix Slices

Serving: about 2-1/2 dozen. | Prep: 15mins | Cook: 0mins | Ready in:

Ingredients

- 2-1/2 cups sliced almonds
- 1/4 cup honey
- 1/8 to 1/4 teaspoon almond extract
- 1-1/4 cups finely chopped dried cherries or dried cranberries
- 1 cup mixed nuts, finely chopped
- 2/3 cup M&M's minis

Direction

- Process almonds till finely ground in a food processor; add extract and honey slowly while processing. Put into big bowl; mix in candies, mixed nuts and cherries. Split mixture in half; form each to 8-inch long log. Tightly wrap in plastic; freeze till firm for 1 hour.
- Unwrap; cut rolls to 1/2-inch slices. Keep in airtight containers between waxed paper pieces.

Nutrition Information

- Calories:
- Total Fat:
- Sodium:
- Fiber:
- Total Carbohydrate:
- Cholesterol:
- Protein:

349. Triple Chocolate Fudge

Serving: 6-3/4 pounds. | Prep: 20mins | Cook: 25mins | Ready in:

Ingredients

- 4 teaspoons plus 1/2 cup butter, divided
- 4-1/2 cups sugar
- 1 can (12 ounces) evaporated milk
- 1 teaspoon salt
- 16 ounces German sweet chocolate, chopped
- 2 cups (12 ounces) semisweet chocolate chips
- 1 package (11-1/2 ounces) milk chocolate chips
- 2 jars (7 ounces each) marshmallow creme
- 4 cups chopped pecans or walnuts, toasted
- 2 teaspoons vanilla extract

Direction

- Line foil over 2 pans of 13x9-inch; use 4 teaspoons of butter to grease the foil. Combine the rest of butter with salt, milk, and sugar in a heavy Dutch oven. Boil over medium heat, whisking constantly. Cook, undisturbed, until mixture reaches soft-ball stage or a candy thermometer registers 234°.
- Take off from the heat. Whisk in chocolate chips and German sweet chocolate until no lumps remain. Fold in vanilla, pecans, and marshmallow creme. Pour mixture into the prepared pans, spread.
- Chill mixture in the fridge until set, for 60 minutes. Take fudge out of the pan using the foil. Remove the foil; divide fudge into squares about 1 inch. Place in airtight containers to store.

Nutrition Information

- Calories: 64 calories
- Protein: 1g protein. Diabetic Exchanges: 1/2 starch
- Total Fat: 3g fat (1g saturated fat)
- Sodium: 17mg sodium
- Fiber: 0 fiber)
- Total Carbohydrate: 9g carbohydrate (8g sugars
- Cholesterol: 2mg cholesterol

350. Triple Nut Candy

Serving: 2 pounds. | Prep: 30mins | Cook: 35mins | Ready in:

Ingredients

- 1 cup walnut halves
- 1 cup pecan halves
- 1 cup Brazil nuts, halved
- 1 teaspoon butter
- 1-1/2 cups sugar
- 1 cup heavy whipping cream
- 1/2 cup light corn syrup

Direction

- Layer the walnuts, pecans and Brazil nuts onto a baking sheet in a single layer. Bake until toasted and golden brown at 350° for about 4-8 minutes, stir only once. Let them cool down on a wire rack. Use foil to line an 8-in. square pan; use butter to grease the foil and put aside.
- Mix together the sugar, cream and corn syrup in a large heavy saucepan. Heat until boiling on medium heat, stir continuously. Stir the toasted nuts into the mixture. Cook, do not stir, until soft-ball stage (a candy thermometer reads 238°).

- Take off from heat. Using a wooden spoon, stir till creamy and thickened. Spread into the prepared pan quickly; cool down. Refrigerate, covered, for 8 hours or overnight.
- Lift the candy out of the pan with foil; discard foil. Slice the candy into squares. For storage, keep in an airtight container in the refrigerator.

Nutrition Information

- Calories: 75 calories
- Protein: 1g protein. Diabetic Exchanges: 1 fat
- Total Fat: 5g fat (1g saturated fat)
- Sodium: 5mg sodium
- Fiber: 0 fiber
- Total Carbohydrate: 7g carbohydrate (6g sugars
- Cholesterol: 5mg cholesterol

351. Tropical Nut Bark

Serving: 1-3/4 pounds. | Prep: 10mins | Cook: 0mins | Ready in:

Ingredients

- 1-1/2 pounds white baking chocolate, chopped
- 2/3 cup coarsely chopped macadamia nuts, toasted
- 1/3 cup sweetened shredded coconut, toasted
- 1/3 cup chopped crystallized ginger
- 1/3 cup dried mangoes, chopped

Direction

- Microwave chocolate in a microwavable bowl until melted; mix until smooth. Mix together mangoes, ginger, coconut and macadamia nuts. Set aside half a cup. Mix the rest of the nut mixture into melted chocolate.
- In a baking sheet lined with waxed paper, spread out mixture. Scatter saved nut mixture on top. Put in the refrigerator for an hour till firm. Break apart the bar into pieces. Keep in a tightly closed container.

Nutrition Information

- Calories: 179 calories
- Protein: 2g protein.
- Total Fat: 11g fat (6g saturated fat)
- Sodium: 46mg sodium
- Fiber: 0 fiber
- Total Carbohydrate: 18g carbohydrate (16g sugars
- Cholesterol: 5mg cholesterol

352. True Love Truffles

Serving: 8 dozen. | Prep: 50mins | Cook: 0mins | Ready in:

Ingredients

- 1 tablespoon plus 3/4 cup butter, divided
- 1-1/2 cups sugar
- 1 can (5 ounces) evaporated milk
- 2 packages (4.67 ounces each) mint Andes candies
- 1 jar (7 ounces) marshmallow creme
- 1 teaspoon vanilla extract
- 22 ounces white baking chocolate, divided
- 1/2 cup semisweet chocolate chips
- Green food coloring, optional

Direction

- Use 1 tablespoon butter to butter 15x10x1-in. pan; put aside. Boil leftover butter, milk and sugar in heavy saucepan on medium heat, constantly mixing. Lower heat; mix and cook till candy thermometer reads soft-ball stage at 236°. Take off heat; mix candies in till mixture blends well and candies melt. Mix vanilla and marshmallow crème in; spread in prepped pan. Cover; refrigerate for an hour.

- Slice to 96 pieces; roll each to ball, it'll be soft. Put onto waxed paper-lined baking sheet.
- Melt 18-oz. white chocolate and the chocolate chips in heavy saucepan/microwave-safe bowl; dip the balls into melted chocolate. Put on waxed paper; let harden. Melt leftover white chocolate; if desired, add food coloring. Drizzle on truffles; keep in airtight container.

Nutrition Information

- Calories: 161 calories
- Sodium: 52mg sodium
- Fiber: 0 fiber)
- Total Carbohydrate: 21g carbohydrate (19g sugars
- Cholesterol: 12mg cholesterol
- Protein: 1g protein.
- Total Fat: 9g fat (5g saturated fat)

353. Truffle Topiary

Serving: 11 dozen. | Prep: 60mins | Cook: 15mins | Ready in:

Ingredients

- 3 packages (12 ounces each) semisweet chocolate chips, divided
- 2-1/4 cups sweetened condensed milk, divided
- 1/2 teaspoon orange extract
- 1/2 to 1 teaspoon peppermint extract
- 1/2 teaspoon almond extract
- 3/4 pound white candy coating, coarsely chopped
- 3/4 pound dark chocolate candy coating, coarsely chopped
- 1/2 cup ground almonds
- 1 each 6- and 8-inch Styrofoam cones or a single 12-inch cone

Direction

- Melt 1 chocolate chips package in a microwave-safe bowl. Add 3/4 cup of condensed milk; stir well. Mix orange extract in; cover. Chill till firm to shape for 45 minutes. Repeat twice more with leftover milk and chips, adding almond extract to 1 portion and peppermint extract to the other.
- Shape truffles: Form chilled mixture to 1-inch balls; put on 3 different waxed paper-lined baking sheets and chill till firm for 1-2 hours.
- In a microwave-safe bowl, melt white candy coating. In coating, dip orange-flavored balls; put on waxed paper. Let harden. Melt leftover candy coating; dip balls again to cover thoroughly. Let them harden.
- Roll almond-flavored truffles into ground almonds.
- The Tree: Brush leftover chocolate on Styrofoam cones if you want. With toothpicks, stick an end in each truffle then other end into cone, covering the whole cone with truffles.

Nutrition Information

- Calories: 83 calories
- Cholesterol: 2mg cholesterol
- Protein: 1g protein.
- Total Fat: 4g fat (3g saturated fat)
- Sodium: 7mg sodium
- Fiber: 1g fiber)
- Total Carbohydrate: 11g carbohydrate (10g sugars

354. Truffle Topiary Centerpiece

Serving: | Prep: 45mins | Cook: 0mins | Ready in:

Ingredients

- Gold spray paint
- 5-inch clay pot
- Floral foam to fit inside pot
- New small flat paintbrush

- 5-inch Styrofoam ball
- Milk chocolate candy coating, melted (about 1/2 cup)
- 12-inch length of 3/8-inch wooded dowel
- Double-sided transparent tape
- 2-1/3 yards of gold metallic cord
- Craft scissors
- White (tacky) glue
- 18-inch square of gold-flecked tulle netting
- Craft wire
- Two large wire-edged bows
- Toothpicks
- 60 to 70 Coconut Truffles (recipe on opposite page)
- 60 to 70 paper or foil candy cups

Direction

- Spray-paint the clay pot gold. Fill pot with the floral foam when dry.
- Cover Styrofoam ball with melted chocolate with a paintbrush; let harden.
- Mark dowel, 1 1/2-in. from other end with a pencil. Put several double-sided tape pieces on dowel between the markings. Cut excess cord away; secure gluing ends.
- Insert long unwrapped dowel's end straight down and up in middle of floral foam. Put pot in middle of the tulle netting; bring netting up on all sides so that you can cover pot. Secure netting to dowel with craft wire right above pot's top; put netting to cover wire. Trim extra netting as desired then attach bows on opposite sides of pot's top. As desired, trim ribbon ends.
- Use pencil to create hole into chocolate-covered Styrofoam ball; center hole inside ball. Push the ball onto dowel's end till wood dowel is covered. Make sure dowel and ball are straight and centered.
- Insert toothpick in top center of ball; leave about 1/3 toothpick exposed. Put truffle in candy cup; push truffle and the cup carefully onto exposed toothpick's end. Repeat till ball is covered completely with truffles.

Nutrition Information

- Calories: 142 calories
- Cholesterol: 9mg cholesterol
- Protein: 1g protein.
- Total Fat: 9g fat (6g saturated fat)
- Sodium: 45mg sodium
- Fiber: 1g fiber)
- Total Carbohydrate: 17g carbohydrate (15g sugars

355. Two Tiered Fudge

Serving: about 2-1/2 pounds. | Prep: 40mins | Cook: 40mins | Ready in:

Ingredients

- CHOCOLATE NUT LAYER:
- 2 teaspoons plus 2 tablespoons butter, divided
- 2-1/4 cups sugar
- 1 cup milk
- 3 ounces unsweetened chocolate
- 1 tablespoon light corn syrup
- 1 teaspoon vanilla extract
- 1/2 cup chopped nuts
- CHERRY VANILLA LAYER:
- 1 teaspoon plus 2 tablespoons butter, divided
- 2-1/2 cups sugar
- 1/2 cup half-and-half cream
- 1/2 cup milk
- 1 tablespoon light corn syrup
- 1/4 teaspoon salt
- 1 teaspoon vanilla extract
- 1/3 cup chopped candied cherries

Direction

- Use foil to line a 9-inch square pan; then butter the foil using 1 teaspoon butter. Put it aside.
- To make the chocolate nut layer, use 1 teaspoon butter to grease a large heavy saucepan's sides; add in the corn syrup, milk, chocolate and sugar. Cook and stir on medium heat until the sugar dissolves. Heat till boiling.

Boil till the mixture reaches soft-ball stage (a thermometer reads 236°), stir from time to time. Take off from heat.

- Add in the remaining butter and vanilla (do not stir). Let it cool down to 110° without stirring. Use a clean dry wooden spoon to stir until fudge begins to thicken; add nuts. Keep on stirring till the fudge thickens and starts to lose its shine, for about 10 minutes. Spread it into the prepared pan right away; put aside.
- To make cherry vanilla layer, use 1 teaspoon butter to grease a clean large heavy saucepan's sides; add in the salt, cream, milk, corn syrup and sugar. Cook and stir on medium heat till the sugar dissolves. Heat till boiling. Boil until mixture reaches soft-ball stage (thermometer reads 236°), stir from time to time. Take off from heat.
- Add in the remaining butter and vanilla (do not stir). Let it cool down to 110° without stirring. Use a clean dry wooden spoon to stir till the fudge begins to thicken; add in the cherries. Continue stirring until fudge becomes thick and begins lose its shine, about 8 minutes. Spread on top of the first layer right away.
- While still warm, score into squares. Use foil to lift the fudge out of pan. Throw the foil; slice the fudge into 1-inch squares. Keep in an airtight container.

Nutrition Information

- Calories: 70 calories
- Sodium: 19mg sodium
- Fiber: 0 fiber)
- Total Carbohydrate: 13g carbohydrate (12g sugars
- Cholesterol: 3mg cholesterol
- Protein: 1g protein.
- Total Fat: 2g fat (1g saturated fat)

356. Walnut Caramel Treats

Serving: 4 pounds. | Prep: 20mins | Cook: 0mins | Ready in:

Ingredients

- 2 teaspoons plus 1/3 cup butter, divided
- 2 packages (11-1/2 ounces each) milk chocolate chips, divided
- 4 tablespoons shortening, divided
- 2 packages (14 ounces each) caramels
- 1/4 cup water
- 3 cups chopped walnuts

Direction

- Line foil on ungreased 9-in. square pan. Use 2 tsp. butter to grease foil; put aside.
- Melt 2 tbsp. shortening and 1 package of chips in a microwave/heavy saucepan; mix until smooth. Put in lined pan; refrigerate for 20 minutes.
- Meanwhile, mix together leftover butter, water and caramels in a big heavy saucepan on medium low heat; cook and stir until smooth and caramels melt. Mix in walnuts; put on chocolate layer. Refrigerate for 45 minutes.
- Melt leftover shortening and chips in a microwave/heavy saucepan; spread on caramel layer. Cover; refrigerate until firm for at least 2 hours.
- Lift candy from pan using fold. Discard foil and cut candy to squares; keep refrigerated.

Nutrition Information

- Calories: 232 calories
- Cholesterol: 10mg cholesterol
- Protein: 5g protein.
- Total Fat: 16g fat (6g saturated fat)
- Sodium: 69mg sodium
- Fiber: 1g fiber)
- Total Carbohydrate: 19g carbohydrate (15g sugars

357. Walnut Caramels

Serving: 3-3/4 pounds (117 pieces). | Prep: 15mins | Cook: 20mins |Ready in:

Ingredients

- 2 teaspoons butter
- 1/3 cup butter, cubed
- 2 cups sugar
- 2 cups heavy whipping cream, divided
- 1 cup light corn syrup
- 1-1/2 cups chopped walnuts
- 1 teaspoon vanilla extract

Direction

- Line foil on a pan, 13x9-inch in size; use 2 teaspoons of butter to grease the foil.
- Mix corn syrup, a cup cream, sugar and cubed butter in a heavy, big saucepan. Cook and mix on moderate heat till a candy thermometer registers 238° for soft-ball stage. Mix in leftover cream very gradually so mixture will not stop boiling.
- Brush down the pan's sides with pastry brush dunked in water to remove sugar crystals. Cook and mix till thermometer registers 245° for firm-ball stage.
- Take off from heat; mix in vanilla and walnuts. Quickly put to lined pan, avoid scraping the saucepan. Rest for about 5 hours up to overnight, till firm.
- Remove candy from pan with foil; peel off foil. Slice caramel with buttered knife into an-inch squares. Use waxed paper to wrap each caramel; twist the ends.

Nutrition Information

- Calories:
- Protein:
- Total Fat:
- Sodium:
- Fiber:
- Total Carbohydrate:
- Cholesterol:

358. White Candy Bark

Serving: 2 pounds. | Prep: 20mins | Cook: 0mins |Ready in:

Ingredients

- 1 tablespoon butter, melted
- 2 packages (10 to 12 ounces each) white baking chips
- 1-1/2 cups walnut halves
- 1 cup dried cranberries
- 1/4 teaspoon ground nutmeg

Direction

- Line foil onto a 15x10x1-inch baking pan. Then brush using butter. Heat white chips in microwave on high until melted. Mix until smooth. Mix in nutmeg, cranberries and walnuts. Scatter into the prepared pan. Refrigerate until firm. Then crack apart into pieces.

Nutrition Information

- Calories: 46 calories
- Protein: 1g protein.
- Total Fat: 3g fat (1g saturated fat)
- Sodium: 6mg sodium
- Fiber: 0 fiber)
- Total Carbohydrate: 5g carbohydrate (1g sugars
- Cholesterol: 1mg cholesterol

359. White Chocolate Coconut Fudge

Serving: 2 pounds. | Prep: 10mins | Cook: 35mins | Ready in:

Ingredients

- 1-1/2 teaspoons plus 1/2 cup butter, divided
- 2 cups sugar
- 1 can (12 ounces) evaporated milk
- 8 ounces white baking chocolate, coarsely chopped
- 1 cup miniature marshmallows
- 1/2 cup sweetened shredded coconut
- 1/2 cup coarsely chopped walnuts
- 1 teaspoon vanilla extract

Direction

- Use foil to line a 9-inch square pan and butter the foil with 1-1/2 teaspoons butter; put aside. Mix the remaining butter, milk and sugar in a big heavy saucepan. Heat up to a boil over medium-low heat, mixing continuously. Cook and mix for 30-40 minutes or until a candy thermometer registers 234° (soft-ball stage).
- Take off from the heat; mix in marshmallows and white chocolate until melted. Mix in vanilla, nuts and coconut. Put into buttered pan. Let sit at room temperature until cool.
- Take fudge out of pan using foil; slice into 1-inch squares. Put in an airtight container to store in the fridge.

Nutrition Information

- Calories: 60 calories
- Total Carbohydrate: 8g carbohydrate (7g sugars
- Cholesterol: 5mg cholesterol
- Protein: 1g protein. Diabetic Exchanges: 1/2 starch
- Total Fat: 3g fat (2g saturated fat)
- Sodium: 17mg sodium
- Fiber: 0 fiber)

360. White Chocolate Latte Cups

Serving: 1-1/2 dozen. | Prep: 30mins | Cook: 20mins | Ready in:

Ingredients

- 1 cup (6 ounces) dark chocolate chips
- 2 teaspoons shortening
- FILLING:
- 3 tablespoons sugar
- 3/4 cup heavy whipping cream
- 1/4 cup coffee liqueur
- 1 teaspoon instant espresso powder
- 14 ounces white baking chocolate, chopped
- Chocolate-covered coffee beans

Direction

- Microwave shortening and chocolate chips until melted; mix until smooth. Brush the inside of eighteen 2-in. foil muffin tin liners with half teaspoon melted chocolate using a narrow pastry brush. Chill for 15 minutes or until set. Keep layering twice. Refrigerate until firm.
- Cook sugar in a big heavy skillet over medium-low heat until melted and has a golden amber color. Mix in cream gradually; cook and mix until sugar has dissolved. Put in espresso powder and liqueur; mix until smooth. Mix in white chocolate until melted. Put into a small bowl; chill, covered, for 1-2 hours or until thickened slightly.
- Peel off foil liners carefully from chocolate cups and dispose. Scoop or pipe filling into the cups; top with coffee beans. Put in an airtight container to store in the fridge.

Nutrition Information

- Calories: 255 calories
- Sodium: 27mg sodium
- Fiber: 0 fiber)

- Total Carbohydrate: 25g carbohydrate (22g sugars
- Cholesterol: 18mg cholesterol
- Protein: 3g protein.
- Total Fat: 16g fat (10g saturated fat)

361. White Chocolate Marshmallow Fudge

Serving: 8-9 dozen. | Prep: 30mins | Cook: 0mins | Ready in:

Ingredients

- 3 cups sugar
- 1 cup evaporated milk
- 1/2 cup butter
- 1 jar (7 ounces) marshmallow creme
- 1-2/3 cups white chocolate chips
- 1 cup chopped pecans or almonds, toasted

Direction

- Put butter, milk and sugar in a heavy saucepan; put over low heat and boil while stirring continuously. Cook until a candy thermometer reads 234 degrees, soft-ball stage.
- Take away from the heat; mix in nuts, chocolate chips and marshmallow crème to melt chocolate and marshmallow. Grease a 13x9-inch pan and spread mixture in the prepared pan. Allow to cool then cut.

Nutrition Information

- Calories: 60 calories
- Cholesterol: 4mg cholesterol
- Protein: 0 protein.
- Total Fat: 3g fat (1g saturated fat)
- Sodium: 15mg sodium
- Fiber: 0 fiber)
- Total Carbohydrate: 9g carbohydrate (7g sugars

362. White Chocolate Peppermint Fudge

Serving: 2 pounds. | Prep: 10mins | Cook: 10mins | Ready in:

Ingredients

- 1-1/2 teaspoons plus 1/4 cup butter, softened, divided
- 2 cups sugar
- 1/2 cup sour cream
- 12 squares (1 ounce each) white baking chocolate, chopped
- 1 jar (7 ounces) marshmallow cream
- 1/2 cup crushed peppermint candy
- 1/2 teaspoon peppermint extract

Direction

- Use foil to line a 9-in. square pan. Use 1-1/2 teaspoons of butter to grease the foil; put aside.
- In a large heavy saucepan, combine the remaining butter, sour cream and sugar. Over medium heat, cook and stir until sugar dissolves. Heat to a rapid boil; cook and stir until candy reaches the soft-ball stage (a candy thermometer reads 234°), for about 5 minutes.
- Take off the heat; mix in marshmallow creme and white chocolate until melted. Fold in the extract and peppermint candy. Transfer into the prepared pan. Refrigerate until firm.
- Lift the fudge out of the pan using the foil. Take off the foil gently; slice the fudge into 1-in. squares. Keep in the refrigerator.

Nutrition Information

- Calories: 60 calories
- Cholesterol: 2mg cholesterol
- Protein: 0 protein.
- Total Fat: 2g fat (1g saturated fat)
- Sodium: 11mg sodium
- Fiber: 0 fiber)

- Total Carbohydrate: 10g carbohydrate (10g sugars

363. White Christmas Candy

Serving: 25 | Prep: 10mins | Cook: 5mins |Ready in:

Ingredients

- 1 (12 ounce) package white chocolate chips
- 2 tablespoons creamy peanut butter
- 2 cups crispy rice cereal (such as Rice Krispies®)
- 1 cup mini marshmallows
- 1 cup lightly salted peanuts
- 1 tablespoon multi-colored sprinkles, or more to taste (optional)

Direction

- In a large microwaveable bowl, combine peanut butter and white chocolate chips.
- Microwave for 1 minute on high power; whisk using a spatula. Keep cooking in 30-second periods in the microwave; whisk until no lumps remain. Fold in peanuts, marshmallows, and rice cereal.
- Drop white chocolate mixture onto a sheet of waxed paper by spoonfuls. Scatter sprinkles over top of each mound. Put aside and allow to cool for half an hour.

Nutrition Information

- Calories: 136 calories;
- Sodium: 87
- Total Carbohydrate: 13.1
- Cholesterol: 3
- Protein: 2.8
- Total Fat: 8.5

364. White Pecan Fudge

Serving: about 3-1/2 pounds (about 6-1/2 dozen). | Prep: 10mins | Cook: 10mins |Ready in:

Ingredients

- 1 tablespoon plus 1/2 cup butter, divided
- 2-1/2 cups miniature marshmallows
- 2-1/4 cups sugar
- 1 cup heavy whipping cream
- 16 ounces white baking chocolate, finely chopped
- 2 teaspoons vanilla extract
- 2 cups chopped pecans

Direction

- Use the foil to line the 9-inch square pan. Grease foil using 0.5 tablespoon of the butter and put aside. Use half tablespoon of the butter to butter sides of the big and heavy saucepan. Chop the leftover butter into the small portions and add into the big heat-proof bowl; put in marshmallows and put aside.
- In buttered saucepan, mix the cream and sugar. Cook and whisk on medium heat till the mixture boils. Cook for 2 minutes with cover to dissolve any of the sugar crystals. Remove the cover; cook on medium heat, no whisking, till the candy thermometer reaches 234 degrees (a soft-ball stage).
- Take out of heat. Add on top of marshmallows and butter; whisk till melted. Put in chocolate. Keep whisking till the mixture and chocolate become smooth. Whisk in the nuts and vanilla. Add to the prepped pan. Chill till firm. Lift from the pan; take off the foil and chop into 1-inch square pieces. Keep in the airtight container at the room temperature.

Nutrition Information

- Calories: 73 calories
- Total Fat: 5g fat (2g saturated fat)
- Sodium: 16mg sodium
- Fiber: 0 fiber)

- Total Carbohydrate: 8g carbohydrate (7g sugars
- Cholesterol: 8mg cholesterol
- Protein: 0 protein.

365. Wonderful Candies Two Ways

Serving: 9 dozen. | Prep: 02hours30mins | Cook: 0mins | Ready in:

Ingredients

- 1 cup butter, melted
- 1 can (14 ounces) sweetened condensed milk
- 3 pounds confectioners' sugar
- COOKIES & CREME BONBONS:
- 1/2 cup cream-filled chocolate sandwich cookie crumbs
- 1 pound white candy coating, melted
- CHOCOLATE-COVERED CHERRIES:
- 54 maraschino cherries (about two 10-ounce jars), patted dry
- 1 pound milk chocolate candy coating, melted

Direction

- Combine the butter and milk in a large bowl. Gradually beat confectioners' sugar into the mixture until it makes a smooth dough. Split it in half; use plastic wrap to cover.
- To make bonbons, into one portion of dough, stir the cookie crumbs. Make 1-in. balls out of the dough. Dip them into the white candy coating; let the excess drip off. Put onto baking sheets lined with waxed paper. Chill till firm.
- To make chocolate-covered cherries, make 1-in. balls out of the remaining portion of dough; flatten them out to 2-in. circles. Use each circle to wrap around a cherry and reshape them gently into a ball. Dip the balls into the milk chocolate coating; let the excess drip off. Put onto baking sheets lined with waxed paper. Refrigerate until firm. For storage, keep in an airtight container.

Nutrition Information

- Calories: 127 calories
- Protein: 0 protein.
- Total Fat: 5g fat (3g saturated fat)
- Sodium: 24mg sodium
- Fiber: 0 fiber)
- Total Carbohydrate: 21g carbohydrate (20g sugars
- Cholesterol: 6mg cholesterol

Index

A

Almond 3,4,5,6,18,41,72,73,78,85,99,102,104,106,133,136,137,150,172,173

Apple 4,74,86

Apricot 4,72,75

B

Baking 63,69,94,112

Banana 4,75

Brazil nut 181

Brie 31

Butter 3,4,5,6,12,27,42,43,47,50,53,54,55,59,60,66,67,78,79,94,95,96,99,115,116,118,119,120,134,135,147,151,152,153,154,158,163,164,167,173

C

Cake 3,21

Caramel 3,4,5,6,11,12,17,29,32,44,51,52,60,66,81,82,83,84,87,96,106,119,124,128,136,155,185,186

Cashew 3,4,5,6,11,22,84,88,107,165

Cheese 5,114

Cherry 3,4,13,14,53,72,85

Chips 152

Chocolate 3,4,5,6,7,13,14,15,16,17,19,23,25,28,31,39,43,48,49,54,59,62,69,75,86,87,88,89,90,91,92,93,94,95,96,97,98,99,100,101,102,107,116,119,121,135,139,141,142,145,150,151,156,159,178,181,187,188

Cinnamon 4,5,6,54,104,105,125,156

Cloves 63

Coconut 3,4,5,6,7,18,19,20,24,25,42,44,73,106,107,108,109,110,111,136,137,148,162,164,179,184,187

Coffee 3,20

Cranberry 3,5,6,22,23,113,114,162

Cream 3,4,5,6,11,15,19,22,23,24,27,43,69,75,81,89,107,114,115,134,139,142,143,144,148,150,152,154,164,171

Crisps 3,5,16,67,138

Crumble 140

D

Date 3,25

E

Egg 3,5,11,15,16,19,25,26,27,31,35,42,43,48,49,125

F

Fat 8,9,10,11,12,13,14,15,16,17,18,19,20,21,22,23,24,25,26,27,28,29,30,31,32,33,34,35,36,37,38,39,40,41,42,43,44,45,46,47,48,49,50,51,52,53,54,55,56,57,58,59,60,61,62,63,64,65,66,67,68,69,70,71,72,73,74,75,76,77,78,79,80,81,82,83,84,85,86,87,88,89,90,91,92,93,94,95,96,97,98,99,100,101,102,103,104,105,106,107,108,109,110,111,112,113,114,115,116,117,118,119,120,121,122,123,124,125,126,127,128,129,130,131,132,133,134,135,136,137,138,139,140,141,142,143,144,145,146,147,148,149,150,151,152,153,154,155,156,157,158,159,160,161,162,163,164,165,166,167,168,169,170,171,172,173,174,175,176,177,178,179,180,181,182,183,184,185,186,187,188,189,190

Fish 71

Fruit 3,5,38,55,126

Fudge 3,4,5,6,7,22,23,30,34,35,37,45,61,72,76,79,80,84,85,91,93,113,115,117,119,120,122,123,124,125,126,127,135,137,14

1,143,149,153,156,158,159,160,161,164,165,166,168,170,171,172,175,177,178,180,181,184,187,188,189

G

Gin 3,4,5,29,57,61,113

H

Hazelnut 4,5,91,92,112,129,131

Heart 5,97

Honey 3,5,32,133,134,135

I

Icing 16

J

Jelly 3,4,32,33,40,74

Jujube 49

Jus 71

L

Lemon 3,10,34

Lime 5,136

M

Macadamia 5,6,136,137,170

Marshmallow 3,4,5,6,7,20,30,31,35,43,54,62,63,68,82,109,123,139,176,188

Marzipan 4,6,63,140

Mascarpone 3,15

Milk 6,141,159,184

Mint 3,4,5,6,24,76,78,116,117,124,129,141,142

Molasses 6,143,162

N

Nougat 5,100,133

Nut 3,4,5,6,8,9,10,11,12,13,14,15,16,17,18,19,20,21,22,23,24,25,26,27,28,29,30,31,32,33,34,35,36,37,38,39,40,41,42,43,44,45,46,47,48,49,50,51,52,53,54,55,56,57,58,59,60,61,62,6

3,64,65,66,67,68,69,70,71,72,73,74,75,76,77,78,79,80,81,82,83,84,85,86,87,88,89,90,91,92,93,94,95,96,97,98,99,100,101,102,103,104,105,106,107,108,109,110,111,112,113,114,115,116,117,118,119,120,121,122,123,124,125,126,127,128,129,130,131,132,133,134,135,136,137,138,139,140,141,142,143,144,145,146,147,148,149,150,151,152,153,154,155,156,157,158,159,160,161,162,163,164,165,166,167,168,169,170,171,172,173,174,175,176,177,178,179,180,181,182,183,184,185,186,187,188,189,190

O

Orange 3,4,6,35,39,40,41,46,94,148,149,150

P

Parfait 6,173

Pecan 3,4,5,6,7,10,20,25,28,51,79,83,96,132,140,154,155,156,157,158,189

Peel 3,10,18,46,64,119,187

Pepper 5,6,7,115,130,147,159,160,176,188

Pie 4,58,68

Pineapple 3,6,44,161

Pistachio 3,4,6,23,77,150,162,167

Pizza 5,97

Praline 5,138

Pulse 24,140

Pumpkin 4,6,54,68,163

R

Raspberry 5,6,119,165

Rice 54,82,103,189

Rum 5,98

S

Salt 3,4,6,44,68,169,170

Strawberry 6,173

Sugar 3,6,21,46,94,116,174,175

Sweets 5,102

T

Toffee
3,4,5,6,16,21,45,46,76,79,102,112,121,131,163,168,170,179

Truffle
3,4,5,6,14,15,22,23,27,28,33,39,41,45,47,48,54,55,57,69,75,81,92,97,98,110,112,121,132,141,143,145,160,176,177,179,182,183,184

Turkey 4,87

W

Walnut 4,5,6,79,85,105,128,138,149,171,185,186

Conclusion

Thank you again for downloading this book!

I hope you enjoyed reading about my book!

If you enjoyed this book, please take the time to share your thoughts and post a review on Amazon. It'd be greatly appreciated!

Write me an honest review about the book – I truly value your opinion and thoughts and I will incorporate them into my next book, which is already underway.

Thank you!

If you have any questions, **feel free to contact at:** *publishing@crumblerecipes.com*

Adele Chun

crumblerecipes.com

Printed in the USA
CPSIA information can be obtained
at www.ICGtesting.com
LVHW062001281124
797896LV00013B/726